Foreword

Welcome to the Second Edition of *The Mixing Engineer's Handbook*. It's been about 7 years since I wrote the original book, and the recording industry has gone through a paradigm shift. Recording budgets have decreased significantly, the number of major studio facilities has dropped to just a handful, and the rise of the digital audio workstation has made it possible for just about anyone to make a record at home for a minimal investment.

That's all the more reason to update this book. Mixing techniques have evolved and adapted to the digital world, and with fewer studios, there are also fewer mentors to learn from. There are also many classic techniques that are more useful than ever that I wanted to preserve before they became lost to rumor and twisted into irrelevance.

So I've added a few chapters and interviews and generally updated the remaining material so that what's contained herein is more relevant to today's mixing.

All that being said, I originally wrote this book probably for the same reason that you're reading it: to get better at mixing. I noticed that over the years, my mixes were somewhat hit or miss. Sometimes they were great, sometimes okay, and sometimes just plain off the mark. I also noticed that much of the time my mixes didn't have the big-time sound that I heard on the radio. I wanted this sound badly, and I figured the only way to get it was to ask questions of the engineers who knew the secret.

While doing research for this book, I found that a common factor among most good mixers was that, for the most part, they all had at least one mentor as a result of coming up through the studio ranks. Most great mixers started as assistants and learned by watching and listening to the greats that they helped. They took a little from all of them as a result.

I hadn't done that, however. Being a musician first and foremost, I learned to engineer thanks to my early interests in electronics in general, and the way the electrons got from my guitar to the speakers of my amplifier specifically. As I became familiar with the recording studio, I was quickly offered all sorts of session work, from recording jingles to Big Band to Jazz to R&B to Hard Rock. However, not wanting to give up being a musician (which I knew I'd have to do), I never took a proper studio job

THE
Mixing Engineer's
HANDBOOK
SECOND EDITION

by
Bobby Owsinski

COURSE TECHNOLOGY
CENGAGE Learning™

Australia • Brazil • Japan • Korea • Mexico • Singapore • Spain • United Kingdom • United States

The Mixing Engineer's Handbook: Second Edition

Publisher and General Manager, Course Technology PTR:
Stacy L. Hiquet

Associate Director of Marketing:
Sarah O'Donnell

Manager of Editorial Services:
Heather Talbot

Marketing Manager:
Mark Hughes

Executive Editor:
Mike Lawson

Project Editor and Copy Editor:
Karen A. Gill

Course Technology PTR Editorial Services Coordinator:
Elizabeth Furbish

Cover Designer and Interior Layout Tech:
Stephen Ramirez

Indexer:
Katherine Stimson

Proofreader:
Carla Spoon

Cover Photo of Allen Sides:
David Goggin

Cover Photo of Andy Johns:
Matt Ward

Cover Photo of Ed Stasium:
Amy Hartman

Library of Congress Catalog Card Number: 2006923223
ISBN 13: 978-1-59863-251-4
ISBN 10: 1-59863-251-5

Course Technology, a division of Cengage Learning
25 Thomson Place
Boston, MA 02210
www.courseptr.com

Printed in Canada
8 9 10 11 12 11 10 09 08

to really learn the trade at the hands of the masters. As a result, my recording skills were always pretty good, but my mixing skills were lacking.

Having taught recording for many years at Berklee College of Music, Trebas Recording Institute, and Nova Institute Multimedia Studies, I soon realized that there were many others like me who were good but not great, not because they weren't capable, but because they didn't have the opportunity or access to the methods of the masters. After all, how often does a George Massenburg or Bruce Swedien record in Lincoln, Peoria, or Santa Fe? And unfortunately, because there are fewer major studios left, there's even less of a chance of that happening today than there used to be.

In almost all cases, the mixers who I talked to were extremely forthcoming, answering just about any question, and offering explicit information as to why and how they work. Professional jealousy just does not exist in this industry, at least in my experience.

This book started out selfishly, because it was meant specifically to meet my needs, but it ended up with useful information for you, too. I hope you will benefit from it as much as I have.

And yes, my mixes have gotten much, much better.

Acknowledgements

Many thanks to all the mixers in this book who were kind enough to give so freely of their time and expertise. Also, a million thanks to Mike Lawson for being my champion. Without you guys, there would be no book.

About the Author

A long-time veteran of the music industry, **Bobby Owsinski** has worked as a producer, recording engineer, guitar and keyboard player, songwriter, and arranger for a variety of major and minor recording artists, motion pictures, and television shows. One of the first to delve into surround sound music mixing, he has worked on a range of surround sound projects and DVD productions for such diverse acts as Elvis, Jimi Hendrix, The Who, Willie Nelson, Neil Young, The Ramones, and Chicago, among many, many others.

Currently a principle in the DVD production house Surround Associates and the content creation companies 2B Media and Fiesta Red Productions, Bobby has penned several hundred audio-related articles for a variety of popular industry trade publications. He has also authored a number of books that are now staples in recording programs in colleges around the world, including *The Mixing Engineer's Handbook*, *The Mastering Engineer's Handbook*, *The Recording Engineer's Handbook*, in addition to *How to Set Up Your Surround Studio* DVD.

Contents

Introduction

This book changed direction several times as it was being written. Because I had met a lot of top engineers over the years, originally I thought that I'd ask them how they mixed purely as background material (a reference, if you will) and simply accumulate their various methods and anecdotes.

The more I got into it, though, the more it became obvious that these interviews were living and breathing on their own and they really should be included in their entirety in the text. Otherwise, a lot of really useful information would be left out. In other words, I decided to let the mixers tell you what they do in their own words.

You might have read some excerpts of these interviews in various trade magazines like *EQ* or *Surround Professional*, but the entire contents of the interviews are contained herein in Part Three of this book.

What You'll Learn in This Book

The Mixing Engineer's Handbook, Second Edition is based on the interviews of more than 20 of the best-mixing engineers in the business.

In this book you will learn

▶ The six elements of a mix and how they relate to each other

▶ How to build your mix

▶ Why the best song arrangements make the best mixes, and how to create those arrangements

▶ How to polish your mixes by layering your effects

▶ Easy-to-remember "golden rules" of EQ

▶ Tips and tricks for a loud and punchy mix

▶ The New York Compression trick

▶ The key to great mixes

▶ How to optimize your monitor setup

▶ Monitoring tricks of the pros

▶ Why a single master mix might not be enough

▶ How mixing in the box is different from using a console

▶ How to get the best-sounding mixes from your DAW

▶ The basics of Internet audio

▶ How to make the best-sounding MP3s and streaming audio files

▶ The fundamentals of mixing 5.1 surround sound

▶ Comprehensive information on all audio file formats and delivery methods currently in use, and those on the horizon

▶ The tips and tricks of the pros in all facets of mixing in all genres of music

Who This Book Is For

Although it wasn't written specifically as a textbook, *The Mixing Engineer's Handbook* has found its way into university, college, and post-secondary recording programs around the world. Its logical description of a subjective process has made it easy for thousands of beginning recording engineers to accelerate their development in the art of music mixing.

There's really something for every recording engineer in this book. Novice mixers will find the book useful for learning the fundamentals of a great mix. Seasoned professionals will also find the tips, tricks, and insights helpful as they pursue the next level of success and craftsmanship. And if the response is anything like it was for the first edition, even the industry's superstars will enjoy reading about the mixing methods and philosophies of their peers.

How This Book Is Organized

This book is divided into three parts. Part One is about the fundamentals of mixing, interjected with comments by interviewed mixers. Part Two pertains solely to mixing in surround sound. Part Three is the entire text of the mixer interviews that the book is based on. This book is organized in a sequential fashion in that whenever a new topic is introduced, you're presented with some background on the subject followed by the fundamentals and then some advanced tips and tricks.

Part One, "Mixing in Stereo," is an in-depth summary of the stereo methods of the mixing engineers.

Chapter 1, "Some Background: The Evolution of Mixing," covers the evolution of mixing and the various mixing styles relating to the major recording centers of New York, Los Angeles, and London.

Chapter 2, "The Mechanics of Mixing," discusses the six elements of a mix and the signs of an amateur mix.

Chapter 3, "Element 1: Balance—The Mixing Part of Mixing," details the way instruments inter-relate, covers level-setting methods, and discusses how to build a mix.

Chapter 4, "Element 2: Panorama—Placing the Sound in the Soundfield," discusses panning placement in the soundfield, panoramic points of interest, panning outside the speakers, and panning tips and tricks.

Chapter 5, "Element 3: Frequency Range—Equalizing," talks about equalization, magic frequencies, EQ methods and rules, the critical relationship between bass and drums, and tips and tricks for each instrument.

Chapter 6, "Element 4: Dimension—Adding Effects," features methods for using delays, reverbs, and modulation effects, in addition to tips and tricks for each instrument and the overall mix.

Chapter 7, "Element 5: Dynamics—Compression and Gating," discusses compression, limiting, gating and de-essing, their uses with various instruments, the New York Compression Trick, mix buss compression, and tips and tricks from the pros.

Chapter 8, "Element 6: Interest—The Key to Great (As Opposed to Merely Good) Mixes," tells you how to find, create, and exploit interest.

Chapter 9, "Monitoring," is often overlooked but is important to achieving a great mix. This chapter looks at setup and placement of monitors, selection of the correct listening level, and listening tips and tricks of the pros.

Chapter 10, "The Master Mix," features sections on mastering, how to get the hottest level, Internet audio, mixdown formats, various file formats and delivery mix methods, alternative mixes, and stems.

Chapter 11, "Mixing in the Box," discusses mixing inside a DAW and how it's different from traditional console mixing, in addition to methods for getting the cleanest sound.

Part Two, "Mixing in Surround," is dedicated to the basics of surround sound mixing. Mixing in surround is an ability that every mixer will need in the near future. Much of the information in this section comes from personal mixing and recording experience and techniques that I've gathered as an editor for *Surround Professional* magazine.

Chapter 12, "Surround Basics," describes the history of surround sound, the different types, the LFE channel, and bass management.

Chapter 13, "Why Is Surround Better Than Stereo?", talks about the advantages of surround sound over stereo, the differences between surround for picture and for movies, surround mixing schools of thought, and the various surround track assignments.

Chapter 14, "Data Compression Used in Surround," discusses the various encoding methods used such as Dolby Digital, DTS, SDDS, and SRS Circle Surround.

Part Three, "The Interviews," includes 22 interview transcripts of the mixing engineers listed in the next section, "Meet the Mixers."

MEET THE MIXERS

Here's the list of the engineers who contributed to this book, along with some of their credits. I've tried to include a representative from every genre of modern music (Punk to Classic Rock to Alternative to Jazz to Classical to R&B to Dance to Remixing to Latin to Rap to Orchestral to Country to TV mixing) so that there's something for everyone. I'll be quoting these people from time to time, so I wanted to introduce them early on so that you'd have some idea of their background when they pop up.

Just remember, whenever a mixer or engineer is referred to in this book, I don't mean your average run-of-the-mill Joe Blow engineer (hard working and well meaning as he is). I mean someone who's made the hits that you've heard and loved and tried to imitate. This book is about how these glorious few think, how they work, and why they do the things they do. And even though we can't hear as they hear, perhaps we can hear through their words.

Joe Chiccarelli: Even though he might not have quite as high a profile as other big-time mixers, engineer/producer Joe Chiccarelli's list of projects are as notable as the best of the best. With credits like Tori Amos, Etta James, Beck, U2, Oingo Boingo, Shawn Colvin, Frank Zappa, Bob Seger,

Brian Setzer, Hole, and many, many more, chances are you've heard Joe's work more times than you know.

Lee DeCarlo: From his days as chief engineer at New York's Record Plant in the heady '70s, Lee DeCarlo has put his definitive stamp on hit records from Aerosmith to John Lennon's famous *Double Fantasy* to releases by Rancid and Zak Wylde.

Jimmy Douglass: After learning at the knee of the legendary Tom Dowd during Atlantic Records' glory days, Jimmy Douglass has gone on to become one of the most sought-after engineer/mixers in R&B, Hip-Hop, and Rock. One of the few engineers who can cross genres with both total ease and credibility, Jimmy has mixed records for artists as varied as Otis Redding, The Rolling Stones, Hall & Oates, Roxy Music, and Rob Thomas to Ludicris, The Roots, Missy Elliott, Destiny's Child, Jay-Z, and TLC.

Benny Faconne: Benny is unique in that he's a Canadian from Montreal, but 99 percent of the things that he works on are Spanish. From Luis Miguel to Ricky Martin to the Latin Rock band Mana to the Spanish remixes for Boys II Men, Toni Braxton, and Sting, Benny's work is heard far and wide around the Latin world.

Jerry Finn: With credits like Green Day, Rancid, the Goo Goo Dolls, and Beck, Jerry represents one of the new generation of mixers who knows all the rules but is perfectly willing to break them.

Jon Gass: Babyface, Whitney Houston, Madonna, Mary J. Blige, N'Sync, Toni Braxton, Mariah Carey, Usher, TLC, Boys II Men, Destiny's Child. Mixer Jon Gass's credit list reads like a Who's Who of R&B greats— and with good reason. Gass's unsurpassed style and technique have elevated him to a most esteemed position among engineers—working with the best of the best on some of the most creative and demanding music around today.

Don Hahn: Although there are a lot of pretty good engineers around these days, not many have the ability to record a 45- to 100-piece orchestra with the ease of someone who's done it a thousand times. Don Hahn can, and that's because he actually *has* done it a thousand times. With an unbelievable list of credits that range from television series like *Star Trek* (*The Next Generation*, *Deep Space Nine*, and *Voyager*), *Family Ties*, *Cheers*, and *Columbo* to such legends as Count Basie, Barbra Streisand, Chet Atkins, Frank Sinatra, Herb Alpert, Woody Herman, Dionne Warwick, and a host of others (actually 10 pages more), Don has recorded the best of the best.

Ken Hahn: There are few people who know television sound the way Ken Hahn does. From the beginning of the television post revolution, Hahn's New York-based Sync Sound has led the way in television sound innovation and the industry's entry into the digital world. Along the way, Ken has mixed everything from *Pee-wee's Playhouse* to concerts by Billy Joel and Pearl Jam and a host of others, while picking up a slew of awards in the process (4 Emmys, a CAS award, 13 ITS Monitor awards).

Andy Johns: Andy Johns needs no introduction because we've been listening to the music that he's been involved with for most of our lives. With credits like Led Zeppelin, Free, Traffic, Blind Faith, The Rolling Stones, and most recently Van Halen (to name just a few), Andy has set a standard that most mixers are still trying to live up to.

Kevin Killen: From Peter Gabriel's seminal *So* to records by U2, Elvis Costello, Stevie Nicks, Bryan Ferry, and Patty Smith, to name just a few, Kevin Killen's cutting-edge work has widely influenced an entire generation of mixers.

Bernie Kirsh: Bernie Kirsh has certainly made his mark as one of the top engineers in the world of Jazz. From virtually all of Chick Corea's records to working on Quincy Jones' groundbreaking *Back on the Block* (which won a Best Engineering Grammy), Bernie's recordings have consistently maintained a level of excellence that few can match.

Nathanial Kunkel: One of the most in-demand mixers in the business with credits that range from James Taylor, Lionel Ritchie, and Sting to Good Charlotte, Fuel, and Insane Clown Posse, Nathanial represents the best of the "next generation" of mixers.

George Massenburg: From designing the industry's most heralded audio tools to engineering classics by Little Feat; Earth, Wind & Fire; and Linda Ronstadt (to name only a few), George Massenburg needs no introduction to anyone even remotely connected to the music or audio business.

Greg Penny: Born into a music business family to bandleader/producer Hank Penny and hit recording artist Sue Thompson, Surround Music Award winner Greg Penny seemed destined for a life in the studio. Indeed, Greg's production aspirations resulted in hits with k.d. lang, Cher, and Paul Young, among others, but a meeting with Elton John while in his teens turned into an award-winning mixing journey with the legend many years down the road.

David Pensado: Mixer David Pensado, with projects by Christina Aguilera, Justin Timberlake, Kelly Clarkson, Pink, Mya, Destiny's Child, Bell Biv DeVoe, Coolio, Take 6, Brian McKnight, Diana Ross, Tony Toni Tone, Atlantic Starr, and many more, has consistently supplied mixes that have not only filled the airwaves, but also rank among the most artful.

Elliot Scheiner: With his work having achieved tremendous commercial success, Elliot Scheiner has also attained something far more elusive in the music business—the unanimous respect of his peers. With a shelf full of industry awards (five Grammys, four Surround Music Awards, Surround Pioneer Award, Tech Awards Hall of Fame, and too many total award nominations to count) from The Eagles, Beck, Steely Dan, Fleetwood Mac, Sting, John Fogerty, Van Morrison, Toto, Queen, Faith Hill, Lenny Kravitz, Natalie Cole, Doobie Brothers, Aerosmith, Phil Collins, Aretha Franklin, Barbra Streisand, and many, many others, Elliot has long been recognized for his pristine stereo and innovative surround mixes.

Ed Seay: Getting his start in Atlanta in the '70s by engineering and producing hits for Paul Davis, Peabo Bryson, and Melissa Manchester, Ed Seay has since become one of the most respected engineers in Nashville since moving there in 1984. With hit-making clients such as Pam Tillis, Highway 101, Collin Raye, Martina McBride, Ricky Skaggs, and a host of others, Ed has led the charge in changing the way that recording is approached in Nashville.

Allen Sides: Although well known as the owner of the premier Oceanway studio complexes in Los Angeles, Allen Sides is also one of the most respected engineers in the business, with credits that include the film scores to *Dead Man Walking*, *Phenomenon*, *Last Man Standing*, *Sunchaser*, the Goo Goo Dolls' *Iris*, and Alanis Morissette's "Uninvited" for the *City of Angels* soundtrack. He's also done records with the Brian Setzer Big Band, Joni Mitchell, Phil Collins, Barry Manilow, and a host of others.

Don Smith: With credits that read like a Who's Who of Rock & Roll, Don has lent his unique expertise to projects such as The Rolling Stones, Tom Petty, U2, Stevie Nicks, Bob Dylan, Talking Heads, The Eurythmics, The Traveling Wilburys, Roy Orbison, Iggy Pop, Keith Richards, Cracker, John Hiatt, The Pointer Sisters, and Bonnie Raitt, among others.

Ed Stasium: Producer/engineer Ed Stasium is widely known for working on some of the best guitar albums in recent memory, including my own personal favorites by the Smithereens, Living Colour, and Mick Jagger. From Marshall Crenshaw to Talking Heads to Soul Asylum to Motorhead to Julian Cope to the Ramones to even Gladys Knight and the Pips and Ben Vereen, Ed has put his indelible stamp on their records as only he can.

Bruce Swedien: Maybe the most revered of all mixers, Bruce has a credit list (in addition to five Grammys) that could take up a chapter of this book alone. Although Michael Jackson would be enough for most mixers' resumes, Bruce can also include such legends as Count Basie, Tommy Dorsey, Duke Ellington, Woody Herman, Oscar Peterson,

Nat "King" Cole, George Benson, Mick Jagger, Paul McCartney, Patti Austin, Edgar Winter, and Jackie Wilson among many, many others.

John X: John X. Volaitis is one of the new breed of engineers who's thrown off his old-school chains and ventured into the world of remixes (known to some as Techno, Trance, Industrial, Ambient, or any one of about 10 other different names). Along with his partner Danny Saber, John has done remixes for such legends as David Bowie, U2, Marilyn Manson, the Rolling Stones, Black Sabbath, Garbage, Korn, Limp Bizkit, and a host of others.

DISCLAIMER: Just because you read this book doesn't automatically guarantee that you'll become a great platinum mixer who makes lots of money and works with big recording artists. You'll get some tips, techniques, and tricks from this book, but you still need ears and experience, which only you can provide. All this book can do is point you in the right direction and help a little along the way!

Keep in mind that just because a number of mixers do things a certain way, that doesn't mean that's the only way to do it. You should always feel free to try something else, because after all, whatever works for you is in fact the right way.

Part One

Mixing in Stereo

CHAPTER 1

Some Background:
The Evolution of Mixing

Before we get into the actual mechanics of mixing, it's important to have some perspective on how this art has developed over the years.

It's obvious to just about everyone who's been around long enough that mixing has changed over the decades, but the whys and hows aren't quite so obvious. In the early days of recording in the 1950s, there really wasn't mixing per se because the recording medium was mono and a big date used only four microphones. Of course, over the years, recording developed from capturing an unaltered musical event to one that was artificially created through overdubs, thanks to the innovation of *Selsync* (the ability to play back off of the record head so that everything stayed in sync), introduced in 1955. The availability of more and more tracks from a tape machine begot larger and larger consoles, which begot computer automation and recall just to manage the larger consoles fed by more tracks. With all that came not only an inevitable change in the philosophy of mixing, but also a change in the way that a mixer listened or thought.

According to the revered engineer/producer Eddie Kramer (engineer for Jimi Hendrix, Led Zeppelin, KISS, and many more), "Everything (when I started recording) was 4-track, so we approached recording from a much different perspective than people do nowadays. My training in England was fortunately with some of the greatest engineers of the day who were basically Classically trained in the sense that they could go out and record a symphony orchestra and then come back to the studio and then do a Jazz or Pop session, which is exactly what we used to do. When I was training under Bob Auger, who was the senior engineer at Pye Studios, he and I used to go out and do Classical albums with a 3-track Ampex machine, three Neumann U47s, and a single mixer of three channels. So with that sort of training and technique under my belt, approaching a Rock n' Roll session was approaching it from a Classical engineering standpoint and making the sound of a Rock band bigger and better than it was. But the fact of the matter was that we had very few tools at our disposal except EQ, compression, and tape delay. That was it."

English mixer Andy Johns, who apprenticed under Kramer and eventually went on to equally impressive credits with The Rolling Stones, Led Zeppelin, Traffic, Van Halen, and others, goes a step further. "You know why *Sgt. Pepper's* sounds so good? You know why *Are You Experienced* sounds so good—almost better than what we can do now? Because, when you were doing the 4 to 4 (bouncing down from one 4-track machine to another), you mixed as you went along. There was a mix on two tracks of the second 4-track machine, and you filled up the open tracks and did the same thing again. Listen to "We Love You" (by the Stones). Listen to *Sgt. Pepper's*. Listen to *Hole in My Shoe* by Traffic. You mixed as you went along. Therefore, after you got the sounds that would fit with each other, all you had to do was adjust the melodies. Nowadays, because you have this luxury of the computer and virtually as many tracks as you want, you don't think that way any more."

And indeed, when more tracks became available and things began to be recorded in stereo (and now 5.1 or even beyond), the emphasis turned from the bass anchoring the record to the big beat of the drums as the main focal point. This was partially because typical drum miking went from just overhead and kick drum mics to the now common occurrence of a mic on every drum. The consoles could accommodate more microphone inputs, and there were plenty of tracks to record on. And because it was possible to spread out the drums over six or eight or even more tracks, you could concentrate on them more during the mix because you didn't have to premix them along with the bass onto only one or two tracks.

People no longer thought of the drums as just another instrument equal to the bass. Now the drums demanded more attention because more tracks were used. At that point (approximately 1975), thanks to the widespread use of the then-standard 24-track tape deck, mixing changed forever. And, for better or for worse, mixing changed into what it is today.

Mixing Styles: LA Versus New York Versus London

Although there's much less of a distinction these days than there used to be, where you live greatly influences the sound of your mix. Up until the late 1980s or so, it was easy to tell where a record was made just by its sound. There's been a homogenization of styles in recent years mostly because engineers now mix in a variety of locations and many have relocated to new areas, transplanting their mixing styles along the way.

There are three major recording styles, and most recordings fall into one of them: New York, LA, and London.

THE NEW YORK STYLE

The New York style is perhaps the easiest to identify because it features a lot of compression that makes the mix punchy and aggressive, just like New Yorkers. In many cases, the compressed instruments—mostly the rhythm section—are even recompressed several times along the way. It seems that every New York engineer that I interviewed—even the transplanted ones—had virtually the same trick, which is to send the drums (sometimes with the bass) into a couple of busses, send that through some compressors, squeeze to taste, and then return a judicious amount of this compressed rhythm section to the mix through a couple of channels. You can enhance this even further by also boosting the high and low frequencies (lots of boost in most cases) to the compressed signal (more on this "New York Compression Trick" in Chapter 7, Element 5: "Dynamics— Compression and Gating"). For an example of this, listen to any of the mixes that Ed Stasium (a proud practitioner of this method) has done, such as the Mick Jagger solo album *She's The Boss*, or anything by The Smithereens or Living Colour.

THE LA STYLE

The LA sound is somewhat more natural. It's less compressed than the New York style and has fewer effects layers than the London style. The LA style has always tried to capture a musical event and augment it a little, rather than re-create it. Some good examples would be any of the Doobie Brothers or Van Halen hits of the 1970s and 1980s.

THE LONDON STYLE

The London sound is a highly layered musical event that borrows some from the New York style in that it's pretty compressed, but it deals with multiple effects layers. This style makes extensive use of what is known as *perspective*, which puts each instrument into its own distinct sonic environment. Although musical arrangement is important to any good mix, it's even more of a distinctive characteristic in a London mix. What this means is that many parts appear at different times during a mix—some for effect, and some to change the dynamics of the song. Each new part is in its own environment and as a result has a different perspective. A perfect example of this is Hugh Padgham's work with The Police, or just about anything produced by Trevor Horn, such as Seal or Grace Jones, or Yes's *Owner of a Lonely Heart*.

Nowadays there's much less of a difference between styles than there was during the 1980s, but variations still do exist. Although the style differences blur on most music, Techno and Dance still have considerable variation divided among the traditional geographic boundaries of London, New York, and Los Angeles.

OTHER STYLES

Increased globalization has affected regional styles. Where once upon a time Philadelphia, Memphis, Ohio, Miami, and San Francisco had sub-styles of the Big Three (New York, LA, and London), all these areas now line up clearly in one of the Big Three camps.

Nashville today is a special case among the regional styles. This style has evolved (some might say devolved) from an offshoot of the NY style during the 1960s and 1970s, to become much more like the LA sound of the 1970s. Says engineer/producer Ed Seay, "Back when I used to listen to my dad's old Ray Price and Jim Reeves Country records, they weren't very far from what Pop was in the early 60s. Very mellow, big vocals, very sub-dued band, very little drums, strings, horns, lush. Mix-wise, there wasn't really too much difference in an Andy Williams record and one of the old Jim Reeves records."

"What happened was that Country got too soft sounding. You'd cut your track and then do some sweetening with some horns and strings. At one time strings were on all the country records, and then it kind of trans-formed into where it's at today, with almost no strings on Country records except for big ballads. For the most part, horns are completely dead. They're almost taboo. Basically it's rhythm track driven and not really very far off from where pop was in the mid to late 70s. The Rondstadt "It's So Easy to Fall in Love" and "You're No Good" where you hear guitar, bass, drums, keyboards, a slide or steel, and then a vocal background—that's pretty much the format now, although fiddle is used also. Ironically enough, a lot of those guys that were making those records have moved here because at this point, this is one of the last bastions of live recording."

The globe-trotting lifestyle of most A-list engineers in the 1990s caused a homogenization of regional styles. Where at one time most studios had house engineers, the market became predominately composed of freelanc-ers who freely traveled from studio to studio, project to project, bouncing between different cities (and therefore styles) as easily as flipping the channel on a TV. Where at one time, an engineer might change studios but remain located in a specific area all his working life, it became com-mon for an engineer to relocate to several major media centers during the course of his career. Because of this movement, a cross-pollination of styles started to blur the distinction between the Big Three in the 1990s.

Today the differences are far fewer than they used to be. Now everyone uses pretty much the same gear, which wasn't true in the heyday of analog. During those heyday years (which really started to wane in about 2001—2002), a studio in each city had a different gear list, from consoles to monitors to tape machines to outboard gear. As a result, everyone had to work a little differently, so the style (and the city's musical environment) was different, too. That's not so anymore. The distinction between mixing styles will be more miniscule as the years progress.

Where the distinction will remain is in the philosophy that's handed down from the A-team mixers of each city to their assistants. Because fewer real studio facilities exist these days, fewer assistants are learning the styles, and the styles are becoming more or less uniform.

But the big difference in mixing styles is still in the layers. There are more effects and element layers from London, fewer but punchier ones from New York, and even fewer, but much more live layers in Los Angeles.

CHAPTER 2

The Mechanics of Mixing

Although most engineers ultimately rely on their intuition when doing a mix, they do consciously or unconsciously follow certain mixing procedures.

Hearing the Final Product

By and large, most mixers can hear some version of the final product in their heads before they even begin to mix. Sometimes this is a result of countless rough mixes during the course of a project that gradually become polished thanks to console or digital workstation automation and computer recall if an engineer is mixing a project that he's tracked. Even if an engineer is brought in specifically to mix, he might not even begin until he has an idea of where he's going.

Engineers who can hear the finished product before they start normally begin a mix the same way. They become familiar with the song either through a previous rough mix or by putting up all the faders (when using a console) and listening for a few passes. Sometimes this is harder than it seems, though. In the case of a complex mix with a lot of tracks (in the old analog days, some tracks shared different elements or synced multitracks), the mix engineer might have to spend some time writing mutes (a *cut pass*) before the song begins to pare down and make sense.

Ed Seay: *I think one of the things that helps me as a mixer, and one thing that helps all of the ones that have made a mark, is what I call "having the vision." I always try to have a vision of the mix when I start. Rather than just randomly pushing up faders and saying, "Well, a little of this EQ or effect might be nice," I like to have a vision as far as where we're going and what's the perspective.*

For better or worse, the engineer's vision will likely change thanks to input from the producer and/or artist. Although it's not unheard of for a major mixer to complete the job unattended by the producer/artists, most mixers actually prefer the input. However, a vast majority would prefer to start the mix by themselves and have the artist come by to offer suggestions five or six hours later, after the mix begins to take shape.

The Overall Approach

Whether they know it or not (and many mixers aren't conscious of how they do it), most great mixers are methodical in the way they approach a mix. Although the method can vary a little depending on the song, the artist, the genre, or even whether the mixer tracked the song from scratch or is just coming in for the mix, the technique remains constant.

Figure out the direction of the song.
Develop the groove and build it like a house.
Find the most important element and emphasize it.

The last point, finding the most important element and emphasizing it, might be the most important in creating an outstanding mix. As famed Latin mixer Benny Faconne so succinctly states, "It's almost like a musician who picks up a guitar and tries to play. He may have the chart in front of him, but soon he has to go beyond the notes in order to get creative. Same thing with mixing. It's not just a thing of setting levels any more, but more about trying to get the energy of the song across. Anybody can make the bass or the drums even out."

Tall, Deep, and Wide

Most great mixers think in three dimensions. They think "tall, deep, and wide," which means making sure all the frequencies are represented, making sure there's depth to the mix, and then giving it some stereo dimension.

The "tall" dimension (which is called *frequency range* later in the book) is the result of knowing what sounds right as a result of having a reference point. This reference point can come from being an assistant engineer and listening to what other first engineers do or simply comparing your mix to some CDs, records, or files that you're familiar with and consider high fidelity.

Essentially, you're trying to make sure that all the frequencies are properly represented. Usually that means that all the sparkly, tinkly highs and fat, powerful lows are there. Sometimes it means cutting some mids. Clarity is what you aim for. Again, experience with elements that sound good really helps as a reference point.

You achieve the effects or "deep" dimension by introducing new ambience elements into the mix. You usually do this with reverbs and delays (and offshoots like flanging and chorusing), but room mics, overheads, and even leakage play an equally big part.

The panning or "wide" dimension is placing a sound element in a soundfield in a way that makes a more interesting soundscape, such that you can hear each element more clearly.

That brings us to the nitty-gritty of the book, where all the elements of a great mix are detailed even further.

Before we can talk about how to make a great mix, it's good to be aware of the signs of one that isn't so great. Does your mix have any of these characteristics?

Signs of an Amateur Mix

No contrast: The same musical texture permeates the entire song.

A frequent lack of focal point: The lyrics have holes where nothing is brought forward in the mix to hold the listener's attention.

Mixes that are noisy: You can hear clicks, hums, extraneous noises, count-offs, and sometimes lip-smacks and breaths.

Mixes that lack clarity and punch: Instruments aren't distinct. The low end is either too weak or too strong.

Mixes that sound distant and are devoid of a feeling of intimacy: The mix sounds distant because of too much reverb or overuse of other effects.

Inconsistent levels: Instrument levels vary from balanced to soft or too loud. Certain lyrics can't be distinguished.

Dull and uninteresting sounds: Generic, dated, or often-heard sounds are used. There's a difference between using something because it's hip and new and using it because everyone else is using it.

The Six Elements of a Mix

Every piece of modern music—meaning Rock, Pop, R&B, Rap, Country, New Age, Swing, Drum and Bass, Trance, and every other genre having a strong backbeat—has six main elements to a great mix:

▶ **Balance:** The volume level relationship between musical elements

▶ **Frequency range:** Having all frequencies properly represented

▶ **Panorama:** Placing a musical element in the soundfield

▶ **Dimension:** Adding ambience to a musical element

▶ **Dynamics:** Controlling the volume envelope of a track or instrument

▶ **Interest:** Making the mix special

Many mixers have only four or five of these when doing a mix, but all these elements *must* be present for a great mix, because they are all equally important.

In music that requires simply re-creating an unaltered acoustic event (Classical or Jazz or any live concert recording), you might need only the first four elements to have a mix be considered great, but dynamics and interest have evolved to become extremely important elements as modern music has evolved.

Let's look at each element individually.

CHAPTER 3

Element 1: Balance—The Mixing Part of Mixing

The most basic element of a mix is balance. A great mix must start here, for without balance, the other mix elements pale in importance. There's more to balance than just moving some faders, though, as we'll see.

The Arrangement—Where It All Begins

Good balance starts with good arrangement. It's important to understand arrangement because so much of mixing is subtractive by nature. This means that the arrangement, and therefore the balance, is changed by the simple act of muting an instrument whose part doesn't fit well with another. If the instruments fit well together arrangement-wise and don't fight one another, the mixer's life becomes immensely easier. But what exactly does "fighting one another" mean?

When two instruments that have essentially the same frequency band play at the same volume at the same time, the result is a fight for attention. Think of it this way: You don't usually hear a lead vocal and a guitar solo at the same time, do you? That's because the human ear can't decide which to listen to and becomes confused and fatigued as a result.

So how do you get around instrument "fighting?" First and foremost is a well-written arrangement that keeps instruments out of each other's way right from the beginning. The best writers and arrangers have an innate feel for what will work, and the result is an arrangement that automatically lies together without much help.

But it's not uncommon to work with an artist or band that isn't sure of the arrangement or is into experimenting and just allows an instrument to play throughout the entire song, thereby creating numerous conflicts. This is where the mixer gets a chance to rearrange the track by keeping what works and muting the conflicting instrument or instruments. Not only can the mixer influence the arrangement this way, but he can also influence the dynamics and general development of the song.

To understand how arrangement influences balance, we have to understand the mechanics of a well-written arrangement.

Most well-conceived arrangements are limited in the number of elements that occur at the same time. An element can be a single instrument like a lead guitar or a vocal, or it can be a group of instruments like the bass and drums, a doubled guitar line, a group of backing vocals, and so on. Generally, a group of instruments playing the same rhythm is considered an *element*. For example, a doubled lead guitar or doubled vocal is a single element, as is a lead vocal with two additional harmonies. Two lead guitars playing different parts are two elements, however. A lead and a rhythm guitar are also two separate elements.

Arrangement Elements

Foundation: The rhythm section. The *foundation* is usually the bass and drums, but it can also include a rhythm guitar or keys if they're playing the same rhythmic figure as the rhythm section. Occasionally, as in the case of power trios, the foundation element consists only of drums because the bass plays a different rhythm figure and become its own element.

Pad: A *pad* is a long sustaining note or chord. In the days before synthesizers, a Hammond organ provided the best pad and was joined later by the Fender Rhodes. Synthesizers now provide the majority of pads, but real strings or a guitar power chord can also suffice.

Rhythm: *Rhythm* is any instrument that plays counter to the foundation element. This can be a double time shaker or tambourine, a rhythm guitar strumming on the backbeat, or congas playing a Latin feel. The rhythm element adds motion and excitement to the track.

Lead: A lead vocal, lead instrument, or solo.

Fills: Fills generally occur in the spaces between lead lines, or they can be a signature line. You can think of a *fill* element as an answer to the lead.

That's not to say that each instrument is a separate element, however. In Bob Seger's radio standard "Night Moves," you hear bass and drums, acoustic guitar, piano, Hammond organ, lead vocal, and background vocals. This is how the elements break out.

BOB SEGER'S "NIGHT MOVES"

Foundation: Bass, drums, acoustic guitar
Pad: Hammond organ
Rhythm: Piano
Lead: Lead vocal
Fills: Background vocal answers, and sometimes the piano fills in the holes

Usually an acoustic guitar falls into the rhythm category because the strumming pushes the band and creates excitement. In "Night Moves," however, the acoustic guitar is pulled back level-wise in the mix so that it melds into the rhythm section, effectively becoming part of the foundation element.

Alanis Morissette's "Thank U" contains several good examples of both rhythm and pads. What's different is that there are two sets of each: one for the intro and chorus, and a different set for the verses.

ALANIS MORISSETTE'S "THANK U"

Foundation: Bass, drums
Pad: Synthesizer in intro and chorus behind the piano; different synths in chorus
Rhythm: Piano; "breath" sample in the verse
Lead: Lead vocal
Fills: Guitar fills in the second verse

Of course, there's so much more going on in this song track-wise, but any additional tracks are either replacing or doubling the preceding elements. The number of elements remains constant.

GARTH BROOKS' "TWO PINA COLADAS"

Foundation: Bass, drums
Pad: Steel guitar
Rhythm: Acoustic guitar and shaker
Lead: Lead vocal
Fills: Electric and acoustic lead guitar; occasional steel fill

This song is different because there's no true pad in the traditional sense. The steel guitar playing softly in the background acts as the pad and shows that it's possible for nontraditional instruments to play that role.

Rules for Arrangements

There are a couple of easy-to-remember rules that make even the densest arrangement manageable.

LIMIT THE NUMBER OF ELEMENTS

Usually no more than four elements should play at the same time. Sometimes three elements can work well. Rarely will five elements simultaneously work.

Kevin Killen: *I had an experience about three years ago on a Stevie Nicks record with Glyn Johns, who's been making records since the 50s. We were mixing without automation, and he would just push the faders up and within a minute or two he would have this great mix. Then he would just say that he didn't like it and pull it back down again and push it back up. I relearned that the great art of mixing is the fact that the track will gel almost by itself if it [is] well performed and reasonably well recorded. I find that the stuff that you really have to work a lot harder on is the stuff that has been isolated and really worked on. The tracks all end up sounding like disparate elements, and you have to find a way to make them bleed together.*

EVERYTHING IN ITS OWN FREQUENCY RANGE

The arrangement, and therefore the mix, fits together better if all instruments sit in their own frequency range. For instance, if a synthesizer and rhythm guitar play the same thing in the same octave, they usually clash. The solution is to change the sound of one of the instruments so that it fills a different frequency range, have one play in a different octave, or have both instruments play at different times but not together.

Lee DeCarlo: *So much of mixing is what you take away, either level-wise or frequency-wise. There are so many things that you have to eliminate in order to make it all sit and work together. Mark Twain once said, "Wagner's music is much better than it sounds." Wagner is a guy that wrote for cellos and French horns doing things in the same register, but it all worked. The only reason that it worked was he kept the other things out of their way. If you have an orchestra and everybody's playing in the same register, it's just going to get away on you. But if you leave holes, then you can fill up the spectrum.*

Ways to Prevent Instrument Fighting

- Change the arrangement and re-record the track.

- Mute the offending instruments so that they never play at the same time.

- Lower the level of the offending instrument.

- Tailor the EQ so that the offending instrument takes up a different frequency space.

- Pan the offending instrument to a different location.

Where to Build the Mix From

Different mixers start from different places when building their mix. This has as much to do with training as it does with the type of material. For instance, most old-time New York mixers and their protégés start from the bass guitar and build the mix around it. Many other mixers work from the drum overheads first, tucking in the other drums as they go along. Many mixers mix with everything up, only soloing specific instruments that seem to exhibit a problem. Still others are completely arbitrary, changing the starting place from song to song depending on whatever instrument needs to be focused on.

Joe Chicarelli: *Usually what I do is put up all the faders first and get a pretty flat balance and try to hear it like a song, then make determinations from there whether to touch up what I have or rip it down and start again from the bottom.*

Jon Gass: *I start with everything on and I work on it like that. The reason is that, in my opinion, the vocal is going to be there sooner or later anyway. You might as well know where it's sitting and what it's doing. All the instruments are going to be there sooner or later, so you might as well just get used to it. And I think that's also what helps me see what I need to do within the first passage.*

John X: *I generally have to start with the loops. You've got to find the main loop or the combination of loops that creates the main groove. Sometimes the loops may have a lot of individual drums, but they're usually not crucial rhythmic elements. They can be accents, and they can be stuff that just pops up in a break here and there.*

Ken Hahn: *It's usually vocals again. I make sure that those are perfect so that it becomes an element that you can add things around. I always clean up the tracks as much as I can because inevitably you want to get rid of rumble and thumps and noises, creaks, mic hits, etc. Then I always start with bass and rhythm.*

Benny Faccone: *It really is like building a house. You've got to get the foundation of bass and drums and then whatever the most important part of the song is, like the vocalist, and you've got to build around that. I put the bass up first, almost like the foundation part. Then the kick in combination with the bass to get the bottom. Because sometimes you can have a really thin kick by itself, but when you put the bass with it, it seems to have enough bottom because the bass has more bottom end. I build the drums on top of that. After I do the bass and drums, then I get the vocal up and then build everything from there. A lot of mixers just put the music up first, but as soon as you put the vocal up, the levels become totally different. After all the elements are in, I spend maybe a couple of hours just listening to the song like an average listener would, and I keep making improvements.*

Ed Seay: *I'll usually go through and push up instruments to see if there's any trouble spots. All this is dependent upon whether it's something that I've recorded or if I'm hearing it fresh and have no idea what it is. If that's the case, then what I'll do is rough mix it out real quick. I'll push it up and see where it's going before I start diving in.*

If it's something that I know what's on the tape, then I'll go through and mold the sounds in a minor way to fit the modern profile that it needs to be. In other words, if it's a real flabby, dull kick drum, it doesn't matter what the vision is. This kick drum's never going to get there. So I'll pop it into a vocal stresser or I'll do whatever I have to do. I'll work through my mix like that and try to get it up into the acceptable range, or the exceptional range, or at least somewhere that can be worked with. It takes a couple of hours to get good sounds on everything and then another couple of hours to get real good balances, or something that plays itself as if it makes sense. Then I'll do some frequency juggling so that everybody is out of everybody else's way.

Wherever you start from, mixers generally agree that the vocal, or whatever is the most prominent or significant melody instrument, has to make its entrance into the mix as soon as possible. The reason for this is two-fold. First of all, the vocal is probably going to be the most important element, so it will take up more frequency space than other supporting instruments. If you wait until late in the mix to put the vocal in, there might not be enough space left, and the vocal will never sit right with the rest of the track.

The second reason has to do with effects. If you tailor all your effects to the rhythm section and supporting instruments, there might be none left when it's time to add in the vocal or most prominent instrument.

Typical Mix Starting Places

- From the bass

- From the kick drum

- From the snare drum

- From the overheads

- From the lead vocal or main instrument

- When mixing a string section, from the highest string (violin) to the lowest (bass)

What Type of Program Material?

The type of program you're mixing frequently affects where you build the mix from. For instance, when you're doing dance music, where the kick is everything, the kick is the obvious choice for a starting point. When you're mixing something orchestral, however, the emphasis is different. According to Don Hahn, "The approach is totally different because there's no rhythm section, so you shoot for a nice roomy orchestral sound and get as big a sound as you can get with the amount of musicians you have. You start with violins, then violas if you have them, cellos, then basses. You get all that happening and then add woodwinds, French horns, trombones, trumpets, and then percussion and synthesizers."

In Jazz, the melody is the starting point, with the bass inserted afterward to solidify the foundation.

Level-Setting Methods

Mixers have debated from the beginning of mixing time about setting levels by using the VU meters. Some mixers feel that they can get in the ballpark by setting the levels with the meters alone, whereas others discount any such method out of hand. The fact of the matter is that for those using the meter method, feel and instinct are still a large part of their technique, making it equally as valid as those who rely on instinct alone.

As with everything else that you read, try the following methods, use what works, and throw away the rest.

Benny Faccone: *I usually start with the bass at about −5 and the kick at about −5. The combination of the two, if it's right, should hit about −3 or so. By the time the whole song gets put together and I've used the computer to adjust levels, I've trimmed everything back somewhat. The bass could be hitting −7 if I solo it after it's all done.*

Don Smith: *I'll start out with the kick and bass in that area (−7VU). By the time you put everything else in, it's +3 anyway. At least if you start that low, you have room to go.*

Ed Seay: *Usually a good place to start is the kick drum at −6 or −7 or so. I'll try to get a bass level that is comparable to that. If it's not exactly comparable on the meter because one's peaking and one's sustaining, I get them to at least sound comparable, because later in mastering, if you affect one, you're going to affect the other. So as long as the ratio is pretty correct between the two, then if you go to adjust the kick, at least it's not going to whack the bass way out as long as they relate together. That's kind of a good starting place for me.*

Lee DeCarlo: *I'll get the snare drum constantly hitting the backbeat of the tune at around −5, and everything gets built around it.*

CHAPTER 4

Element 2: Panorama—Placing the Sound in the Soundfield

One of the most overlooked or taken-for-granted elements in mixing is *panorama*, or the placement of a sound element in the soundfield. To understand panorama, first we must understand that the stereo sound system (which is two channels for our purposes) represents sound spatially. Panning lets us select where in that space we place the sound.

In fact, panning does more than just that. Panning can create excitement by adding movement to the track and adding clarity to an instrument by moving it out of the way of other sounds that might be clashing with it. Correct panning for a track can also make it sound bigger, wider, and deeper.

So what is the proper way to pan? Are there rules? Well, just like so many other things in mixing, although panning decisions might sometimes seem arbitrary, there's a method to follow and a reason behind the method.

Imagine that you're at the movies and watching a Western. The scene is a panorama of the Arizona desert, and right in the middle of the screen is a cowboy sitting on his horse in a medium shot from his boots up. A pack of Indians (we'll say six) is attacking him, but we can't see them because the cowboy is in the shot directly in front of them. If we can't see them, their impact as a suspense builder is limited, and they cost the production money that just went to waste. Wouldn't it be better if the director moved the Indians to the left out of the shadow of the cowboy so we could see them? Or maybe even spread them out across the screen so the attack seems larger and more intimidating?

Of course, that's what we do with the pan control (sometimes called *pan pot*, which is short for potentiometer, the name of the electronic component used to pan the signal). It allows the engineer (the director) to move the background vocals (Indians) out of the way of the lead vocal (cowboy) so that in this case we can hear (see) each much more distinctly.

Phantom Center

Stereo, which was invented in 1931 by Alan Blumlien at EMI Records (the patent wasn't renewed in 1959 when the format was taking off—doh!), features a phenomenon known as the phantom center. The phantom center means that the output of the two speakers combines to provide an imaginary speaker in between. This imaginary image can sometimes shift as the balance of the music shifts from side to side, which can be disconcerting to the listener. As a result, film sound has always relied on a third speaker channel in the center to keep the sound anchored. This third channel never caught on in music circles until recently, mostly because consumers had a hard enough time finding a place for two speakers, let alone three. (See Part 2, "Mixing in Surround.")

The Three Points of Panoramic Interest

Three panoramic areas in the mix seem to get the most action.

THE CENTER AND THE EXTREME HARD LEFT AND RIGHT

The center is obvious in that the most prominent music element (usually the lead vocal) is panned there, but so is the kick drum, the bass guitar, and even the snare drum. Although putting the bass and kick up the middle makes for a musically coherent and generally accepted technique, its origins are really from the era of vinyl records.

When stereo first came into widespread use in the mid-1960s, it was common for mixers to pan most of the music from the band to one side while the vocals were panned opposite. This was because stereo was so new that the recording and mixing techniques for the format hadn't been discovered or refined yet, so pan pots were not available on mixing consoles. Instead, a three-way switch was used to assign the track to the left output, right output, or both (the center).

Music elements tended to be hard-panned to one side, which caused some serious problems in that if any low-frequency boost was added to the music on just that one side, the imbalance in low-frequency energy caused the cutting stylus to cut right through the groove wall when the master lacquer disc (the master record) was cut. The only way around this was to decrease the amount of low-frequency energy from the music to balance the sides or to pan the bass and kick and any other instrument with a lot of low-frequency information to the center. In fact, a special equalizer called an elliptical EQ was used during disc cutting specifically to move all the low-frequency energy to the center if anything with a lot of low frequencies was panned off-center.

Likewise, as a result of the vast array of stereo and pseudostereo sources and effects that arrived on the market over the years, mixers began to pan these sources hard left and right as a matter of course. Because the mixer's main task is to make things sound bigger and wider, it was an easy choice to pan one of these stereo sources or effects hard left and hard right. Suddenly things sounded huge! The problem surfaced later when almost all keyboards and effects devices came with stereo outputs. (Many are actually pseudostereo, with one side just chorused a little sharp and then flat against the dry signal.) Now there was a temptation to pan all these "stereo" sources hard left and right on top of one another. The result was "big mono."

David Pensado: *I think that there are three sacred territories in a mix that if you put something there, you've got to have an incredibly good reason. That's extreme left, center, and extreme right. I've noticed that some mixers will get stereo tracks from synthesizers and effects, and they just instinctively pan them hard left and hard right. What they end up with is these big train wrecks out on the ends of the stereo spectrum. Then they pan their kick, snare, bass, and vocals center, and you've got all this stuff stacked on top of each other. If it were a visual, you wouldn't be able to see the things behind the things in front. So what I do is take a stereo synthesizer track, and I'll just toss one side because I don't need it. I'll create my own stereo by either adding a delay or a chorus or a predelayed reverb or something like that to give it a stereo image. I'll pan maybe the dry signal to 10:00, and then I'll pan the effects just inside the extreme left side. I would never put it hard left because then there are too many things on top of it. I would pan it at 9:00, and then pan the dry signal to say 10:30, something like that.*

Big Mono

Big mono occurs when you have a track with a lot of pseudostereo sources that are panned hard right and hard left. In this case, you're not creating much of a panorama because everything is placed hard left and right, and you're robbing the track of definition and depth because all these tracks are panned on top of one another.

The solution is to throw away one of the stereo tracks (throw away the chorused one, but keep the dry one) and make your own custom stereo patch either with a pitch shifter or delay. (See Chapter 6, "Element 4:

Dimension—Adding Effects.") Then instead of panning hard left and right, find a place somewhat inside those extremes.

One possibility is to pan the left source to about 10:00 while panning the right to about 4:00. Another more localized possibility is to put the left to 9:00 and the right all the way to 10:30. This gives the feeling of localization without getting too wide.

Ed Seay: *One of the things I don't like is what I call "big mono," where there's no difference in the left and the right other than a little warble. If you pan that left and right wide, and then here comes another keyboard, and you pan that left and right wide, and then there's the two guitars, and you pan them left and right wide, by the time you get all this stuff left and right wide, there's really no stereo in the sound. It's like having a big mono record, and it's just not really aurally gratifying. So to me, it's better to have some segregation, and that's one of the ways I try to make everything heard in the mixes. Give everybody a place on the stage.*

Panning Outside the Speakers

Some mixers like to use the phantom images afforded by some external processors to pan an instrument outside the speakers. In this case, the phase differences make the instrument seem to come from *outside* the speakers instead of *from* them. Although some find this effect disconcerting, it can be effective under the right circumstances.

Tricks and Tips

Although there are not as many tips and tricks for panning as there are for the other mix elements, here are some that are surprisingly effective.

PANNING IN DANCE MUSIC

David Sussman:
(New York Dance Remixer) *For a dance club record, it's best not [to] go extremely wide with important elements, which would be kick, snares, hi-hats, and cymbals. Because of the venues where the song is being played, if you pan a pretty important element on the left side, half the dance floor's not hearing it. So it might be best to keep important elements either up the middle or maybe at 10:30 and 1:30. Lead vocals are almost always up the middle.*

PANNING IN MONO (YES, THAT'S RIGHT!)

Don Smith: *I check my panning in mono with one speaker, believe it or not. When you pan around in mono, all of a sudden you'll find that it's coming through now and you've found the space for it. If I want to find a place for the hi-hat, for instance, sometimes I'll go to mono and pan it around and you'll find that it's really present all of a sudden, and that's the spot. When you start to pan around on all* *your drum mics in mono, you'll hear all the phase come together. When you go to stereo, it makes things a lot better.*

PANNING FOR CLARITY

Joe Chiccarelli: *The only thing I do is, once I have my sounds and everything is sitting pretty well, I'll move the pans around a tiny bit. If I have something panned at 3 o'clock and it's sitting pretty well, I'll inch it a tiny sliver from where I had it just because I found it can make things clearer that way. When you start moving panning around, it's almost like EQing something because of the way that it conflicts with other instruments. I find that if I nudge it, it might get out of the way of something or even glue it together.*

CHAPTER 5

Element 3: Frequency Range— Equalizing

Even though an engineer has every intention of making his tracks sound as big and as clear as possible during tracking and overdubs, the frequency range of some or all of the tracks is often still somewhat limited when it comes time to mix. This could be because the tracks were recorded in a different studio using different monitors, used a different signal path, or were highly influenced by the producer and musicians. As a result, the mixing engineer must extend the frequency range of those tracks.

In the quest to make things sound bigger, fatter, brighter, and clearer, the equalizer is the chief tool that most mixers use. But perhaps more than any other audio tool, the use of the equalizer requires a skill that separates the average engineer from the master.

Allen Sides: *What I would say is that I tend to like things to sound sort of natural, but I don't care what it takes to make it sound like that. Some people get a very pre-conceived set of notions that you can't do this or you can't do that. Like Bruce Swedien said to me, he doesn't care if you have to turn the knob around backwards; if it sounds good, it is good—assuming that you have a reference point that you can trust, of course.*

What Are You Trying to Do?

There are three primary goals when equalizing:

▶ Make an instrument sound clearer and more defined.

▶ Make the instrument or mix bigger and larger than life.

> ▶ Make all the elements of a mix fit together better by juggling frequencies so that each instrument has its own predominate frequency range.

Magic Frequencies

Before we examine some methods of equalizing, it's important to note the areas of the audio band and the effect they have on what we hear. We can break down the audio band into six distinct ranges, each one having enormous impact on the total sound:

▶ **Sub-Bass:** This is the very low bass between 16 and 60Hz that encompasses sounds that are often felt more than heard, such as thunder in the distance. These frequencies give the music a sense of power even if they occur infrequently. Too much emphasis on this range makes the music sound muddy.

▶ **Bass:** The bass between 60 and 250Hz contains the fundamental notes of the rhythm section, so EQing this range can change the musical balance, making it fat or thin. Too much boost in this range can make the music sound boomy.

▶ **Low Mids:** The midrange between 250 and 2000Hz contains the low-order harmonics of most musical instruments and can introduce a telephone-like quality to the music if boosted too much. Boosting the 500 to 1000Hz octave makes the instruments sound horn-like, whereas boosting the 1 to 2kHz octave makes them sound tinny. Excess output in this range can cause listening fatigue.

▶ **High Mids:** The upper midrange between 2 and 4kHz can mask the important speech recognition sounds if boosted, introducing a lisping quality into a voice and making sounds formed with the lips such as *m*, *b*, and *v* indistinguishable. Too much boost in this range, especially at 3kHz, can also cause listening fatigue. Dipping the 3kHz range on instrument backgrounds and slightly peaking 3kHz on vocals can make the vocals audible without having to decrease the instrumental level in mixes where the voice would otherwise seem buried.

▶ **Presence:** The presence range between 4 and 6kHz is responsible for the clarity and definition of voices and instruments. Boosting this range can make the music seem closer to the listener. Reducing the 5kHz content of a mix makes the sound more distant and transparent.

▶ **Brilliance:** The 6 to 16kHz range controls the brilliance and clarity of sounds. Too much emphasis in this range, however, can produce sibilance on the vocals.

Range		Description	Effect
Sub-Bass	16 to 60Hz	Sense of power	Too much makes the music sound muddy
Bass	60 to 250Hz	Contains fundamental notes of rhythm section; makes music fat or thin	Too much makes the music boomy
Low Mids	250 to 2kHz	Contains the low-order harmonics of most instruments	Boosting 500 to 1kHz sounds hornlike; 1 to 2kHz sounds tinny
High Mids	2kHz to 4kHz	Contains speech recognition sounds like *m*, *b*, and *v*	Too much causes listener fatigue
Presence	4kHz to 6kHz	Responsible for clarity and definition of voices and instruments	Boosting makes music seem closer
Brilliance	6kHz to 16kHz	Controls brilliance and clarity	Too much causes vocal sibilance

Leo di Gar Kulka. "Equalization—The Highest, Most Sustained Expression of the Recordist's Heart." *Recording Engineer/Producer*, Vol. 3, Number 6. November/December 1972.

For those of you who have an easier time visualizing the audio spectrum in one-octave increments (like those found on a graphic equalizer), here's an octave look at the same chart.

Octave	Popular Definition
63Hz	Bottom
125Hz	Boom, thump, warmth
250Hz	Fullness or mud
500Hz	Honk
1kHz	Whack
2kHz	Crunch
4kHz	Edge
8kHz	Sibilance, definition, "ouch!"
16kHz	Air

EQ Methods

Because each specific song, instrument, and player is unique, it's impossible to give anything other than some general guidelines as to equalization methods. Also, different engineers have different ways of arriving at the same end, so if the following doesn't work for you, keep trying. The method doesn't matter—only the end result.

Before these methods are outlined, it's really important that you observe the following:

LISTEN!

Open up your ears and listen carefully to all the nuances of the sound. It's all important.

Make sure you're monitoring at a comfortable level—not too loud and not too soft. If it's too soft, you might be fooled by the nonlinearity of the speakers and overcompensate. If it's too loud, certain frequencies might be masked or overemphasized by the nonlinearities of the ear itself (thanks to the Fletcher-Munson curves), and again you will overcompensate.

Equalize to make an instrument sound clearer and more defined.

Even some sounds that are recorded well can be lifeless thanks to certain frequencies being overemphasized or others being severely attenuated. More often than not, the lack of definition of an instrument is because of too much lower midrange in approximately the 400 to 800Hz area. This area adds a "boxy" quality to the sound.

1. Set the Boost/Cut knob to a moderate level of cut. (8 or 10dB should work.)

2. Sweep through the frequencies until you find the frequency where the sound has the least amount of boxiness and the most definition.

3. Adjust the amount of cut to taste. Be aware that too much cut causes the sound to be thinner.

4. If required, add some "point" to the sound by adding a slight amount (start with only a dB; add more to taste) of upper midrange (1 to 4kHz).

5. If required, add some "sparkle" to the sound by adding a slight amount of high frequencies (5 to 10kHz).

6. If required, add some "air" to the sound by adding a slight amount of the brilliance frequencies (10 to 15kHz).

PLEASE NOTE:

Always try attenuating (cutting) the frequency first. This is preferable because all equalizers add phase shift as you boost, which results in an undesirable coloring of sound. Usually, the more EQ you add, the more phase shift is also added and the harder it is to fit the instrument into the mix. Many engineers are judicious in their use of EQ. That being said, anything goes! If it sounds good, it *is* good.

ALTERNATE METHOD

1. Starting with your EQ flat, remove *all* of the bottom end by turning the low frequency control to full cut.

2. Using the rest of your EQ, tune the mid-upper midrange until the sound is thick yet distinct.

3. Round it out with a supporting lower-mid tone to give it some body.

4. Slowly bring up the mud-inducing bottom end enough to move air, but not so much as to make the sound muddy.

5. Add some high frequency for definition.

Ed Seay: *I just try to get stuff to sound natural, but at the same time be very vivid. I break it down into roughly three areas: mids and the top and the bottom. Then there's low mids and high mids. Generally, except for a very few instruments or a few microphones, cutting flat doesn't sound good to most people's ears. So I'll say, "Well, if this is a state-of-the-art preamp and a great mic and it doesn't sound that great to me, why?" Well, the mid range is not quite vivid enough. Okay, we'll look at the 3k, 4k range, maybe 2500. Why don't we make it kind of come to life like a shot of cappuccino and open it up a little bit? But then I'm not hearing the air around things, so let's go up to 10k or 15k and just bump it up a little bit and see if we can kind of perk it up. Now, all that sounds good, but our bottom is kind of undefined. We don't have any meat down there. Well, let's sweep through and see what helps the low end. Sometimes, depending on different instruments, a hundred cycles can do wonders for some instruments. Sometimes you need to dip out at 400 cycles because that's the area that sometimes just clouds up and takes the clarity away. But a lot of times adding a little 400 can fatten things up.*

Equalize to make the instrument or mix bigger and larger than life.

"Bigness" usually comes from the addition of bass and sub-bass frequencies in the 40 to 250Hz range. This will come from a region below 100Hz, a region above 100Hz, or both.

1. Set the Boost/Cut knob to a moderate level of boost. (8 or 10dB should work.)

2. Sweep through the frequencies in the bass band until you find the frequency where the sound has the desired amount of fullness.

3. Adjust the amount of boost to taste. Be aware that too much boost makes the sound muddy.

4. Go to the frequency either one-half or twice the frequency that you used in step 2 and add a moderate amount of that frequency. For example, if your frequency in step 2 was 120Hz, go to 60Hz and add a dB or so. If your frequency was 50Hz, go to 100 and add a bit there.

PLEASE NOTE:

It's usually better to add a small amount at two frequencies than a large amount at one.

Be aware that making an instrument sound great while soloed might make it impossible to fit together with other instruments in the mix.

Rule of Thumb

• The fewer the instruments in the mix, the bigger each one should be.

• Conversely, the more instruments in the mix, the smaller each one needs to be for everything to fit together.

Equalize to make all the elements of a mix fit together better by juggling frequencies so that each instrument has its own predominate frequency range.

1. Start with the rhythm section (bass and drums). The bass should be clear and distinct when played against the drums, especially the kick and snare.

You should be able to hear each instrument distinctly. If not, do the following:

A. Make sure that no two equalizers are boosting at the same frequency. If they are, move one to a slightly higher or lower frequency.

B. If an instrument is cut at a certain frequency, boost the frequency of the other instrument at that same frequency. For example, if the kick is cut at 500Hz, boost the bass at 500Hz.

2. Add the next most predominant element, usually the vocal, and proceed as above.

3. Add the rest of the elements into the mix one by one. As you add each instrument, check it against the previous elements as above.

REMEMBER:

1. The idea is to hear each instrument clearly, and the best way for that to happen is for each instrument to live in its own frequency band.

2. After frequency juggling, an instrument might sound terrible when soloed by itself. That's okay. The idea is for it to work in the track.

3. You probably will have to EQ in circle where you start with one instrument, tweak another that's clashing, return to the original one, and then go back again over and over until you achieve the desired separation.

Jon Gass: *I really start searching out the frequencies that are clashing or rubbing against each other. Then I work back toward the drums. But I really try to keep the whole picture in there most of the time as opposed to really isolating things too much.*

If there are two or three instruments that are clashing, that's probably where I get more into the solo if I need to kind of hear the whole natural sound of the instrument. I'll try to go more that way with each instrument unless there's a couple that are really clashing, then I'll EQ more aggressively. Otherwise, I'm not scared to EQ quite a bit.

Ed Seay: *Frequency juggling is important. You don't EQ everything in the same place. You don't EQ 3k on the vocal and the guitar and the bass and the synth and the piano, because then you have such a buildup there that you have a frequency war going on. So sometimes you can say, "Well, the piano doesn't need 3k, so let's go lower, or let's go higher." Or, "This vocal will pop through if we shine the light not in his nose, but maybe toward his forehead." In so doing, you can make things audible, and everybody can get some camera time.*

Easy-to-Remember Golden Rules of Equalization

▶ If it sounds muddy, cut some at 250Hz.

▶ If it sounds honky, cut some at 500Hz.

▶ Cut if you're trying to make things sound better.

▶ Boost if you're trying to make things sound different.

▶ You can't boost something that's not there in the first place.

The Relationship Between Bass and Drums

Perhaps the most difficult task of a mixing engineer is balancing the bass and drums (especially the bass and kick). Nothing can make or break a mix faster than how these instruments work together. It's not uncommon for a mixer to spend hours on this balance (both level and frequency), because if the relationship isn't correct, the song will never sound big and punchy.

Andy Johns: *The way that I really learned about music is through mixing, because if the bass part is wrong, how can you hold up the bottom end? So you learn how to make the bass player play the right parts so you can actually mix.*

So how do you get this mysterious balance?

In order to have the impact and punch that most modern mixes exhibit, you have to make a space in your mix for both of these instruments so they won't fight each other and turn into a muddy mess. While simply EQing your bass high and your kick low (or the other way around) might work at its simplest, it's best to have a more in-depth strategy.

So to make them fit together, try the following:

1. EQ the kick drum between 60 to 120Hz as this will allow it to be heard on smaller speakers. For more attack and beater click, add between 1 to 4kHz. You may also want to dip some of the boxiness between 300–600Hz. EQing in the 30–60Hz range will produce a kick that you can feel, but it may also sound thin on smaller speakers and probably won't translate well to a variety of speaker systems. Most 22" kick drums like to center somewhere around 80Hz.

2. Bring up the bass with the kick. The kick and bass should occupy slightly different frequency spaces. The kick will usually be in the 60–80Hz range, whereas the bass will emphasize higher frequencies anywhere from 80 to 250 (although sometimes the two are reversed depending upon the song). Shelve out any unnecessary bass frequencies (below 30Hz on kick and 50Hz on the bass, although it varies according to style and taste) so they're not boomy or muddy. There should be a driving, foundational quality to the combination of these two together.

A common mistake is to emphasize the kick with either too much level or EQ and not enough on the bass guitar. This gives you the illusion that your mix is bottom light, because what you are doing is shortening the duration of the low frequency envelope in your mix. Since the kick tends to be more transitory than the bass guitar, this gives you the idea that the low frequency content of your mix is inconsistent. For Pop music, it is best to have the kick provide the percussive nature of the bottom while the bass fills out the sustain and musical parts.

3. Make sure the snare is strong; otherwise, it'll lose drive when everything else is added in. This usually calls for at least some compression. (See Chapter 7, "Element 5: Dynamics—Compression and Gating.") You may need a boost at 1k for attack, 120 to 240Hz for fullness, and 10k for snap. As you bring in the other drums and cymbals, you might want to dip a little of 1k on these to make room for the snare. Also make sure that the toms aren't too boomy. (If so, shelve below 60Hz.)

4. If you're having trouble with the mix because it's sounding cloudy and muddy on the bottom end, turn the kick drum and bass off to determine what else might be in the way in the low end. You might not realize that there are some frequencies in the mix that aren't really musically necessary. With piano or guitar, you're mainly looking for the mids and top end to cut through, while the low end is just getting in the way, so it's best to clear some of that out with a hi-pass filter. When soloed, it might sound too thin, but with the rest of the mix, the bass will sound so much better, and you're not really missing that low end from the other instruments. Now the mix sounds louder, clearer, and fuller. Be careful not to cut too much from the other instruments, as you might lose the warmth o f the mix.

5. For Dance music, be aware of kick-drum-to-bass melody dissonance. The bass line over the huge sound systems in today's clubs is very important and needs to work very well with the kick drum. But if your kick has a frequency of A at around 50 or 60Hz and the bass line is tuned to A#, it's going to clash. Tune your kick samples to the bass lines (or vice versa) where needed.

Benny Faccone: *I put the bass up first, almost like the foundation part. Then the kick in combination with the bass to get the bottom. Because sometimes you can have a really thin kick by itself, but when you put the bass with it, it seems to have enough bottom because the bass has more bottom end. I build the drums on top of that.*

For bass, I use a combination of a low frequency, usually about 50Hz, with a limiter so it'll stay tight but still give it the big bottom. Add a little 7k if you want a bit of the string sound, and between 1.5 and 3k to give it some snap.

For the kick, I like to have bottom on that, too. I'll add a little at 100 and take some off at 400, depending on the sound. Sometimes I even take all the 400 out, which makes it very wide. Then add some point at 3 or 5k.

On the snare, I give it some 10k on the top end for some snap. I've been putting 125Hz on the bottom of the snare to fill it out a little more.

Jerry Finn: *I'll get the drums happening to where they have some ambience, then put the vocal up and get that to where that's sitting right. Then I'll start with the bass and make sure that the kick and the bass are occupying their own territory and not fighting each other.*

Instrument	Magic Frequencies
Bass guitar	Bottom at 50 to 80Hz, attack at 700Hz, snap at 2.5kHz
Kick drum	Bottom at 80 to 100Hz, hollowness at 400Hz, point at 3 to 5kHz
Snare	Fatness at 120 to 240Hz, point at 900Hz, crispness at 5kHz, snap at 10kHz
Toms	Fullness at 240 to 500Hz, attack at 5 to 7kHz
Floor tom	Fullness at 80Hz, attack at 5kHz
Hi-hat and cymbals	Clang at 200Hz, sparkle at 8 to 10kHz
Electric guitar	Fullness at 240 to 500Hz, presence at 1.5 to 2.5kHz, attenuate at 1kHz for 4x12 cabinet sound
Acoustic guitar	Fullness at 80Hz, body at 240Hz, presence at 2 to 5kHz
Organ	Fullness at 80Hz, body at 240Hz, presence at 2 to 5kHz
Piano	Fullness at 80Hz, presence at 3 to 5kHz, honky-tonk at 2.5kHz
Horns	Fullness at 120Hz, piercing at 5kHz
Voice	Fullness at 120Hz, boomy at 240Hz, presence at 5kHz, sibilance at 4 to 7kHz, air at 10 to 15kHz
Strings	Fullness at 240Hz, scratchy at 7 to 10kHz
Conga	Ring at 200Hz, slap at 5kHz

Tricks and Tips

More than any other element, the EQ tricks and tips are specific to the instrument. Remember that the frequencies stated are approximations that will change slightly depending on the player, instrument, environment, and song.

GENERAL TIPS

▶ Use a narrow Q (bandwidth) when cutting and a wide Q when boosting.

▶ If you want something to stick out, roll off the bottom; if you want it to blend in, roll off the top.

FOR SNARE

To find the "point" on the snare, boost the upper midrange starting at about +5 or 6dB at 2kHz or so. Open up the bandwidth (if that parameter is available) until you get the snare to jump out, and then tighten the bandwidth until you get only the part of the snare sound that you want most. Then fine-tune the frequency until you need the least amount of boost to make it jump out of the mix.

FOR DRUMS

Dave Pensado: *A lot of the music I do has samples in it, and that gives the producer the luxury of pretty much getting the sound he wanted from the start. In the old days, you always pulled out a little 400 on the kick drum. You always added a little 3 and 6 to the toms. That just doesn't happen as much anymore because when I get the project—even with live bands—the producer's already triggered the sound he wanted off the live performance, and the drums are closer.*

FOR KICK

▶ Try to boost 4kHz, cut 250 to 300Hz, and then boost the low frequency around 60 to 100Hz to find the drum's resonance.

▶ One fairly common effect used in R&B is to bring a 32Hz tone back to a channel on the board, gate it, and trigger the gate with the kick. Blend and compress both the original kick and 32Hz tone to taste.

▶ For a Metal kick, use 3kHz or so on the kick drum to function as the "nail in the paddle."

▶ For a kick meant for a club, emphasize the 200–300Hz range without the extreme low end. The club system makes up the difference, so if you mix the bottom of it the way you like to hear it in a club, you're probably going to overload the house system.

▶ If your bass has a lot of sine wave in it and your kick is an 808, they may mask each other. If the kick sounds lower than the bass, add a sample with some mid or top punch. If the kick is higher than the bass, you can add some distortion or use MaxxBass (see Figure 5.1) to add higher harmonics to the bass. Make sure you check both on small speakers.

Figure 5.1
Waves MaxxBass.

FOR BASS

▶ The ratio between the low bass (80–120Hz) and the mid bass (130Hz–200Hz) is important. Try using two fairly narrow peaking bands—one at 100Hz and another at 140Hz—boosting one and cutting the other slightly. If the bass is too "warm," sometimes reducing the upper band can make it more distinct without removing the deeper fundamentals that live in the 100Hz band.

▶ Also try boosting some of the 800Hz area because this can provide clarity without getting too "snappy" sounding.

▶ A four-band parametric allows you to put several bands below 200Hz. The low frequencies around 40–70Hz might be attenuated, the frequencies from 80–120Hz are where the fundamental lies, and the frequencies from 130–200Hz are the overtones and cabinet/neck/body resonances.

▶ Muddy bass can mean a lot of things, but at a minimum, it usually involves a lack of presence of the higher harmonics. Most bass tracks have a sweet spot between 600 and 1.2k where the lower-order harmonics sing.

▶ Take a low-cut filter and center it at 250Hz so that all the lows of the bass are attenuated. Then take a bell filter and boost it 4dB with a narrow band and sweep around the 80 to 180Hz region to find where your bass frequencies fit best in the track. When you find it, widen the bandwidth and boost more if necessary. If you want more density on the bottom, you might need to use another bell filter, which should tighten up the low end, add space for a kick drum, and make your mix less boomy.

▶ Hi-pass filter the bass anywhere from 50 to 125Hz. It's amazing how much that can help the bass tighten up sometimes.

▶ This is an often-used method that works on NS-10Ms only! (See Figure 5.2.) Turn up the NS-10Ms to the point where the surround of the woofer on the NS-10M is "crinkling." Then bring up the hi-pass filter until the woofer looks normal. Drop the volume and continue mixing as usual.

▶ *Anything* with low-frequency content (below 500Hz) affects the bass. This includes kick, bass, keyboards, (male) vocals, double bass, celli, low-tuned guitars, and so on. Cut the low end (anywhere below 80 to 120Hz) from tracks that don't really need lots of bass. Doing that helps those tracks to cut through while leaving space for the bass and the kick.

▶ Removing the 250Hz region information from other instruments—such as guitars, keyboards, and even vocals—is often more useful than cutting it from the bass.

Figure 5.2
Yamaha NS-10Ms.

▶ Here's another method to achieve more definition from a bass guitar. First, make a duplicate of the bass track, and then process the duplicate track in Pro Tools or another DAW with the Moogerfooger Lo-Pass plug-in. (See Figure 5.3.) Set the plug-in's Mix parameter to 10, the Resonance to 1, and the overall Amount to 1. Then turn up the Frequency control until you get a well-defined subtone. Group both bass tracks to a separate bus, and create a new aux track. Be sure to assign the inputs to the same bus. Then, on the original bass track in Pro Tools, use an EQ plug-in to roll some of the low subs out. Next, blend the original bass track with the Moogerfooger track to create a fat, solid composite bass sound. The aux track becomes the bass master track. Finally, EQ and compress that aux track to fine-tune the bass sound to taste. You can also use the same tip on kick drums.

Figure 5.3
Bomb Factory Moogerfooger
Lo-Pass Filter plug-in (courtesy of
Bomb Factory).

▶ With Hip-Hop music, the bass tends to be a "feel" bass with a lot of information in the 30–60Hz range. Many Hip-Hop records raise the low-frequency target area slightly higher to the 70–100Hz range and elongate the duration to create the illusion that there is a lot of bass information so that it can sound full on smaller monitors. Be careful not to over-EQ, though. Clubs and cars with huge bass drivers are already hyped in this frequency range.

▶ With Rock bass, the idea is to create an aggressive in-your-face bass sound. For this, you focus mainly on the amp sound. Boost anywhere between 50–100Hz for the bottom end, dip between 400–800Hz to allow the guitars and vocal to have more room to speak musically, and boost between 1.5–2.5kHz for midrange. Be aware that mixing the DI sound with the amp sound can cause phasing problems in the midrange.

FOR FATTER GUITARS

▶ Boost midrange a lot (9dB or so), and sweep the frequencies until you hear the range where the guitar sounds thick but yet still bright enough to cut through. Then back the boost down to about +4 or so until the guitar cuts through the mix without being too bright.

Don Smith: *I use EQ different from some people. I don't just use it to brighten or fatten something up; I use it to make an instrument feel better. Like on a guitar, making sure that all the strings on a guitar can be heard. Instead of just brightening up the high strings and adding mud to the low strings, I may look for a certain chord to hear more of the A string. If the D string is missing in a chord, I like to EQ and boost it way up to +8 or +10 and then just dial through the different frequencies until I hear what they're doing to the guitar. So I'm trying to make things more balanced in the way they lay with other instruments.*

▶ Above 10kHz on guitars accentuates finger noise and tiny string movements. 5k–8k gives the guitar more cut. 1k to 5k gives the guitar more presence.

▶ Consider filtering the guitar. If you leave too much low end in a distorted electric guitar, it competes with the rhythm section, and much above 8k competes with the cymbals.

Benny Faccone: *For guitars, usually 1.5k gives it that present kind of sound. Pianos and keyboards vary so much that it all depends on how it feels in the track.*

FOR VOCALS
Boost a little 125 to 250Hz to accentuate the voice fundamental and make it more "chesty" sounding. 2 to 4kHz accentuates the consonants and makes the vocal seem closer to the listener.

Ed Seay: *On a vocal, sometimes I think, "Does this vocal need a diet plan? Does he need to lose some flab down there?" Or sometimes we need some weight on this guy, so let's add some 300 cycles and make him sound a little more important.*

Dave Pensado: *I think of EQ as an effect much the same way you would add chorus or reverb to a particular instrument or vocal. Like, I might have a vocal where I think it's really EQed nicely, and then I'll add a little more 3k just to get it to bite a* *little more. Then it just makes me feel like the singer was trying harder, and it brings out a little bit of passion in his or her voice. So I tend to be most effective when I do the standard equalizing, then take it to the next level, thinking of it as an effect.*

Benny Faccone: *For vocals, it really depends if it's male or female. If they sing really low, I don't add as much bottom end. Usually I always take some off at about 20Hz to get rid of rumble. But anything on up, it really all depends on the singer. I might add a little bit in the 4–6k range in there.*

CHAPTER 6

Element 4: Dimension—Adding Effects

The fourth element of a mix is *dimension*, which is the ambient field where the track or tracks sit. Dimension can be captured while recording but usually has to be created or enhanced when mixing by adding effects such as reverb, delay, or any of the modulated delays such as chorusing or flanging. Dimension might be something as simple as re-creating an acoustic environment, but it also could be the process of adding width or depth to a track or trying to spruce up a boring sound.

Actually, there are really four reasons why a mixer would add dimension to a track:

- **To Create an Aural Space**

- **To Add Excitement**

Joe Chiccarelli: *I try to start out with a flat track, then find the tracks that are boring and add some personality to them.*

- **To Make a Track Sound Bigger, Wider, or Deeper**

Lee DeCarlo: *Everything has to be bigger always. Now, a lot of times I'll do stuff with no effects on it whatsoever, but I don't particularly like it. Effects are makeup. It's cosmetic surgery. I can take a very great song by a very great band and mix it with no effects on it at all and it'll sound good, and I can take the same song and mix it with effects and it'll sound fantastic! That's what effects are for. It's just makeup.*

- **To Move a Track Back in the Mix (Give the Impression It's Farther Away)**

Dave Pensado: *The way I think of it is the pan knob places you left to right, while the effects tend to you place you front to rear. That's a general statement, but it's a good starting point. In other words, if you want the singer to sound like she's standing behind the snare drum, leave the snare drum dry and wet down the singer, and it'll sound like the singer is standing that far behind the snare drum. If you want the singer in front of the snare drum, leave him dry and wet down the snare drum.*

One of the reasons why we record elements in stereo is to capture the natural ambience (or dimension) of an instrument. Because we can't record everything this way due to track or storage limitations, we must create this aural space artificially.

Ed Seay: *Sometimes (I add effects for) depth and sometimes you just want it to sound a little bit more glamorous. Other times you just want it to sound appropriate. Well, appropriate to what? If it's an arena rock band, then all this room stuff is going to make it sound like they flunked out of the arena circuit and they're now doing small clubs. But if you got a band where that's more of an in-your-face, hard-driving thing, you want to hear the room sound.*

I've done records where I didn't use any effects or any verb, but quite often just a little can make a difference. You don't even have to hear it, but you can sense it when it goes away. It's just not quite as friendly sounding, not quite as warm. Obviously, an effect is an ear-catcher or something that can just kind of slap somebody and wake them up a little bit in case they're dozing off there.

Although there are no specific rules for dimension, there are some guidelines:

- **As a General Rule of Thumb, Try to Picture the Performer in an Acoustic Space and Then Realistically Re-Create That Space Around Him.**

This method usually saves some time over simply experimenting with different effects presets until something excites you (although if that method works best for you…). Also, the created acoustic space needn't be a natural one. In fact, as long as it fits the music, the more creative the better.

- **Smaller Reverbs or Short Delays Make Things Sound Bigger.**

Reverbs with decays under a second (usually much shorter than that) and delays under 100 milliseconds (again, usually a lot shorter than that) tend to create an acoustic space around a sound, especially if the reverb or delay is stereo.

Many times a reverb is used with the decay turned down as far as it will go. This setting is sometimes the most difficult for a digital reverb to reproduce, resulting in a metallic sound. If this occurs, you can try lengthening the decay time a little or trying a different preset and hope for a smoother, less tinny sound, or you can try another unit or plug-in that performs better under these conditions.

EQing Reverbs

From the early days of reverb chambers and plates, it's always been common to EQ the reverb returns, although the reasons for doing this have changed over the years. Back when plates and chambers were all that was available, usually some high-frequency EQ at 10 or 115kHz was added because the plates and chambers tended to sound dark and the reverb tended to get lost in the mix without the extra high-frequency energy.

Nowadays, EQ is added to reverb to help create some sonic layering. Here are some points to consider when EQing a reverb return. The type of reverb (digital, real plate, and so on) doesn't matter as much as how it is applied, and that depends on your ears and the song.

Equalization Tips for Reverbs and Delays

- To make an effect stick out, brighten it up.

- To make an effect blend in, darken it up. (Filter out the highs.)

- If the part is busy (like with drums), roll off the low end of the effect to make it fit.

- If the part is open, add the low end to the effect to fill in the space.

- If the source part is mono and panned hard to one side, make one side of the stereo effect brighter and the other darker. (Eddie Van Halen's guitar on the first two Van Halen albums comes to mind here.)

Sonic Layering of Effects

Sonic layering means that each instrument or element sits in its own ambient environment, and each environment is usually artificially created by effects. The idea here is that these sonic atmospheres don't clash with one another, just like with frequency ranges.

The following sidebar features some suggestions so that the sonic environments don't clash.

Layering Tips for Reverbs and Delays

- Layer reverbs by frequency with the longest being the brightest and the shortest being the darkest.

- Pan the reverbs any way other than hard left or right.

- Return the reverb in mono and pan accordingly. Reverbs don't need to be returned only in stereo to sound big.

- Get the bigness from reverbs and depth from delays, or vice versa.

- Use a bit of the longest reverb on all major elements of the track to tie all the environments together.

Although layering reverbs is all well and good, a couple of additional tips help in the final setup:

■ **Long Delays, Reverb Predelays, or Reverb Decay Push a Sound Farther Away If the Level of the Effect Is Loud Enough.**

As stated before, delays and predelays longer than 100ms (although 250 is where it really kicks in) are distinctly heard and begin to push the sound away from the listener. The trick between something sounding big or just distant is the level of the effect. When the decay or delay is short and the level loud, the track just sounds big. When the decay or delay is long and loud, the track just sounds far away.

Jon Gass: *I hardly ever use long halls or long reverbs. I use a lot of gear but it's usually for tight spaces. Sometimes in the mix it doesn't sound like I'm using anything but I might use 20 different reverb type boxes, maybe not set on reverbs, just to create more spaces. I think that helps with the layering and adding textures to things. Though you may not hear it in the mix, you can feel it.*

■ **If Delays Are Timed to the Tempo of the Track, They Add Depth Without Being Noticeable.**

Most engineers set the delay time to the tempo of the track. (See the "Calculating the Delay Time" sidebar on how to do this.) This makes the delay pulse with the music and adds a reverb type of environment to the sound. It also makes the delay seem to disappear as a discrete repeat but still adds a smoothing quality to the element.

Don Smith: *I usually start with the delays in time, whether it's 1/8 note or 1/4 note or dotted value or whatever. Sometimes on the drums I'll use delays very subtly. If you can hear them, then they're too loud, but if you turn them off, you definitely know they're gone. It adds a natural slap like in a room, so to speak, that maybe you won't hear but you feel. And, if the drums are dragging, you can speed the delays up just a nat so the drums feel like they're getting a lift. If they're rushing, you can do it the other way by slowing the delays so it feels like they're pulling the track back a bit.*

Delays are measured tempo-wise using musical notes in relation to the tempo of the track. In other words, if the song has a tempo of 120 beats per minute (bpm), then the length of time it takes a quarter note to play would be 1/2 second (60 seconds/120bpm = .5 seconds). Therefore, a quarter-note delay should be .5 seconds or 500 milliseconds (.5 × 1000ms per second), which is the way almost all delay devices are calibrated.

But 500ms might set the source track too far back in the mix. Divide that in half for an eighth-note delay (500ms/2 = 250ms). Divide in half again for a sixteenth-note delay (250ms/2 = 125ms). Divide again for a thirty-second-note delay (125/2 = 62.5ms, or rounded up to 63). That still might not be short enough for you, so divide again for a sixty-fourth-note delay (62.5/2 = 31.25, or rounded to 31ms). Again, this might not be short enough, so divide again for a one hundred twenty-eighth-note delay (31ms/2 = 15.625, rounded up to 16ms). This still might not be short enough, so divide again for a two hundred fifty-sixth-note delay if there is such a thing (16ms/2 = 8ms).

Such small increments like 8 and 16ms might not seem like much, but they're used all the time to make a sound bigger and wider. Even a short delay like this fits much more smoothly into the track if it's timed.

Bruce Swedien: *I think that's (early reflections of a sound) a much overlooked part of sound because there are no reverb devices that can generate that. It's very important. Early reflections will usually occur under 40 milliseconds. It's a fascinating part of sound.*

It's also possible (and sometimes even preferable) to use other note denominations such as triplets or dotted eighths, sixteenths, and so on. You can figure these out using the following formula:

Delay time × 1.5 = dotted value

Example: 500ms (quarter note 120bpm delay) × 1.5 = 750ms (dotted quarter note)

Delay time × .667 = triplet value

Example: 500ms (quarter note 120bpm delay) × .667 = 333.5ms (quarter note triplet)

As with the straight notes (quarter, eighths, and so on), you can continually divide the preceding values in half until you get the desired denomination.

Calculating the Delay Time

After engineers know the beats per minute (see the "Calculating the Delay Time" sidebar), they usually determine the delay time by looking at a chart that identifies the delay time at any bpm, a utility program or tap function found on some digital workstations, or by using a tap function found on many effects devices (like the Lexicon PCM 80 or 90). If none is available, engineers can still determine the delay time by using a little math.

60,000 (the number of milliseconds in a minute) / song tempo in bpm = quarter-note delay in milliseconds

You can determine all the other values from this by doing the following:

▶ Dividing by 2 for lower denominations

▶ Multiplying any of the above by 1.5 for dotted values

▶ Multiplying any of the above by 667 for triplet values

Calculating the Delay Time

1. Start a stopwatch when the song is playing and count 25 beats.

2. Stop the stopwatch on the twenty-fifth beat and multiply the time by 41.81.

The result is the delay time in milliseconds for a quarter-note delay

or

60,000 ÷ song tempo
(in beats per minute)

The result equals the delay time in milliseconds for a quarter-note delay.

The timing of the delays and reverbs is the missing element for most beginning mixers, but it makes a huge difference in how polished the final mix sounds. Here are some things to keep in mind:

- **If Delays Are Not Timed to the Tempo of the Track, They Stick Out.**

Sometimes you want to hear a delay distinctly, and the best way to do that is to make sure that the delay is *not* exactly timed to the track. Start by putting the delay in time with the track. Then slowly alter the timing until you achieve the desired effect.

- **Reverbs Work Better When They're Timed to the Tempo of the Track.**

Reverbs are timed to the track by triggering them off of a snare hit and adjusting the decay parameter so that the decay dies by the next snare hit. The idea is to make the decay "breathe" with the track.

The best way to achieve this is to make everything as big as possible at the shortest setting first and then get gradually longer until it's in time with the track.

The *predelay* of a reverb (the space between where the note of the source track dies off and the reverb begins) can change the sound of the reverb considerably and is usually timed to the tempo of the track. Back in the days of real plates and chambers, predelay was achieved by using a tape slap (see Figure 6.1). This was the natural echo that occurred when you played back off the repro head of a tape machine while recording onto it. The gap between the record and playback head gave a noticeable delay, and early engineers used this to their advantage. Because the early tape machines didn't have a way to vary their speed, it wasn't possible to time the delay to the tempo of the track. The best that you could do was to select a 7 1/2ips or 15ips tape slap. (Note that ips stands for inches per second.)

Figure 6.1
Predelay using tape slap.

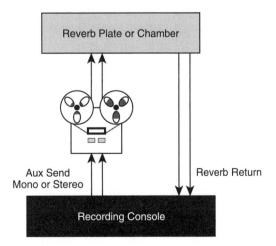

TAPE-BASED DELAY

Because Figures 6.1 refers to predelay coming from a tape machine, here are the delay times based on the commonly used tape speed:

7 1/2ips = 250ms

15ips = 125ms

Times are approximate because the gap between the record and playback head is slightly different on each model of tape machine. The speed, and therefore the delay time, can usually be changed by about 10 percent on the 1980s and 1990s tape machines.

Re-Amping

One of the ways that a natural environment is re-created is a process known as *re-amping*. This is accomplished by sending a signal of an already recorded track (say a guitar) back out to an amplifier in the studio and then miking it from a distance to capture the ambience of the room. It's even better if the ambience is recorded in stereo.

Bruce Swedien: *What I will do frequently when we're layering with synths and so on is to add some acoustics to the synth sounds. I think this helps in the layering in that the virtual direct sound of most synthesizers is not too interesting, so I'll send the sound out to the studio and use a coincident pair of mics to blend a little bit of acoustics back with the direct sound. Of course, it adds early reflections to the sound, which reverb devices can't do. That's the space before the onset of reverb where those early reflections occur.*

True Tape Flanging

Even though a multitude of digital effects boxes on the market have a flanging preset, almost nothing sounds like the real thing. *Flanging,* another name for an artificially induced comb filter, got its name from the fact that the effect is achieved by actually slowing down a reel of tape by holding your finger on the edge of the reel flange (the metal piece on each side of the tape that holds the reel together). The public first noticed the effect on The Small Faces 1966 hit "Itchycoo Park" (it's actually been reported to have been invented by Les Paul in the 1950s), but The Beatles, Jimi Hendrix, and many others of that time used it extensively.

THE VINTAGE METHOD

1. Play the recording to be processed on Deck 1.

2. Split Deck 1's output to Deck 2 and Deck 3.

3. Mix Deck 2's and Deck 3's outputs together and record on Deck 4 (the master).

4. Set Decks 1, 2, and 3 in Repro Monitor mode. Set Deck 4 in Input Monitor mode.

5. Start Decks 2, 3, and 4 in Record. Start Deck 1 in Play.

6. Put your finger on a flange of a supply reel on Deck 2 or 3 and flange away.

7. Splice the flanged master into the original master.

See Figure 6.2 for an example of the Vintage method.

Figure 6.2
Vintage tape flanging.

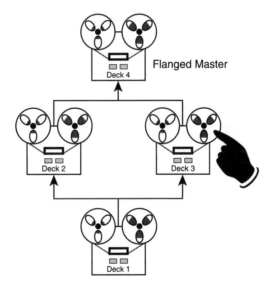

The flanged master is two generations away from the original master. The first generation is in the recording to Decks 2 and 3, and the second generation is the recording that saves your flanging work on Deck 4.

Remember that you need to drop the output level of the two machines 1.5dB each because you will add 3dB to the final level when you combine the signals of the two decks. Otherwise, the level jumps when you cut the flanged portion back into the original master.

THE DAW METHOD

Although it's really easy to dial in a flange plug-in on just about any digital workstation, here's a manual method that simulates the earlier tape machine methods that can work just as well or even better, depending on the program:

1. Make a copy of the region where you want the flange to occur, and copy it to another track.

2. Select the Pitch Shift process and dial in anywhere from –3 to –10 cents (if it's measured in semitones) on the copied track. Make sure the Time Correction is selected so that the selection to be flanged stays at the same length.

3. Nudge the flange track backward a millisecond or two.

4. Play both tracks together. You'll hear a flanging similar to the tape machine methods. For a deeper effect, increase the Pitch Shift effect.

Tricks and Tips

As in the previous "Tricks and Tips" sections of the book, the effect settings depend on the player, instrument, environment, and song. You should vary them to find what works best for your mix.

FOR FATTER LEAD OR BACKGROUND VOCALS

Use some chorusing (short modulated delays) panned hard left and right to fatten up the sound. Also, use different EQ and reverb settings on the delays. (Make sure you check the mix in mono to be sure that the delays aren't canceling.) Then ride the chorusing effect, adding and subtracting to it according to what sounds best.

FOR OUT-OF-TUNE VOCALS

► If you have something against Autotune and just want to cover up an out-of-tune vocal, use a stereo pitch shifter with one side tuned slightly high and the other tuned slightly low. Pan these left and right. The more out of tune the vocal, the more you might want to detune the pitch up and down. This does an effective job of taking the listener's attention off the sour notes.

► If a vocal effect is too prominent, bring up the delay or reverb to where you can hear it, and then back off the level 2dB. Then add a decibel of 800–1KHz to either the send or return of the delay unit.

▶ To get a dry vocal to jump out, use a bandwidth limited (about 400Hz to 2.5KHz) short delay or two in the neighborhood of 12ms to the left and 14ms to the right (or just a tad off-center, like 10 and 2 o'clock). Bring up the delay until you can hear it in the mix, and then back off of it to where you can't. Occasionally mute the returns to make sure they're still bringing the vocals out as they sit well into the rest of the balance. You can also time the delays to an eighth note on one side and a quarter note on the other.

▶ Pan a delayed signal behind the vocal and then send it to a harmonizer, detuning both sides a bit so that the delay sounds wide.

▶ Automate the delay or reverb return so that in the sparse parts of the arrangement—particularly in the beginning of the song—the vocal is dryer and more upfront and intimate, which also makes the effect more subtle.

▶ Try mixing various reverbs. Set up three for a typical mix: short, medium, and long. (The specifics of the actual lengths vary with the songs.) On a nonballad vocal, favor the short and medium over the long. The short (try a .3 to .6sec room or plate) one thickens the sound as you describe without a slap effect. Blending in the medium (1.2 to 1.6sec plate or hall) creates a smooth transition that is quite dense but still decays fairly fast. Add a little of the longer one (2 to 3+ second hall) for whatever degree of additional decay you want. The three combined sound like one thick, meaty reverb that sticks to the vocal and does not muddy it up with excess length and diffusion. It sounds good even when used sparingly in the modern relatively dry style. In a way, this approach is the opposite of adding predelay to a reverb.

FOR ELECTRONIC KEYBOARDS

You can achieve a nice delay effect that simulates a small room by using a stereo delay and setting the delay times to 211 and 222ms.

FOR FATTER GUITARS

▶ Delay or offset the guitar about 12ms (or whatever the tempo dictates) and hard pan both the guitar and delay. This sounds like two people playing perfectly in sync, but it sounds bigger and still keeps a nice hole in the middle for the vocals.

▶ Pan the guitar track and the delay to the center (or put your monitors in mono), and then slowly increase the delay time until it sounds bigger. Increase it a little more for good measure. You'll probably find the result to be 25–30ms.

▶ For years, LA session guitarists have automatically dialed up a stereo delay of 25ms on one side and 50ms on the other.

Allen Sides: *I'm a big fan of the RMX16 [see Figure 6.3], not for drums, but for vocals and guitars and stuff. I love the Non-Lin setting for guitars and things. Let's say that you had a couple of discrete guitars that were playing different lines and you try putting them in the middle and they get on top of each other. If you put them left and right, they're too discrete. The RMX Non-Lin set at 4 seconds with a 10-millisecond predelay and an API EQ on the send with about +4 at 12K shelf and −2 at 100Hz going into it does a wonderful job of creating a left/right effect, but it still spreads nicely. It works great for that.*

Figure 6.3
AMS RMX16 reverb.

▶ With a singer/acoustic guitar player, try to picture the performer in an acoustic space and then realistically re-create that space around him. This lends itself to a medium-sized room or a small plate, with perhaps a little more verb on the voice than the guitar. If the vocal is wet and the guitar dry (leakage aside), it's difficult for them to share a common acoustic space.

▶ Put a guitar on a stand in front of an amp, and tune it to an open variant of the key that your song is in. Send the original guitar track into the studio and into the amp where it will cause the second guitar to vibrate in resonance. Either use this with a direct box, or plug it into another amp in an isolation (sometimes just called iso) booth. The second guitar is not an exact double, but it can make the first guitar sound huge and ethereal if you place it right.

TOMMY LEE "THUNDER DRUMS"

For this to work, the bass drum has to sound tight to begin with and have a decent amount of beater present. Then gate all the drums, with the gate timed to the track. Set a reverb on the cathedral or large hall setting, and then add a little to each drum. Pan the reverb returns to sit the reverb behind each part of the kit.

ROBOT VOICE

Use sharp cutoff filters, slight pitch shift, and then deep flange to make the sound more metallic. Doubling is optional. Then, most importantly, use the voice as an external key to gate SMPTE code in time with the voice. Mix in the gated code gently.

EXPLODING SNARE

If the snare has been miked from the bottom, add a short slap from 50 to 125ms with a touch of feedback on the bottom head. Bring the slap back on a second channel. Using an aux, send the signal from both top and bottom snare mikes and the slap to a short reverb of a second or less (timed to the song). Adjusting the proportions, phase, and EQ lets you fit the snare into almost any situation.

CHAPTER 7

Element 5: Dynamics— Compression and Gating

In years past, the control of the volume envelope of a sound (*dynamics*) would not have been included as a necessary element of a great mix. In fact, dynamics control is still not a major part of Classical and Jazz mixing. But in today's modern music, the manipulation of dynamics plays a major role in the sound. In fact, just about nothing else can affect your mix as much and in so many ways as compression.

Jerry Finn: *I think that the sound of modern records today is compression. Audio purists talk about how crunchy compression and EQ [are], but if you listen to one of those Jazz or Blues records that are done by the audiophile labels, there's no way they could ever compete on modern radio even though they sound amazing. And unfortunately, all the phase shift and pumping and brightening and stuff that's imparted by EQ and compression is what modern records sound like. Every time I try to be a purist and go, "You know, I'm not gonna compress that," the band comes in and goes, "Why isn't that compressed?"*

Dynamics Controllers

Dynamics are controlled by the use of compression, limiting, de-essing, and gating. For those of you new to mixing or for those who need a review or clarification, here's a brief description of each. See the Glossary or any number of recording texts for more complete information.

Compression

Compression is an automated level control using the input signal to determine the output level. You set compression by using the Threshold and Ratio controls.

Figure 7.1
*Precision Limiter (courtesy of
Universal Audio).*

Compressors work on the principle of gain ratio, which is measured on the basis of input level to output level. (See Figure 7.1.) This means that for every 4dB that goes into the compressor, 1dB will come out, for a ratio of 4 to 1 or 4:1. If a gain ratio of 8:1 is set, then for every 8dB that goes into the unit, only 1 will come out of the output. Although this could apply to the entire signal regardless of level, a compressor is usually not set up that way. A Threshold control determines at what signal level the compressor will begin to operate. Therefore, threshold and ratio are interrelated, and one affects the way the other works. Some compressors (like LA2-As and UREI LA-3s—see Figures 7.2 and 7.3) have a fixed ratio, but on most units, the control is variable.

Figure 7.2
*Universal Audio LA2-A (courtesy of
Universal Audio).*

Figure 7.3
*UREI LA-3 (courtesy of Universal
Audio).*

Most compressors also have attack and release parameters. These controls determine how fast or slow the compressor reacts to the beginning (attack) and end (release) of the signal. Many compressors have an Auto mode that sets the attack and release in relation to the dynamics of the signal. Although Auto works relatively well, it still doesn't allow for the precise settings required by certain source material. Some compressors (like the dbx 160 series—see Figure 7.4) have a fixed attack and release, which gives it a particular sound.

Figure 7.4
dbx 160x compressor.

When a compressor operates, it decreases the gain of the signal, so there is another control called Make-Up Gain or Output that allows the signal to be boosted back up to its original level or beyond.

Most compressors also have an additional input and output called a sidechain, which is an input and output back into a compressor for connecting other signal processors to it. The connected processor only gets the signal when the compressor exceeds threshold and begins to compress. Sidechains are often connected to EQs to make a de-esser, which softens the loud *SSS* and *PPP* sounds from a vocalist when he exceeds the compressor's threshold. But you can connect delays, reverb, or anything you want to sidechain for unusual, program level-dependent effects. Sidechains are not needed for typical compressor operations, so many manufacturers don't include sidechain connectors. See Figure 7.5.

Figure 7.5
Illustration courtesy of Alesis Studio Electronics.

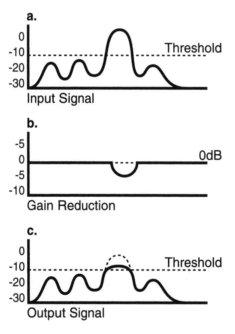

Diagram A shows an input signal before compression.

Diagram B shows what the compressor does—turning down the volume when your signal crosses the threshold.

Diagram C shows the new output level. (The original signal is shown as a dotted line.)

Limiting

You can use the same box to change compression and limiting. The difference is how the parameters are set. Any time you set the compression ratio to 10:1 or more, the result is considered *limiting*. A limiter is essentially a brick wall for level, allowing the signal to get only to a certain point and little more. Think of it like a governor that's sometimes used on trucks to make sure that they don't go over the speed limit. After you hit 65 mph (or whatever the speed limit in your state is), no matter how much more you depress the gas pedal, you won't go faster. It's the same with a limiter. When you hit the predetermined level, no matter how much you try to go beyond it, the level pretty much stays the same.

Limiting is usually used in sound reinforcement for speaker protection. (There are some limiters on powered studio monitors, too.) It's not used much in mixing, with the following exception. Most modern digital limiters (either hardware or software) have a function known as *look ahead* that allows the detector circuitry to look at the signal a millisecond or two before it hits the limiter. This means that the limiter acts extremely fast and just about eliminates overshoot of the predetermined level, which can be a problem with analog limiters (refer to Figure 7.1).

Many engineers who feel that the bass guitar is the anchor for the song want the bass to have as little dynamic range as possible. In this case, limiting the bass by 3 to 6dB (depending on the song) with a ratio of 10:1, 20:1, or even higher will achieve that.

De-Essing

One of the major problems when tracking vocals is a predominance of *S*s that comes from a combination of mic technique, the mic used (usually a condenser), and mostly from the use of severe compression or limiting. Sometimes this isn't much of an issue until it's time to mix, when a compressor is put on the vocal to even out the level and all of the sudden every *S* from the singer is so loud that it takes your head off. This effect is what's known as *sibilance*. As you can imagine, it's undesirable.

You can combat sibilance with a *de-esser*, which is a unit that compresses just the *S* frequencies, which are between 4 and 6kHz.

A de-esser can be made up of a compressor and equalizer plugged into the sidechain as stated earlier, or it can be a dedicated unit designed just for this purpose. The de-esser usually only has two controls: Threshold and Frequency. (See Figure 7.6.) The Threshold control is similar to that on a compressor/limiter in that it sets the level when the de-essing process begins. The Frequency control allows you to fine-tune exactly the frequency where the *Ss* stick out.

Figure 7.6
dbx 902 de-esser.

Gating

Although gates are not used nearly as much in the studio now that digital workstations and console automation are so prevalent, they are still used both in the studio and in sound reinforcement. A *gate* (like the one shown in Figure 7.7) keeps a signal turned off until it reaches a predetermined threshold level. Then the gate opens and lets the sound through. You can set the gate to turn the sound completely off when it drops below the threshold, or you can just lower the level a predetermined amount. Depending on the situation, turning the level down a bit sounds more natural than turning it completely off, although completely turning the sound off can be a great effect in the right situation.

Figure 7.7
Drawmer 201 Expander/Gate
(courtesy Drawmer Electronics).

You usually use a gate (sometimes called a *noise gate* or *expander*) to cover up some problems on a track, such as noises, buzzes, coughs, or other low-level noises off-mic. On loud guitar tracks, for instance, you can use a gate to effectively eliminate amplifier noise when the guitar player is not playing. On drums, you can use gates to turn off the leakage from the tom mics because they tend to muddy up the other drum tracks. Or you can use a gate to tighten up the sound of a floppy kick drum by decreasing the after-ring.

In addition, expander/gates can have a sidechain, or just an additional input called a *key* or *trigger* input, which allows the gate to open when triggered from another instrument, channel, or processor. This can be really useful, as you'll see in the "Tricks and Tips" section at the end of this chapter.

Some expander/gates have a setting called *duck* mode. This is actually another use for the sidechain, but this time the gate stays open until it sees a signal on the key/trigger input and lowers the level of the gate. An example of this occurs in an airport when you hear music over the sound system that is decreased automatically (or ducked) when an announcement comes on.

Just like compressors, modern hardware gates are fast, but plug-ins can be designed so that the sidechain "looks" at the signal a millisecond or two before it arrives at the gate's main input, allowing the gate to start opening just before the transient arrives. This look-ahead facility is only an advantage when dealing with sounds that have a fast attack, so it is usually switchable or variable when it is provided.

Why Add Compression?

If there is one major difference between the sound of a demo or semipro recording and a finished professional mix, it's the use of compression. As a matter of fact, the difference between one engineer's sound and another's is more often than not his use of compression.

George Massenburg: *The big difference between engineers today is the use of the compressor. At one time or another I tried to compress everything, because I was building a compressor and I wanted to see how it did on every instrument. I'm a little off on compression now because there are so many people that overuse it. Everything is squeezed to death.*

There are two reasons to add compression to a track or mix: to control the dynamics, or to add an effect.

COMPRESSION TO CONTROL DYNAMICS
Controlling dynamics means keeping the level of the sound even. In other words, it refers to lifting the level of the soft passages and lowering the level of the loud ones so that there is not much difference between them.

Here are a few instances where this would be useful:

▶ **On a bass guitar:** Most basses inherently have certain notes that are louder than others and some that are softer than others. Compression evens out these differences.

▶ **On a lead vocal:** Most singers can't sing every word or line at the same level, so some words get buried as a result. Compression allows you to hear every word.

▶ **On a kick or snare drum:** Sometimes a drummer doesn't hit every beat with the same intensity. Compression can make all hits sound the same.

When controlling dynamics, a small amount of compression (2 to 4dB or so at a 2:1 to 4:1 ratio) is usually used to limit the peaks of the signal.

Benny Faccone: *I like to compress everything just to keep it smooth and controlled, not to get rid of the dynamics. Usually I use around a 4:1 ratio on pretty much everything I do. Sometimes on guitars I go to 8:1. On the kick and the snare, I try not to hit it too hard because the snare really darkens up. It's more for control, to keep it consistent. On the bass, I hit that a little harder, just to push it up front a little more. Everything else is for control more than sticking it right up in your face.*

COMPRESSION AS AN EFFECT

Compression can radically change the sound of a track. A track that is compressed with the right unit and with the correct settings can seem closer and have more aggression and excitement. You can modify the volume envelope of a sound to have more or less attack, which can make it sound punchy, or a longer decay, to make it sound fatter.

Andy Johns: *I use compression because it's the only way that you can truly modify a sound because whatever the most predominant frequency is, the more you compress it, the more predominate that frequency will be. Suppose the predominate frequencies are 1 to 3k. Put a compressor on it, and the bottom end goes away, the top end disappears, and you're left with "Ehhhh" [makes a nasal sound]. So for me, compressors can modify the sound more than anything else. If it's a bass guitar, you put the compressor before your EQ, because if you do it the other way around, you'll lose the top and mids when the compressor emphasizes the spot that you EQed. If you compress it first [and] then add bottom, then you're gonna hear it better.*

The New York Compression Trick (Parallel Compression)

One of the little tricks that seem to set New York mixers apart from everyone else is something I call the *New York Compression Trick*. It seems like every mixer who's ever mixed in New York City comes away with this maneuver. Even if you don't mix in NYC, after you try it, you just might find yourself using this trick all the time because it is indeed a useful method to make a rhythm section rock.

Here's the trick:

1. Buss the drums, and maybe even the bass, to a stereo compressor.

2. Hit the compressor fairly hard—at least 10dB or more if it sounds good.

3. Return the output of the compressor to a pair of fader inputs on the console or two additional channels in your DAW.

4. Add a pretty good amount of high end (6 to 10dB at 10kHz or so) and low end (6 to 10dB at 100Hz or so) to the compressed signal.

5.   Then bring up the fader levels of the compressor until it's tucked just under the present rhythm section mix to where you can just hear it.

The rhythm section then sounds bigger and more controlled without sounding overly compressed.

Joe Chiccarelli: *What I will do a lot is buss my drums to another stereo compressor, usually a Joe Meek SC2, and blend that in just under the uncompressed signal. Sometimes what I'll do if everything sounds good but the bass and kick drum aren't locked together or big enough to glue the record together, I'll take the kick and bass and buss them together to a separate compressor, squish that a fair amount, and blend it back in. I'll add a little bottom end to that if the record still isn't big enough on the bottom. This helps fit the bass and kick lower on the record and gets it out of the way of the vocal.*

Compression on Individual Instruments

In these days with consoles that contain compressors on every channel, it's common for at least a small amount of compression to be used on every instrument (depending on the music, of course). Once again, compression is used on individual instruments to either control the dynamic range or as an effect.

Ed Seay: *To me, the key to compression is that it makes the instrument sound like it's being turned up, not being turned down. If you choose the wrong compressor or you use it the wrong way, then your stuff can sound like it's always going away from you. If you use the correct compressor for the job, you can make it sound like, "Man, these guys are coming at you." It's very active and aggressive.*

John X: *I use it a lot. Not always in great amounts, but I tend to try to get some handle on the peaks. Loops I rarely mess with. If somebody's got a loop and a certain groove that they like, I almost always leave those things alone because they start getting real squirrelly if you mess with them. All of a sudden the groove can change radically. Anything else, I don't mind slammin' the hell out of as long as it sounds the way I want it to sound. I don't even have a rule about it.*

Compression on the Mix Buss

Along with compressing individual tracks, many engineers place a stereo compressor across the mix buss to affect the entire mix. Originally this came about when artists began asking why their mixes sounded different in the studio from what they heard on the radio or when their record (it was still vinyl in those days) came from the pressing plant. Indeed, the radio and record sounded different because an additional round or two of compression was added in both mastering and broadcast. To simulate what this would sound like, mixing engineers began to add a touch of compression across the mix buss. The problem was that everybody liked it, so the majority of records now have at least a few decibels of compression added to the stereo mix despite the fact that it will probably be recompressed at mastering and yet again if played on the radio or television.

Joe Chiccarelli: *Compression is like this drug that you can't get enough of. You squish things, and it feels great and it sounds exciting, but the next day you come back and it's like the morning after and you're saying, "Oh God, it's too much." So I've been trying to really back it off, especially with stereo buss compression.*

In the case of buss compressors, not all are up to the task. Because only 2 or 3dB of compression might be all that's added (although it can be a lot more), the compressor actually adds an intangible sonic quality. Current favorites are the Fairchild 670 (at a hefty $25,000 each or so, and it's mono—see Figure 7.8), the Manely Vari-mu (see Figure 7.9), and the Neve 33609 (see Figure 7.10).

Figure 7.8
Fairchild 670 compressor (long out of production—courtesy of Universal Audio).

Figure 7.9
Manely Vari-mu compressor (courtesy of Manely Labs).

Figure 7.10
Neve 33609 (Courtesy Neve).

Don Smith: *Generally, the stereo buss itself will go through a Fairchild 670 (serial #7). Sometimes I'll use a Neve 33609 depending on the song. I don't use much; only a dB or 2. There's no rule about it. I'll start with it just on with no threshold just to hear it.*

The SSL Mix Buss Compressor

The sound of many (some say the majority of) records in the 1980s and 1990s comes from the sound of the built-in mix buss compressor on an SSL console (see Figure 7.11). This is an aggressive compressor with a distinct sonic signature. Some have even gone so far as to call the compressor In button (meaning in the signal path) the "good" button because it makes everything sound better.

Figure 7.11
SSL Buss Compressor plug-in
(courtesy KS Waves).

If you get a chance to work on an SSL (any vintage—they all have a mix buss compressor) or the outboard rack-mount version and knock-off Alan Smart, here's the time-honored settings to use as a starting point.

Typical SSL Buss Compressor Settings

Attack: All the way slow

Release: All the way fast

Ratio: 4:1

Threshold: To taste

Kevin Killen: *I tend to be quite modest on compression because my rationale is that you can always add more but you can never take it off. Since it will probably be applied at a later point during mastering and broadcast, I tend to err on the side of caution.*

Since SSLs hit the marketplace, I know what a temptation it is to set up the quad buss compressor even before you start your mix. I tried that for a while, but I found out that I didn't like the way it sounded. What I came up with instead was almost like sidechain compression where you take a couple of groups on the console and you assign various instruments to them, and use a couple of compressors across the buss and mix it in, almost as an effect, instead of using compressors across the inserts. You actually get a sense that there is some compression, yet you can ride the compression throughout the song, so if there's a section where you really want to hear it, like in the chorus, you can ride the faders up.

Setting the Compressor

In most modern music, you use compressors to make the sound punchy and in your face. The trick to getting the punch out of a compressor is to let the attacks through and play with the release to elongate the sound. Fast attack times reduce the punchiness of a signal, whereas slow release times make the compressor pump out of time with the music.

Because the timing of the attack and release is so important, here are a few steps to help set it up. Assuming that you have some kind of constant meter in the song, you can use the snare drum to set up the attack and release parameters. This method works the same for other instruments.

1. Start with the slowest attack and fastest release settings on the compressor.

2. Turn the attack faster until the instrument (snare) begins to dull. Stop at that point.

3. Adjust the release time so that after the snare hit, the volume goes back to 90–100 percent normal by the next snare beat.

4. Add the rest of the mix back in and listen. Make slight adjustments to the attack and release times as needed.

The idea is to make the compressor breathe in time with the song.

Lee DeCarlo: *I just get the bass and drums so they just start to pump to where you can actually hear them breathing in and out with the tempo of the song. What I'll do is put the drums and bass in a limiter and just crush the hell out of it. Then*

I'll play with the release and the attack times until I can actually make that limiter pump in time with the music. So when the drummer hits the snare, it sucks down and you get a good crest on it, and when he lets go of the snare, the ambience of the bass and the drums suck and shoot back up again. You can actually hear a [breathing sound] going on that was never there before. But it was there—it's just that you're augmenting it by using that limiter.

Jerry Finn: *I would say 10 or 12dB and at a ratio anywhere from like 4:1 to 8:1. My compression technique is something I actually learned from Ed Cherney. He was telling me about compressing the stereo buss when I was assisting him, but I use the same technique on everything. I set the attack as slow as possible and the release as fast as possible so all the transients are getting through and the initial punch is still there, but it releases instantly when the signal drops below threshold. I think that's a lot of the sound of my mixes. It keeps things kinda popping the whole time. Also, you can compress things a little bit more and not have it be as audible.*

AMOUNT OF COMPRESSION

The amount of compression you add is usually to taste, but generally speaking, the more compression, the greater the effect. Less compression (6dB or less) is more for controlling dynamics than for the sonic quality. It is common for radical amounts of compression to be used. 15 or 20dB is routinely used for electric guitars, room mics, drums, and even vocals. As with most everything else, it depends on the song.

Nathaniel Kunkel: *There are times when there's singing when they're not in compression at all, but if my limiter hits 15 or 20dB of compression and I don't hear it, I don't think about it for an instant more.*

Tricks and Tips

As in the previous "Tricks and Tips" sections of the book, the dynamics settings depend on the player, instrument, environment, and song. Vary them to find what works best for your mix.

FOR SNARE

► It's often useful to gate the effects send on the snare so it only triggers with forceful hits. Send the snare direct out of its channel to another channel on the board and gate this new channel. This gated channel generally is not sent to the main mix, but it can be. You can then EQ the gated channel and send it to a reverb or effects unit. By adjusting the threshold, you can more easily control the signal sent to the effects unit. This simple technique allows a different effect to be placed on the snare during harder hits and prevents leakage to the effect during things such as tom hits and kick drum beats.

To avoid sending high-hat bleed from the snare into a reverb, gate only the signal going to the reverb and leave the actual snare track ungated.

▶ To make the snare drum sound bigger, gate either room ambience or reverb and trigger it from the snare. (Send the snare signal to the trigger/key input of the gate.)

▶ To compress the snare drum to get more sustain, bring up the snare on two tracks—one for the attack sound and another to gate the snare. Then compress the snare with a fast attack and fast release time.

▶ To remove snare leakage from the overheads without making the hi-hat sound too ambient, compress the overhead mics and key them from the snare by sending the snare signal into the sidechain input of the overhead compressor.

▶ Instead of adding more high-end EQ to the snare, try compressing it instead. This allows you to elongate the snare drum's duration and create the illusion that it is brighter.

Ed Stasium: *What I do a lot is take a snare drum and go through an LA-2, just totally compress it, and then crank up the output so it's totally distorted and edge it in a little bit behind the actual drum. You don't notice the distortion on the track, but it adds a lot of tone in the snare, especially when it goes [makes an exploding sound]. Actually, something I've done for the last 20 years is to always split the kick drum and snare drum on a mult and take the second output into a Pultec (see Figure 7.12) into a dbx160VU and into a Drawmer 201 gate. Then I pretty much overemphasize the EQ and compression on that track and use it in combination with the original track.*

Figure 7.12
Pultec Equalizer plug-in (courtesy of Universal Audio).

FOR DRUMS

▶ When gating drums, set the Range control so that it attenuates the signal only about 10 or 20dB. This lets some of the natural ambience remain and prevents the drums from sounding choked.

► 808 kicks are inherently mushy, especially if you want to add low end to them. Multing the kick, compressing it with a fast attack and release compressor, and mixing the compressed signal back in with the original can help punch it up.

► To make the rhythm section feel tighter, feed the bass through a gate with only 2 or 3dB of attenuation when the gate is closed. Trigger the gate from the kick drum so that the bass is slightly louder on each kick drum beat.

When the groove doesn't quite lock or the bass player is playing on top of the beat and the drummer is lying back, put a gate on the bass and key it from the kick drum. The bass only plays when the kick drum is played, so the rhythm section will sound incredibly tight. Set the sustain and release so that they sound more natural and less staccato because the kick is a transient instrument and the bass is not—or leave it staccato if that works well.

► You can also use the previous technique to get more space and rhythm in a big chorus by gating the rhythm guitar track keyed from the hi-hat. It also works for synth parts where you can turn a pad into a rhythmic idea.

FOR PIANO

If you liked the early Elton John piano sound, put the piano into two LA-2As or similar compressors and compress the signal at least 10dB. Then put the output into two Pultecs or similar equalizers. Push 14kHz all the way up and set 100Hz to about 5. The effect should be a shimmering sound. The chords hold and seem to chorus.

FOR VOCALS

► A good starting point for a lead vocal is a 4:1 ratio, medium attack and release, and the threshold set for about 4 to 6dB of gain reduction.

Don Smith: *I'll experiment with 3 or 4 compressors on a vocal. I've got a mono Fairchild to Neve's to maybe even a dbx 160 with 10dB of compression to make the vocal just punch through the track.*

► Use the 1176 (hardware or plug-in—Figure 7.13) on fast attack (clockwise), release set to medium (5), and 8 or 12:1 just to clip the peaks 4 to 5dB. Then feed it to an LA2 (again, hardware or software) just for gentle gain riding of 2 to 3dB if possible. This is great for singers, where a single compressor or limiter isn't enough.

As an option to the previous trick, if you have access to another 1176 or have enough DSP to insert a second one, set the first one on fastest attack and an 8:1 ratio, and set the second on a slightly slower attack and a 4:1 ratio. With both set for about 10dB of compression, you'll have a silky, smooth, in-your-face vocal.

Figure 7.13
UREI 1176 compressor/limiter (courtesy of Universal Audio).

▶ To make your compressor into a de-esser:

1. Insert the compressor on the vocal as usual.

2. Attach an EQ to the sidechain in and out.

3. Press the Key Listen switch on the compressor (assuming you have one).

4. Set it for very high Q and maximum boost, and then sweep through the 3 to 5kHz range until you hear the Ss at their loudest level. With a Key Listen, make it sound as nasty as possible. These are the frequencies you're going to smooth out, and what you're sending to the sidechain input isn't in the signal path. (Just don't forget to turn Key Listen off.) If you don't have a Key Listen, vary the frequencies until you tame the Ss.

5. Set the compressor to a ratio of at least 4:1.

As a slight variation on the previous trick, delay the main signal a few milliseconds relative to the sidechain. That gives the compressor time to lower the gain before the Ss appear.

▶ For tighter background vocals, patch the best-phrased harmony line into the key insert of a gate across a stereo submix of the harmonies. This ensures that all the vocal entrances and exits remain tight.

▶ If the room was recorded with your drum tracks, compress the room mics hard (10 to 20dB) to increase the room sound. Most of the time that will sound tighter and better than any outboard verb, unless the room doesn't sound that great to begin with.

FOR BASS

▶ Using a dbx 160X set at a ratio of infinity:1 (the highest ratio), set the threshold for a 3 or 4dB reduction. This keeps the bass solid and unmoving in the mix.

▶ With a bass track that has no definition to the notes, try an 1176 with the attack set to around noon and the release set to around 3 or 4 o'clock. With an 8:1 ratio and a fair amount of gain reduction, this helps put a front end on the notes that should have articulated when the part was played.

▶ With a bass track where the notes don't sustain long enough, you can often create something resembling sustain with a long (more clockwise) release on an 1176.

▶ If a bass player is using a pick, it can create uncontrollable audio transients in the midrange, so you might need to limit the transients before you compress. The attack and release times have to be fast during limiting and medium to slow for compression. Sometimes you might need to put in a multiband compressor across the bass to target specific frequency areas.

FOR GUITAR

▶ Higher ratios of compression around 8 or 10:1 sometimes work well, with the threshold set so that the guitar cuts through the track. Time the attack and release to the pulse of the song.

Don Smith: *I may go 20:1 on a (UREI) 1176 with 20dB of compression on a guitar part as an effect. In general, if it's well recorded, I'll do it just lightly for peaks here and there.*

▶ Here's a trick to get guitars sounding like they're 40 feet wide but stay out of the way of the vocal. If a guitar has an ambient track, pan the ambience to follow the main sound. Then attach a compressor across the ambience tracks keyed off the lead vocal. When the lead vocal is present, the ambience goes away. When the lead vocal stops, the ambience comes back.

▶ Pan doubled guitars hard left and right. Patch the input of a compressor to an aux send and send a little of both guitars to it. Bring the output of the compressor back into the mixer panned to the center. When you spread out the guitars like this, they don't have to be as loud to have presence.

▶ If you notice that the guitar is getting lost in places, try compressing in the 2:1 to 4:1 range with medium attack and release times. This allows the rhythmic transients to go through unobstructed while raising the sustain resonance of the guitar.

▶ The idea is to have Rock guitars big and in your face. You can accomplish that by limiting the transients out of the signal with ratios 10:1 or higher. Make sure that the sustain parts of the signal return to unity gain.

CHAPTER 8

Element 6: Interest—The Key to Great (As Opposed to Merely Good) Mixes

Although having control of the previous five elements might be sufficient for many types of audio jobs and might be just fine to get a decent mix, most popular music requires a mix that can take it to another level. Although it's always easier with great tracks, solid arrangements, and spectacular playing, a great mix can take simply okay tracks and transform them into hit material so compelling that people can't get enough of them. That's been done on some of your all-time favorite songs.

Ed Seay: *The tough part, and the last stage of the mix, is the several hours it takes for me to make it sound emotional and urgent and exciting so that it's just not a song, it's a record. It's not making it just sound good; it's making it sound like an event. Sometimes that means juggling the instruments or the balances or adding some dynamics help. That's the last stage of when I mix, and that's the part that makes it different or special.*

How can we get to that point?

More than being just technically correct, a mix must be as interesting as a good movie. It must build to a climax while having points of tension and release to keep the listener subconsciously involved. Just as a film looks larger than life, a great mix must sound larger than real life. The passion and the emotion must be on a level where the listener is sucked in and forced to listen.

That brings us back to where we started.

> Figure out the direction of the song.
>
> Develop the groove and build it like a house.
>
> Find the most important element and emphasize it.

The Direction of the Song

The first thing that the mixer must do before delving headfirst into the mix is determine the direction of the song. That direction is determined by both the artist and the performances. For instance, if the song is folksy in nature, it probably won't need big, bombastic drums and long reverbs and delays. But if the artist is a loud arena rock band, you probably won't want a close intimate sound.

Although it's absolutely possible to change the direction of the song and have a hit (the dance version of Amy Grant's 1990's hit "Baby, Baby" comes to mind), usually a song works best with one artist only one way. A good example of this is Marvin Gaye's "Heard It Through the Grapevine," which has been a hit by many artists in innumerable styles. The direction of Creedence Clearwater is different from the direction of Gladys Knight and the Pips, yet it works equally well for both. The direction is a function of the artist and the performance.

Develop the Groove and Build It Like a House

All good music—regardless of whether it's Rock, Jazz, Classical, Rap, or some new space music that we haven't heard yet—has a strong groove.

> The *groove* is the pulse of the song and how the instruments dynamically breathe with it.

A common misconception of a groove is that it must have perfect time. A *groove* is created by tension against even time. This means that it doesn't have to be perfect, just even, and that not all the performances have to have the same amount of evenness. In fact, the groove feels stiff it it's too perfect. This is why perfect quantization of parts and lining every hit up in a workstation frequently takes the life out of a song. It's too perfect because there's no tension. It's lost its groove.

We usually think of the groove as coming from the rhythm section, especially the drums, but that's not always the case. In The Police's "Every

Breath You Take," the rhythm guitar establishes the groove, whereas in most songs from Motown's golden age by the Supremes, Temptations, and Four Tops, the groove was established by James Jamerson's bass.

The trick for the mixer is to find what instrument defines the groove and then build the rest of the mix around it.

Find the Most Important Element and Emphasize It

Equally as meaningful, and in some cases even more important than the groove, is finding whatever element is the most important to the song. In some cases (like Dance and Rap music), the most important element is the groove. Yet in other genres (like Country), the most important element is the lead vocal.

Even though the most important element is often the lead vocal, it doesn't have to be. The most important element could be a riff as in The Stone's "Satisfaction" and "Start Me Up" or the Rick James loop from Hammer's "Can't Touch This." The most important element is always the part that is so compelling that it forces you to listen to the song.

Whatever part is most important, the mixer must identify it and emphasize it in the mix so that the mix can be elevated to extraordinary.

Ed Seay: *I try to find what's important in the mix. I try to find out if the lead vocal is incredibly passionate, then make sure that the spotlight shines on that. Or if the acoustics are sitting there but they're not really driving the thing and they need to. If, for instance, the mix needs eighth notes, but they're going [sound effect] and it's not really pushing the mix, sometimes playing with compression on the acoustics or auditioning different kinds of compression [can] make it sound like, "Boy this guy was into it." Maybe pushing and pulling different instruments. Somebody's got to be back, and sometimes it's better when things are back and other things are farther up front. It's just basically playing with it and trying to put into it that undefinable thing that makes it exciting. Sometimes it means making sure your cymbals or your room mics are where you can actually feel the guy, or sometimes adding compression can be the answer to making the thing come alive. Sometimes hearing the guy breathe like the old Steve Miller records did. They had that [breathing]. With a little of that, you might say, "Man, he's working. I believe it." It's a little subconscious thing, but sometimes that can help.*

Like most other creative work that requires some divine inspiration for success, you can't underestimate talent and experience.

Monitoring

A mixer depends on his monitoring conditions and methods more than just about any other parameter. If the monitors don't work with the environment or if the mixer doesn't interact well with the monitors, all the other tips and techniques are for naught.

Basic Monitor Setup

One thing frequently overlooked when auditioning near-field monitors is placement of the monitors. This can make an enormous difference in the frequency balance and stereo field, and it's important to address it before you get into any serious listening. Here are a few things to experiment with before you settle on the exact placement.

CHECK THE DISTANCE BETWEEN THE MONITORS

If the monitors are too close together, the stereo field becomes smeared with no clear spatial definition. If the monitors are too far apart, the focal point or "sweet spot" is too far behind you, and you hear the left or the right side but not both together. A rule of thumb is that the speakers should be as far apart as the distance from the listening position. That is, if you are 4 feet away from the monitors, start by moving them 4 feet apart so that you make an equilateral triangle between you and the two monitors. (See Figure 9.1.) You can use a simple tape measure to get it close and adjust the monitors either in or out from there.

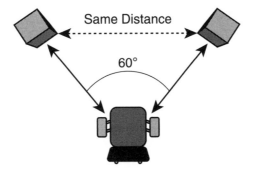

Figure 9.1
Set the monitors in an equilateral triangle.

Equilateral Triangle

CHECK THE ANGLE OF THE MONITORS

Improper angling causes smearing of the stereo field, as evidenced by a lack of instrument definition. Mixers determine the correct angle strictly by taste, with some preferring the monitors to be angled directly at their mixing position and others preferring the focal point (the point where the sound from the tweeters converges) anywhere from 3 to 5 feet behind them to eliminate some of the "hype" of the speakers.

To set the angle of the monitors, place them in the equilateral triangle fashion, as shown in Figure 9.1. A great trick for getting excellent left/right imaging is mounting a mirror over each tweeter and adjusting the speakers so that your face is clearly seen in both mirrors at the same time when you are in your mixing position.

CHECK THE MOUNTING OF THE MONITORS

Monitors that are mounted directly on top of a console meter bridge without decoupling are subject to comb filter effects, especially in the low end. That is, the sound travels through the console and the floor and reaches your ears before you hear the direct sound from the monitors through the air, causing phase cancellation. (The console and floor are denser than the air.) This can be more or less severe depending on whether the speakers are mounted directly on the metal meter bridge or are mounted on a piece of carpet or similar material covering the metal meter bridge (very popular). The best way to decouple the monitors is to use the same method you use when soffit-mounting your main monitors. If you set the near fields on a 1/2 or 3/4-inch piece of open cell neoprene (soft rubber), decoupling will no longer be an issue.

Instead of mounting the nearfields on the console, a better solution is to mount them on stands just directly behind the meter bridge. Not only does this improve the low-frequency decoupling, but it greatly decreases the unwanted reflections off the console.

CHECK THE SETTING OF THE MONITOR PARAMETERS

Many monitors are meant to be used in an upright position, yet users frequently lay them on their sides. This results in a variety of acoustic anomalies that deteriorate the sound. Also, with powered monitors, be sure that the parameter controls of both monitors are set correctly for the application and are the same on each.

CHECK THE POSITION OF THE TWEETERS

Most mixers prefer that the tweeters of a two- or three-way system are on the outside, thereby widening the stereo field. Occasionally, tweeters to the inside work but usually smear the stereo image. Experiment with both, however, because you never know.

CHECK THE CONSOLE

The angle of the console; the type of materials used for the panels, knobs, and switches; the type of paint; and the size and composition of the arm-rest all make a difference in the sound due to reflections causing phase cancellation. If the sound of the nearfields on top of the meter bridge is unacceptable, try moving the nearfields toward you with extenders or put them on stands behind the console. (Don't forget to decouple them.)

Mixing Volume

One of the greatest misconceptions about music mixers (especially the great ones) is that they mix at high volume levels. In fact, quite the opposite is generally true. Most mixers find that they get better balances that translate well to the real listening world by monitoring at conversation level (79dB SPL) or lower.

High SPL levels for long periods of time are generally not recommended for the following reasons:

▶ Exposure to high volume levels for long periods of time can cause long-term physical damage.

▶ High volume levels for long periods of time not only causes the onset of ear fatigue, but also general physical fatigue. This means that you might effectively be able to work only 6 hours instead of the normal 8 (or 10 or 12) that's possible with lower levels.

▶ The ear has different frequency response curves (remember the Fletcher-Munson curves?) at high volume levels that overcompensate on both the high and low frequencies. This means that your high volume mix generally sounds pretty limp when played at softer levels.

> ▶ Balances tend to blur at higher levels. What works at higher levels doesn't necessarily work when played softer. However, balances that are made at softer levels always work when played louder.

This isn't to say that you should do all mixing at the same level and all mixing should be soft. In fact, music mixers (as opposed to film, which always has a constant SPL level) tend to work at a variety of levels—up loud for a minute to check the low end and moderate while checking the EQ and effects. But the final balances are nearly always done quietly.

Don Smith: *I like to listen loud on the big speakers to get started, and occasionally thereafter, and most of the time at about 90dB. When the mix starts to come together, it comes way down, sometimes barely audible. I turn it down way low and walk around the room to hear everything.*

Allen Sides: *Generally speaking, when I put up the mix, I'll put it up at a fairly good level, maybe 105, and set all my track levels and get it punchy and fun sounding. And if I listen loud, it's only for very short periods of time. It's rare that I would ever play a track from beginning to end loud. I might listen to 20 seconds or 30 seconds of it here and there, but when I'm actually down to really detailing the balance, I'll monitor at a very modest level. I would say at a level that we could have a conversation and you could hear every word I said.*

Ed Seay: *I mix at different levels. I try not to mix too loud because it'll wear you down and fool your perspective. I don't find it extremely valuable to listen loud on big wall monitors very often. The only reason I'll go up there is to check bottom end.*

Sometimes it's very valuable to turn things down, but there's an up and down side to both. If you listen too soft, you'll add too much bass. If you listen too loud, you'll turn the lead vocals down too much. What I like to do is make it sound good on all three unrelated systems. Then it's got to relate to the rest of the world.

George Massenburg: *I'll monitor way loud to see what rocks. I'll monitor at a nominal level to get sounds together. Then I'll monitor about 5dB over background noise to hear all the elements into focus. If a mix works at 30dB SPL, 25dB SPL, it'll almost always work a lot louder. If you can hear everything at that low a level, then when you turn it up, you'll have a very even balance. That's the way to get everything in the same plane, by listening extremely low.*

Jon Gass: *Like the SSL up on one (the Control Room Monitor level control) is what I mix on most of the time. It's really quiet, but I can mix long and not get fatigued. Sure, I do the NS10 thing, and then towards the end of the mix I'll go really loud on the NS10s and do some adjusting, and I'll go extremely loud on the big ones and do some more adjusting just to fine-tune.*

Nathanial Kunkel: *I listen quietly as much as I can. It's hard to check kick drum level when it's quiet, so certainly you have to push it up every once in a while, but I fatigue pretty quickly when listening at loud levels. I can make better emotional and timbre decisions before I fatigue.*

Elliot Scheiner: *I'm still using NS10s for stereo and 5 of them for surround, and generally when I'm mixing I monitor at about 40dB. I just find that I can definitely hear the balances better at a lower level so I can hear if I've got a little too much or not enough of something. That comes from wanting to hear every instrument. If I can hear it when it's soft, then it's probably going to be there at any level. You don't beat yourself up, and I'd like to believe that I can still hear a little bit because I've monitored so softly for so long. I might go to 80 or 85 when I'm putting the kick and the bass in just to hear where they're sitting comparatively, but once I establish that, I'll go right down to 40 or so.*

David Pensado: *I usually listen to NS10s kind of medium, and Auratones I listen at the same volume you would listen to TV. I found that on the NS10s, in order for them to really work, it's best to have them stay at one level for most of the mix. Then near the end of the mix, check your levels and your EQ with the NS10s about 20% lower and again about 20% higher, and you'll make adjustments that you'll really be pleased with when you hear it on the radio. The big speakers I use mostly to show off for clients and to just have fun. I like to turn it up, and if my body is vibrating properly, then I'm happy with the low end. A lot of engineers use them to hype the client, but I also use them to hype myself! If I'm cranking and I'm not getting excited, then I just keep on working.*

Ken Hahn: *I personally monitor about as low as most people would accept. I tend to go that way because inevitably, if you get it sounding good at a low level, it just sounds that much better at higher levels. It sort of forces you to do a lot more manual gain riding at low level because otherwise stuff just doesn't poke through. I'm sort of doing my own form of manual compression, and I've found that usually works better than the other way around.*

Allen Sides: *Yeah, there's also a question of dryness versus liveness versus deadness in regards to monitor volume. Obviously when you turn it down, your ambiance determines how loud it sounds to you to some degree. And if you're monitoring at a loud level and it's very dry, it can be very impressive sounding. When you turn down, it might not be quite so full sounding, so obviously there's a balance there.*

Listening in Mono

Because sooner or later your mix will be played back in mono, it's best to check what will happen before you're surprised later. Listening in mono is a time-tested operation that allows the mixer to discern several things:

► Phase coherency

► Balances

► Panning

PHASE COHERENCY

When you combine a stereo mix into mono, any elements that are out of phase drop in level or completely cancel out. This could be because the left and right outputs are wired out of phase (pin 2 and pin 3 of the XLR connector are reversed), which is the worst-case scenario, or perhaps because an out-of-phase effect causes the lead vocal or solo to disappear. In any event, it's prudent to listen in mono once in a while just to make sure that a mono disaster isn't lurking in the wings.

BALANCES

Many engineers listen to their mix in mono strictly to balance elements because they feel that they hear the balance better this way. Listening in mono is also a great way to tell when an element is masking another.

Joe Chiccarelli: *I listen in mono an awful lot and find it's great for balances. You can easily tell if something's fighting.*

Andy Johns: *People don't listen in mono anymore, but that used to be the big test. It was harder to do, and you had to be a bloody expert to make it work. In the old days, we did mono mixes first then did a quick one for stereo. We'd spend 8 hours on the mono mix and half an hour on the stereo.*

PANNING

Although not many engineers are aware that they can improve their stereo panning while listening in mono, this is in fact a good way to achieve a level of precision not available in stereo.

Don Smith: *I check my panning in mono with one speaker, believe it or not. When you pan around in mono, all of a sudden you'll find that it's coming through now and you've found the space for it. If I want to find a place for the hi-hat, for instance, sometimes I'll go to mono and pan it around, and you'll find that it's really present all of a sudden, and that's the spot. When you start to pan around on all your drum mics in mono, you'll hear all the phase come together. When you go to stereo, it makes things a lot better.*

Choosing a Monitor

Which speaker is best for you to monitor on? Certainly there are plenty of choices, and there is no single favorite among the great mixers. Probably the closest to a standard we've ever had is the Yamaha NS-10M, closely followed by the Auratone. (See Figure 9.2.) Because NS10s are no longer made, they're becoming less and less of a standard. Auratones had fallen out of favor since their peak of popularity during the 1970s, but most mixers still use them as an additional reference (although sometimes only one in mono).

Figure 9.2
An Auratone after a session with too much low end.

THINGS TO LISTEN FOR IN A MONITOR

Even frequency balance: While listening to a piece of music that you know well, check to see if certain frequencies are exaggerated or attenuated. This is especially important in the cross-over area (usually about 1.5 to 2.5kHz). Listen to cymbals on the high end, vocals and guitars for the midrange, and bass and kick drum on the low end.

Frequency balance that stays the same at any level: The less often the frequency response changes as the level does (especially when playing softly), the better. In other words, the speaker should have roughly the same frequency balance when the level is soft as when it's loud.

High output level without distortion: Be sure that there's enough clean level for your needs. Many powered monitors have built-in limiters that stop the speaker or amplifier from distorting but also might keep the system from getting as loud as you find necessary.

The number of monitor references that are used is an important aspect to getting a mix right. Although a mixer might do most of his work on a single system, it's common to check the mix on at least two (maybe more) other sources. Usually this is the main soffit-mounted monitors, the nearfield monitors of choice (which might be NS10s), and an alternative, which could be Auratones, NS10s, or just about anything else. Couple that with the ever-present boom box, car stereo, or stereo in the lounge, and the average of all these systems should make for a good mix.

Before the trend turned toward powered monitors, many engineers also brought their own amplifiers to the studio. This is because the amp/

speaker combination is a delicate one, with each speaker having a much greater interdependence on the power source than most of us realize. In fact, the search for the perfect amplifier took almost as long as the search for the perfect monitor. All of this has dwindled in recent years, thanks to monitors with built-in amplifiers perfectly matched to its drivers.

Jerry Finn: *When I was an assistant, a lot of the engineers that I liked working with had Tannoy SRM10Bs. When I went independent, I searched high and low and finally found a pair. I carry those around with me wherever I go, as well as a Hafler Transnova amp, which gets frowned upon sometimes amongst the guys that are into the more hi-fi kind of thing. But I tried 20 amps, and that just sounded the best.*

Even though NS10s reside in just about every studio, there are two complete camps consisting of lovers who wouldn't mix without them and haters who never touch them. It would certainly be folly to use these speakers just because everyone else is (because they're not all using them, for one thing). In fact, it's not a good idea to use anything unless you're really in love with it. You'll have to listen to these monitors for countless hours, so you might as well like what you hear.

In my frequent speaker auditions for *EQ Magazine* over the course of five years, I've found that you can easily get used to just about any speaker if you use it enough and learn its strengths and weaknesses. It also helps to have a solid reference that you're sure of to compare the sound with. For instance, if you know how things sound in your car, adjust your mixes so they work when you play them there. I usually use mastering engineer Eddy Schreyer at Oasis Mastering as my reference. When I do a mix on a new set of speakers, he'll tell me, "You're off a dB at 5k, a dB and a half at 150, and –2 at 40." I'll then adjust accordingly.

Listening Tricks and Tips

Most everyone wants to hear what their mix sounds like on different speakers and in different environments to get a more consumer-oriented perspective. Here are some of the age-old standards:

► The car

► The boom box

► Through the control room door

Jon Gass: *One of my favorite ones is to turn on the vacuum cleaner and lay it up against the wall in the front of the room. Sounds a little strange, but I just kind of want to see if the mix is still cutting through at all.*

Andy Johns: *Obviously, the idea is to make it work on all systems. You listen on the big speakers, the NS10s, out in the car, plus your own speakers, then you go home and listen again. This is a lot of work, but it's the only way to go.*

Don Smith: *I mix a lot at my house now, where I sit outside a lot on my patio. If I mix in a studio with a lounge, I'll go in there with the control room door shut and listen like that. I definitely get away from the middle of the speakers as much as possible.*

Ed Seay: *What I'll do about an hour before printing the mix is prop open the control room door and walk down the hall or into the lounge where the music has to wind its way out the door. I find that very valuable because it's not like hitting mono on the console. It's like a true acoustic mono. It's real valuable to see if you hear all the parts, and it's real easy to be objective when you're not staring at the speakers and looking at the meters.*

Good television commercial producers use a similar technique: Flip to a single mono Auratone, lower the volume to just perceptible, and see if it still sounds like a record. Then raise the volume a tiny bit, walk out into the hall, and see if you still like it.

George Massenburg: *I'm a big one for the hallway. I hate cars. Through the control room doors is always an important thing for me, because I almost never do loud playbacks. I like listening around the corner and on a blaster.*

Joe Chiccarelli: *I'll walk out of the control room and listen to it right outside the door. It's interesting to hear what it sounds like through the crack in the door. Things pop out. Ghetto blasters are good things for sure as well.*

CHAPTER 10

The Master Mix

Gone are the days of manual mixing, where the hands of not only the engineer but the producer and all the band members manned a fader, a mute button, or a pan control to get the perfect mix. Gone are the days of massive amounts of takes of your mix to get your "keeper." Thanks to the digital workstation and the advanced state of console automation, the mix is (or at least it should be) perfect before it ever gets committed to hard disc, DAT, optical disc, analog tape, solid state memory, or any other format yet to be devised.

Regardless of the ultimate delivery method to the record label, mastering, and ultimately the public, the mixing engineer is faced with several decisions both right before and right after achieving a mix that lights up the speakers.

Competitive Level

As far back as the 1950s, mixers have strived to make their mixes hotter than their competitors. That's because if two songs are played back to back, listeners sometimes perceive the louder one as sounding better. But the delivery medium to the consumer determined the limitation of how loud a mix could actually be. In the days of vinyl records, if a mix was too loud, the stylus vibrated so much that it lifted out of the groove and the record skipped. When mixing too hot to analog tape, the sound began to softly distort and the high frequencies disappeared. When digital audio and CDs came along, any attempt to mix beyond 0dB Full Scale resulted in terrible clipping.

But over the years, mixes have become hotter in perceived level, mostly because of new digital technology that has resulted in better limiters. Today's digital look-ahead limiters make it easy to set a maximum level (usually at −.1 or −.2dB FS) and never worry about digital overs or distortion again.

That being said, raising the competitive level (the mix level that's as loud as your competitor's mix) used to be left to the mastering engineer. The mix engineer handed off an approved mix that was acceptable, and the level was raised from there, regardless of whether the ultimate delivery medium to the consumer was a record, cassette, CD, or DVD. Part of the voodoo of the mastering engineer was his ability to make your mix louder than you were able to.

But that doesn't cut it these days. Artists, producers, and A&R people want the mix to immediately sound not only like a record but also as loud as anything commercially released from the first rough mix onward. This is one of the reasons that the famous mix buss compressor on any SSL console became so popular. It was built like a typical mastering compressor to give your mix that radio sound as soon as you inserted it into the signal path.

Today, with many powerful plug-in compressor/limiters available, it's all too easy to raise the level of your mix as loud as it will go. However, just because you *can* do it doesn't mean that you *should*.

Hypercompression

Too much buss compression or over-limiting either when mixing or mastering results in what's become known as *hypercompression*. You should avoid hypercompression at all costs for the following reasons:

▶ It can't be undone later.

▶ It can suck the life out of a song, making it sound weaker instead of punchier.

▶ Lossy codecs (see the later section by the same title) like MP3 have a hard time encoding hypercompressed material and insert unwanted side effects as a result.

▶ Hypercompression leaves the mastering engineer no room to work.

A hypercompressed track has no dynamics, leaving it loud but lifeless and unexciting. On a DAW, it's a constant waveform that fills up the DAW region. Figure 10.1 shows how the levels have changed on recordings over the years.

Figure 10.1
From little compression to
hypercompression.

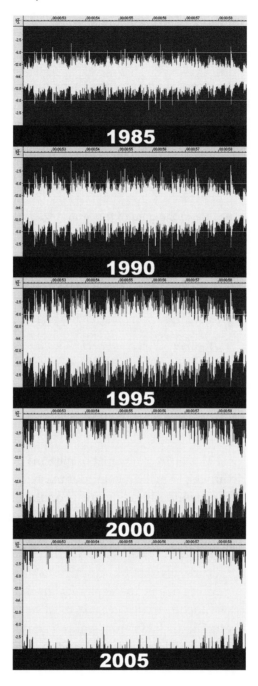

That being said, it's important to attain relatively hot levels on mixes so that clients can roughly compare them to existing records. Here are some tips from mastering engineers on how to do that.

The real key is to have a compressor that has a low compression ratio (1.5 or 2 to 1) and slow attack and release strapped across your mix buss. This gives you what's known as *relative level*. The compressor then feeds a limiter (preferably a look-ahead digital one) set to clamp down at −.1 or

–.2dB FS to prevent digital overs. You then use make-up gain to taste. Be careful not to add too much!

Tips for Hot Levels

- Set a compressor at a 1.5 or 2:1 ratio with a slow attack and release.

- Set the compressor for up to 5dB *or less* compression.

- Feed the compressor into a limiter set to a maximum of –.1 or –.2dB FS to prevent digital overs.

- Raise the gain of the limiter to taste.

- Don't hypercompress.

Mastering

Technically speaking, mastering is the intermediate step between taking a mix from the studio and preparing it for replication. But it's really much more. *Mastering* is the process of turning a collection of songs into a record by making them sound like they belong together in tone, volume, and timing (spacing between songs).

Mastering is not a set of plug-ins or a device that you run some music through to make it come out mastered. It's an art form that, when done conscientiously, relies mostly on the mastering engineer's skill, experience with various genres of music, and good taste.

In the early days of vinyl, mastering was a black art practiced by technical curmudgeons who mysteriously transferred music from the electronic medium of tape to the physical medium of vinyl. There was a high degree of difficulty in this because the level applied to the vinyl lacquer was so crucial; too low a level, and you could get a noisy disc. Hit it too hard, and you could destroy the disc and maybe the cutting stylus, too (expensive at $15,000 in 1950–1960s dollars).

Along the way, mastering (sometimes called *transfer*) engineers found ways to make the discs louder (and therefore less noisy) by applying equalization and compression. Producers and artists began to notice that certain records actually sounded louder than others on the radio, and if it played louder, it sounded better and maybe even sold better. Hence, a new breed of mastering engineer was born, this one with some creative control and ability to influence the final sound of a record rather than being just a transfer jock from medium to medium.

Today's mastering engineer doesn't practice the black art of disc cutting much, but he's no less the wizard as he continues to shape and mold a project.

PURPOSE OF MASTERING

Mastering is considered the final step in the creative process because it is the last chance to polish and fix the project. A principal function of mastering is making sure that the first impressions can open doors for the artist because most people audition music before they buy it. It's interesting to note that just about all the major record labels and most of the larger indie labels still choose to master their projects with major mastering houses.

A project that has been mastered (especially at a top-flight mastering house like Oasis Mastering, seen in Figure 10.2) simply sounds better. It sounds complete, polished, and finished. The project that sounded like a demo now sounds like a record. This is because the mastering engineer added judicious amounts of EQ and compression to make your project bigger, fatter, richer, and louder. He matched the levels of each song so that all of them have the same apparent level. He fixed the fades so that they're smooth. He inserted the *spreads* (the time between each song) so that the songs now flow seamlessly together on a CD or playlist. He sequenced the songs so that they fall in the correct order. He edited out any bad parts so well that you didn't even notice. He made all the songs blend together into a cohesive unit. He proofed your master before it went to the replicator to make sure it was free of glitches and noise. He also made and stored a backup clone in case anything should happen to your cherished master, and he took care of all the shipping or uploading to the desired replication facility or distributor. And all this happened so quickly and smoothly that you hardly knew it was happening.

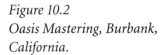

Figure 10.2
Oasis Mastering, Burbank, California.

So why can't you just use the mastering plug-ins on your workstation instead of going to a high-priced commercial mastering facility? Besides what we've already talked about, there are lots of reasons why a real commercial mastering house produces a better product than home or self-mastering. The mastering house is better equipped. It has many things available that you probably won't find in a typical DAW room, such as a high-quality digital transfer console and A/D and D/A converters, ultra-smooth compressors and equalizers, and an exceptional monitoring system in a precision listening environment. In fact, the monitor system alone at these facilities sometimes costs more than entire home studios. But cost isn't the point here; quality is. You can rarely hear what you need to hear in even the biggest and best studios to make the adjustments that you need.

But the mastering engineer is the real key to the process. This is all he does day in and day out. He has big ears because he masters for at least eight hours every day and knows his monitors the way you know your favorite pair of shoes. Also, his reference point of what constitutes a good, balanced mix is finely honed thanks to working hours and hours on the best- and worst-sounding mixes of each genre of music.

Although it might seem like I'm trying to discourage you from doing your own mastering, that's really not the case. In fact, what I'm trying to do is give you a reference point, and that reference point is how the pros operate and why they're so successful. From there, you can determine whether you're better served by doing it yourself or using a pro.

THINGS TO REMEMBER BEFORE MASTERING

If you decide to use a mastering engineer, here are some tips to help you get the most out of your mastering session:

▶ **Don't over-EQ when mixing:** It's better to be a bit dull and let your mastering engineer brighten things up. In general, mastering engineers can do a better job for you if your mix is on the dull side rather than too bright.

▶ **Don't overcompress when mixing:** You might as well not even master if you've squashed it too much already. Hypercompression deprives the mastering engineer of one of his major abilities to help your project. Squash it for your friends. Squash it for your clients. But leave some dynamics for your mastering engineer.

▶ **Document everything:** You'll make it easier on yourself and your mastering engineer if you've documented everything well, and you'll save yourself some money, too. The documentation you're expected to provide includes any flaws, digital errors, distortion, bad edits, fades, shipping instructions, and record company identification numbers. If your songs reside on hard disc as files, make sure that each file is properly identified (especially if you're not there).

▶ **Don't be afraid to put down any glitches, channel imbalances, or distortion:** The mastering engineer won't think less of you if something got away (you wouldn't believe the number of times it happens to everybody), and explaining that is a whole lot easier than wasting a billable hour trying to track down an equipment problem when the problem is actually on the mix master.

▶ **Check your phase when mixing:** It can be a real shock when you get to the mastering studio and the engineer begins to check for mono compatibility and the lead singer disappears because something is out of phase. Even though this was more of a problem in the days of vinyl and AM radio, it's still an important point because many so-called stereo sources (such as television) are either pseudostereo or only stereo some of the time. Check your phase and fix it if necessary before you get to the studio.

▶ **Go to the session if at all possible:** Most engineers and producers go to the first few sessions when checking out a new mastering engineer to see if he has the same musical and technical sensibilities. After that, a bond of trust develops and they simply send the mix master with instructions. That being said, you should go to all the mastering sessions if possible because it will always sound a bit different (and probably better) than what it sounded like during mix-down. Attending the session also allows for some final creative decisions that only you can make. ("The kick is a little loud; see if you can de-emphasize it a bit." "Let's squash the whole mix a little more to make this tune punchier.")

▶ **Come prepared:** Make sure all documentation, shipping instructions, and sequencing are complete before you get to the studio.

Sequencing (the order that the tunes appear on the CD or vinyl record) is especially important, and deciding that beforehand saves you a bunch of money in mastering time. Many engineers/producers have the mistaken impression that after the final mix is finished, it's off to the mastering studio. There should be one additional session, however, known as the *sequencing session*. On this day, you do any editing that is required (it's cheaper to do it here than during mastering) and listen to the various sequence possibilities. This is really important if you will be releasing in multiple formats such as CD and vinyl (yes, there are still some die-hards) or different countries or territories because they will probably require a different song order due to the two sides of the record.

▶ **Have your songs timed out:** This is important because you want to make sure that your project can easily fit on a CD, if that's your release format. Most CDs have a total time of just under 80 minutes (78:33 to be exact), although it's possible to get an extended time CD. (Be careful, though, because you might have replication problems.) Obviously, the available time decreases if you choose to include additional files on the ROM section of the disc.

▶ **Vinyl records might be around for a while (but in limited quantities), so the following applies if you intend to cut vinyl:** Cumulative time is important because the mastering engineer must know the total time per side before he starts cutting due to the physical limitations of the disc. You are limited to a maximum of about 25 minutes per side if you want the record to be nice and loud.

Because you can only have 25 minutes or less on a side, it's important to know the sequence before you get there. Cutting vinyl is a one-shot deal with no undos like on a workstation. It costs you money every time you change your mind.

Mix-Down Formats

There used to be few options when it came to a mix-down format. You mixed to either 1/4-inch or later 1/2-inch tape, and you selected either 15ips or 30ips (inches per second—the speed that the tape is pulled across the heads). Now, with improved internal mix and buss algorithms in workstations, better A/D and D/A converters, and higher sample rates, many of those die-hard tape mixers have now changed to digital files as their mix format of choice, but there's still plenty of tape proponents who won't mix on anything else (although their numbers are diminishing rapidly).

ANALOG TAPE

Once the only thing that many major mixers would consider, there are still many mixers who prefer to mix to the now-old-fashioned 1/2-inch two-track analog tape at 30ips. Even though the sonic differences aren't as clear-cut as they once were, there are still a couple of really good reasons to use analog tape.

▶ **The sound, of course:** Because of the natural tape compression that happens as more and more level is pumped onto the tape, many mixers feel that an analog mix has a sort of "glue" that a digital mix doesn't have. Most mixers make an analog and a digital mix at the same time and ultimately choose the one that sounds best for the particular song.

▶ **Archival purposes:** Although many distrust the longevity of the various digital formats, it's almost universally agreed that analog will be able to maintain its integrity long enough to find a new long-term replacement. After all, tapes made in the early 1950s still play and generally sound better than many recent digital formats.

Even though sample rates and bit depths are increasing all the time, many feel that an analog master made today can better fulfill the needs of the future than a digital file format made today that has a limited sample rate and bit depth.

DIGITAL

Sample rate and word length determine the quality of a digital audio signal. To understand the significance of sample rate and word length and how they affect quality, a brief discussion is in order.

The analog audio waveform is measured by an analog to digital converter (called A to D, ADC, or A/D converter) in amplitude at discrete points in time, and this is called *sampling*. The more samples per second of the analog waveform that are taken, the better digital representation of the waveform that occurs, resulting in greater bandwidth for the signal. Audio on a CD has a sampling rate of 44,100 times per second (or 44.1kHz), which, thanks to a law of digital audio called the *Nyquist Theory*, yields a maximum bandwidth of about 22kHz. A sampling rate of 96kHz gives a better digital representation of the waveform because it uses more samples and yields a usable audio bandwidth of about 48kHz. A 192kHz sample rate yields a bandwidth of 96kHz. Therefore, the higher the sampling rate, the better the representation of the signal and the greater the bandwidth.

A digital word is somewhat the same in that more is better. The more bits in a digital word, the better the dynamic range. Every bit means 6dB of dynamic range. Therefore, 16 bits yields a maximum dynamic range of 96dB, 20 bits equals 120dB DR, and 24 bits equals the theoretical maximum of 144dB DR.

From this, you can see that a high-resolution 96kHz/24 bit (usually just abbreviated 96/24) format is far closer to sonic realism than the current CD standard of 44.1/16. The higher the sample rate, the greater the bandwidth and the more accurate the sound. The longer the word length (more bits), the greater the dynamic range and the more accurate the sound.

What all this means is that the mixer now has the choice of sonic resolutions to mix to that was never available before. For the highest fidelity, you can choose a stereo mix at 192/24 (and even higher in the future), although most people probably won't hear it at that resolution (more on this later). Thanks to the optical disc mediums like DVD, Blu-Ray, HD-DVD, and whatever else comes along, mixers are no longer tied to the old CD-quality standard of 44.1kHz at 16 bits.

It's always best to mix to the highest resolution possible, even if the ultimate delivery medium is to be a lower-resolution CD or MP3, both for archival purposes and because a high-res master makes for a better-sounding, lower-resolution delivery.

Standard Audio File Formats

▶ **LPCM (Linear Pulse Code Modulation):** This is the process of sampling an analog waveform and converting it to digital bits that are represented by binary digits (1s and 0s) of the sample values. When LPCM audio is transmitted, each 1 is represented by a positive voltage pulse, and each 0 is represented by the absence of a pulse. (See Figure 10.3.) LPCM is the most common method of storing and transmitting uncompressed digital audio. Because it is a generic format, most audio applications can read it, which is similar to the way that any word processing program can read a plain-text file. LPCM is used by audio CDs and digital audio tape formats (DATs or DA-88s) and is represented in a file format on a DAW by AIFF, WAV, or SD2 files.

Figure 10.3
Pulse Code Modulation (A) Analog signal is (B) sampled to produce pulses corresponding to the wave-form amplitude, which is then (C) encoded into a digital signal.

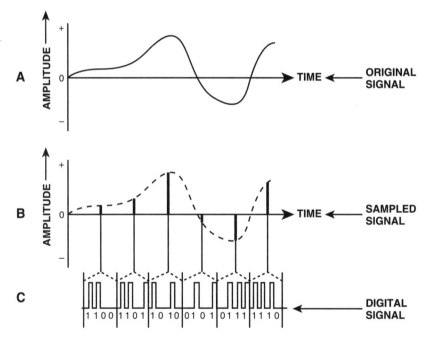

▶ **AIFF Audio Interchange File Format (.aif):** This is a file format for storing LPCM digital audio data. It supports a variety of bit resolutions, sample rates, and channels of audio. Apple Computer developed this format, which is the standard for Macintosh computers, although all platforms can read just about any file format these days. AIFF files generally end with .aif.

▶ **Waveform Audio (.wav):** This is another file format for storing LPCM digital audio data. Created by Microsoft and IBM, WAV was one of the first audio file types developed for the PC. Wave files are indicated by a .wav suffix in the file name and are often spelled wav (instead of wave) in writing. The .wav file format supports a variety of bit resolutions, sample rates, and channels of audio.

▶ **Broadcast Wave (.bwf):** This is a special version of the standard .wav audio file format that the European Broadcast Union developed in 1996. BWFs contain an extra "chunk" of data, known as the *broadcast extension chunk*, that contains, among other things, information on the author, title, origination, date, and time of the audio content. Perhaps the most significant aspect of BWFs is the feature of time stamping, which allows files to be moved from one DAW application to another and easily aligned to their proper point on a timeline or edit decision list.

▶ **Sound Designer II (SDII, or sometimes seen abbreviated as SD2):** This is a mono or stereo audio file format for storing LPCM, originally developed by Digidesign for its DAW software applications. It is the successor to the original monophonic Sound Designer I audio file format. Files store sample rate and bit depth information. When you use SDII on a PC, the file must use the extension of .sd2. SD2 files are quickly losing favor to the AIFF and WAV formats.

Data Compression

Data compression isn't at all like the audio compression that we've been talking about so far in this book. *Data compression* is the process of using psychoacoustic principles to reduce the number of bits required to represent the signal. This is similar to letting the air out of a bicycle tire. It's still a tire, yet you can now fit it into a little box that it couldn't possibly fit into when it was inflated.

Data compression is currently used because the normal LPCM files are so big that they're not easy to transfer or store online. Data compression reduces the amount of physical storage space and memory required to store a sound; therefore, it reduces the time required to transfer a file.

Data compression can be *lossy*, meaning the sound quality will be negatively affected by compression, or *lossless*, meaning there will be no change in sound quality when decoded. Data compression uses a variety of *codecs* (which stands for compressor/decompressor), all having a different sound and a different purpose.

Lossy Codecs

Lossy compression is built around perceptional algorithms that remove signal data that louder signal data is masking or covering up. Because this data is thrown away and never retrieved, it's known as lossy.

Depending on the source material and the codec parameter settings, lossy compression can be either completely inaudible or somewhat noticeable and objectionable. It should be noted that even when lossy compression is audible, it still does a remarkable job of recovering the audio signal and can still sound quite good.

MP3

MP3 is officially known as MPEG-1 Audio Layer 3. The MP3 file (.mp3), is a common, compressed WAV file. MPEG-1 files are about one-twelfth the size of WAV files. This is why MP3 players can accommodate thousands of songs on a tiny chunk of storage space.

AAC

AAC stands for Advanced Audio Coding and was developed by the MPEG group that includes Dolby, Fraunhofer (FhG), AT&T, Sony, and Nokia—companies that have also been involved in the development of audio codecs such as MP3 and AC3 (see the later section "Dolby Digital [.ac3]"). For a number of years, many cell phones from the big manufacturers such as Nokia, Motorola, and Sony Ericsson have supported AAC playback. Sony has also added support for playing back AAC files on its PSP player.

AAC can have better audio quality than MP3 at equivalent or slightly lower bit rates. Here is a list of just some of the advantages that AAC has over MP3 (even when the MP3 is encoded with the newest LAME encoder):

▶ Sample frequencies from 8Hz to 96kHz (MP3 is 6Hz to 48kHz)

▶ Up to 48 channels

▶ Higher coding efficiency, resulting in better quality at a lower bit rate

▶ Much better handling of frequencies above 16 kHz

▶ Better handling of transients

AAC is wrapped in the MPEG-4 container (.mp4, .m4a, and so on) and is rapidly gaining support. The Apple iPod is fully compatible with AAC in MPEG-4.

MPEG-4

First of all, it's important to understand that MPEG-4 is a new standard and has nothing to do with MP3. The MPEG-4 technology works by splitting content into its individual elements. A small movie can, for instance, be seen as audio, video, titles, and subtitles: four different elements that together form the complete movie. If you want the best quality using the lowest amount of disc space, you need to analyze each element and choose the appropriate compression format. For example, if in the movie someone is only making a phone call, you could use an audio compression format that needs less quality than when you see an orchestra playing in an opera house in the same movie. If the person is making a phone call and he only moves his lips, you need less movie quality than when you're showing an entire moving orchestra playing a powerful song.

MPEG-4 has several different extensions:

▶ **.mp4:** Official extension for both audio and video files.

▶ **.m4a:** Introduced by Apple for Apple Lossless Audio Coding files, .m4a can safely be renamed to .mp4.

▶ **.m4p:** Digital Rights Management (DRM) protected files sold in iTunes.

▶ **.m4e:** Renamed .sdp files used by Envivio for streaming.

▶ **.m4v**, **.mp4v**, **.cmp**, **.divx**, **.xvid:** Video-only, raw MPEG-4 video streams.

▶ **.3gp, .3g2:** Used by mobile phones. Also stores content that is not defined in .mp4.

Windows Media Audio (.wma)

Windows Media Audio (.wma) is a proprietary compressed audio file format that Microsoft developed as a competitor to the MP3 format. With the introduction of Apple's iTunes Music Store, Windows Media Audio has positioned itself as a competitor to the Advanced Audio Coding format that Apple uses. Numerous consumer devices, ranging from portable handheld music players to portable CD player and set-top DVD players, support the playback of WMA files.

The most current version of the format includes specific codecs for lossless, multichannel surround sound and voice encoding in addition to the main lossy codec. Both constant and variable bit rate encoding are supported.

A WMA file is almost always encapsulated in an Advanced Systems Format (ASF) file. The resulting file might have the file name suffix .wma or .asf, with the .wma suffix used only if the file is strictly audio. The ASF file format specifies how metadata about the file is to be encoded, which is similar to the ID3 tags that MP3 files use. ASF is patented in the United States.

Ogg Vorbis (.ogg)

This is another compressed source code similar to MP3. Like WMA, it is more efficient at data compression, so the files are smaller. Ogg Vorbis is also open source (free to all, unlicensed, no strings attached). Whereas most MP3 encoders compress data at a constant bit rate, Ogg uses a variable bit rate. This means that if you are copying chunks of silence into MP3 format using a constant bit rate, the compression bit rate stays the same, as if you were compressing the sound of an entire orchestra. But if you are copying chunks of silence into Ogg, the rate varies with the need, and your compression rate will drop to nothing.

μ-Law

The μ-law (pronounced *mu-law*) file format is an international standard for compressing voice-quality audio. It has a compression ratio of 2 to 1. Because it's optimized for speech, in the United States, it is a standard compression technique for telephone systems. In Europe, a-law is used. On the Internet, μ-law uses the .au file format, also known as *Sun audio format.*

Dolby Digital (.ac3)

Dolby Digital is the standard audio codec for the DVD-Video disc. It's used not so much to save disc space (although it does that nicely) but to send a lot of data when the bandwidth is limited and leave room for larger video bandwidth. Dolby Digital (sometimes called AC-3, which is the perceptual coding system used in Dolby Digital) takes up to six channels (5.1) of 48kHz/24-bit information and compresses it at about an 11 to 1 ratio to a maximum bit rate of 640kbps, although 384 is the average data rate used.

DTS Coherent Acoustics

DTS Coherent Acoustics is the full name for the audio format standard usually known as just *DTS*. It offers variable compression ratios targeting a wide variety of bit rates and has a base specification that allows for up to 5.1 channels of audio with a 48kHz sampling rate. An extended specification allows an additional two channels or additional high-frequency data to be transmitted, with a full DTS system receiving eight channels at 192kHz sampling rate. DTS is an optional format for the DVD-Video disc and compresses at about a 3 to 1 ratio at an average data rate of 1.4Mbps. Because there is less data compression, many prefer the sound of DTS-encoded product to Dolby Digital, but any differences depend greatly on the program material.

The company that created the DTS codec, Digital Theater Systems, is co-owned and was co-founded by film director Steven Spielberg, who wasn't satisfied by state of the art in cinema audio when the company was founded. Work on the format started in 1991, but Spielberg debuted the format with his 1993 production of *Jurassic Park.*

The extension used for a DTS-encoded file is .cpt, .dts, or .wav. Generally speaking, most newer professional DVD authoring workstations prefer the .cpt file type, which is somewhat compacted compared to the .dts file. The .cpt file has a marker for the start time of the project. The .wav files are primarily intended for standalone audio discs to be used as 5.1 music discs or check discs so that you don't have to author a DVD.

Dolby-EX or DTS-ES

These are the Dolby and DTS seven-channel, 6.1 audio encoding formats that include a rear center speaker.

Dolby Digital Plus

This is a new audio codec based on Dolby Digital that is designed to be backward compatible with the existing Dolby Digital codec in use today. Dolby Digital Plus is capable of 14 channels (13.1) at a data rate of up to 6Mbps. Dolby Digital Plus is a standard audio format for HD-DVD video and is also an optional format for the Blu-ray Disc.

Lossless Codecs

Lossless audio formats provide compression of about 2 to 1, but no data or quality is lost in the compression. When uncompressed, the data is identical to the original.

FLAC (Free Lossless Audio Codec)

FLAC supports linear PCM samples with a resolution between 4 and 32 bits, sample rates from 1Hz to 1,048,570Hz in 1Hz increments, and from 1 to 8 channels per stream separately, or if required, multiplexed together in a suitable file container.

With FLAC, you do not specify a bit rate like with some lossy codecs. The resulting bit rate is roughly proportional to the amount of information in the original signal, and the result can be from around 100 percent of the input rate (if you're encoding a spectrally dense sound like noise) to almost 0 when encoding silence. FLAC is stored with a .flac extension.

MLP (Meridian Lossless Packing)

This is the compression standard used on the DVD-Audio disc to store up to six channels of high-resolution 96/24 audio or two channels of 192/24. MLP's main feature is that it never discards signal information during data compression (which is why it's "lossless"); therefore, it doesn't affect the audio quality. MLP provides a compression ratio of about 1.85 to 1 (about 45 percent), and its licensing is administered by Dolby Laboratories.

DTS-HD

This is a set of extensions to DTS' Coherent Acoustics audio coding system. As a mandatory technology in the next-generation optical disc standards, a DTS decoder is built into every HD-DVD or Blu-ray Disc player. DTS Digital Surround (DTS' core 5.1 technology) has been selected as mandatory audio technology for both Blu-ray Disc (BD) and High Definition-Digital Versatile Disc (HD-DVD).

Dolby TrueHD

This is Dolby's next-generation lossless technology developed for high-definition disc-based media. Dolby TrueHD can support more than eight audio channels of 96/24 audio at a bit rate up to 18Mbps, although HD-DVD and Blu-ray Disc standards currently limit their maximum number of audio channels to eight.

Apple Lossless

Also known as *Apple Lossless Encoder*, *ALE*, or *Apple Lossless Audio Codec* (*ALAC*), this is an audio codec developed by Apple Computer for lossless encoding of digital music.

Apple Lossless data is stored within an MP4 container with the file name extension .m4a. ALAC-compressed files are about 60 percent the size of the originals, which is similar to other lossless formats. Compared to most other formats, Apple Lossless is not as difficult to decode, making it practical for a limited-power device such as an iPod. The Apple Lossless Encoder was introduced as a component of both QuickTime and iTunes.

Mixing for Internet Distribution

Mixing for Internet distribution, which means mixing using lossy codecs, requires a totally different approach from the previous generations of mixers. Although audio quality is still important, fast downloads thanks to smaller file sizes are paramount. The following section gives you some tips on how to keep the quality up and file size down.

MP3 ENCODING

Encoding an MP3 of your mix requires a bit of thought, some knowledge, and some experimentation. The idea is to encode the smallest file with the highest quality, which is, of course, the tricky part. Here are some tips to get you started in the right direction so that you won't have to try every possible parameter combination. Remember, though, that just because the settings work on one particular song or type of music, they might not work on another.

The Source File

Lossy coding makes the quality of the master mix more of an issue because high-quality audio is damaged much less by lossy encoding than by low-quality audio. Therefore, it's vitally important that you start with the best audio quality (highest sample rate and most bits) possible.

It's also important to listen to your encode and perhaps even try different parameter settings before settling on the final product. Listen to an encode, A/B it to the original, and make any additional changes you feel are necessary. Sometimes a big, thick wall of sound encodes terribly, and you need to ease back on the compression and limiting of the source track. Other times, heavy compression can make it through better than with a mix with more dynamics. You can make a few predictions after you've been encoding files for a while, but you can never be certain. Listening and adjusting is the only sure way.

Here are some things to consider if your mix is intended for lossy encoding:

▶ Start with the highest quality audio file possible.

▶ Filter out the top end at whatever frequency works best. (Judge by listening.) MP3 has the most difficulty with high frequencies. Cutting these frequencies liberates lots of bits (literally) for encoding the lower and mid frequencies. You trade some top end for better quality in the rest of the spectrum.

▶ A busy mix can lose punch after encoding. Sparse mixes, like acoustic jazz trios, seem to retain more of the original audio oomph.

▶ Make sure your level is reasonably hot. Use the "Tips for Hot Levels," or normalize if you must, but it's far better to record at a good level in the first place.

▶ Don't squander bandwidth. Your song might compress a lot better at 32kHz than at 44.1kHz because the encoding algorithm can concentrate on the more critical midrange.

▶ Don't squash everything. Leave some dynamic range so that the encoding algorithm has something to look at.

▶ Use multiband compression (like a Finalizer) or other dynamic spectral effects sparingly. They just confuse the algorithm.

▶ Set your encoder for "maximum quality," which allows it to process for best results. It takes longer, but it's worth it.

▶ Remember: MP3 encoding almost always results in the post-encoded material being hotter than the original material. Limit the output of the material intended for MP3 to −1dB instead of the commonly used −.1 or −.2dB.

The Encoder

Unfortunately, not all MP3 encoders are created equally and provide the same quality output, so getting a good one is the biggest advantage you can give yourself.

One MP3 encoder to consider is LAME, which is an open source application. LAME is an acronym for **LAME A**in't an **MP3 E**ncoder, although the current version is a standalone encoder. The consensus as of 2006 seems to be that LAME produces the highest quality MP3 files for average bit rates of 128kbps and higher.

Bit Rate

Regardless of the encoder, one parameter matters most in determining the quality of the encode, and that's bit rate. *Bit rate* is the number of bits of encoded data used to represent each second of audio. Lossy encoders provide several options for bit rate. Typically, the rates chosen are between 128 and 320kbps. By contrast, uncompressed audio as stored on a compact disc has a bit rate of about 1400kbps.

MP3 files that are encoded with a lower bit rate result in smaller files and therefore download faster, but they generally play back at a lower quality. With a bit rate too low, *compression artifacts* (that is, sounds that were not present in the original recording) might appear in the reproduction. A good demonstration of compression artifacts is provided by the sound of applause, which is hard to compress because it is random. As a result, the failings of an encoder are more obvious and are audible as ringing.

Conversely, a high bit rate encode almost always produces in a better-sounding file, but it also results in a larger file, which might take an unacceptable amount of time to download.

Bit Rate Settings

For average signals with good encoders, many listeners consider a bit rate of 128kbps, providing a compression ratio of approximately 11 to 1, to be near enough to compact disc quality. However, listening tests show that with a bit of practice, many listeners can reliably distinguish 128kbps MP3s from CD originals. Many times when that happens, listeners reconsider and then deem the 128kbps MP3 audio to be of unacceptably low quality. Yet other listeners, and the same listeners in other environments (such as in a noisy moving vehicle or at a party), consider the quality quite acceptable.

► **128kbps:** Lowest acceptable bit rate, but might have marginal quality depending on the encoder, some artifacts, small file size

► **160kbps:** Lowest bit rate considered usable for high-quality file

▶ 320kbps: The highest quality, largest file size, but might be indistinguishable from CD

Constant Versus Average Versus Variable Bit Rate

Three modes are coupled to bit rates that affect the final sound quality of the encode:

▶ **Variable Bit Rate Mode (VBR):** Maintains a constant quality while raising and lowering the bit rate depending on the complexity of the program. Size is less predictable than with ABR, but the quality is usually better.

▶ **Average Bit Rate Mode (ABR):** Varies the bit rate around a specified target bit rate.

▶ **Constant Bit Rate Mode (CBR):** Maintains a steady bit rate regardless of the complexity of the program. CBR mode usually provides the lowest quality encode, but the file size is predictable.

At a given bit rate range, VBR provides higher quality than ABR, which in turn provides higher quality than CBR. The exception to this is when you choose the highest possible bit rate of 320kbp. In that case, depending on the encoder, the mode might have little bearing on the final sound quality.

Other Settings

There are some additional parameter settings that can influence the quality of the final encode. These include the following:

▶ **Mid-Side Joint Stereo (MS Joint Stereo):** This encodes all the common audio on one channel and the difference audio (stereo minus the mono information) on the other channel. This is intended for low bit rate material and to retain surround information from a surround mix source. It is not needed or desired for stereo source files.

▶ **Intensity Joint Stereo:** Intended for lower bit rates, Intensity Joint Stereo combines the left and right channels by saving some frequencies as mono and placing them in the stereo field based on the intensity of the sound. You should not use this setting if the stereo audio contains surround-encoded material.

▶ **Stereo Narrowing:** Again, this is intended for lower bit rates. It allows narrowing of the stereo signal to increase overall sound quality.

It's better not to check any of the preceding parameters when encoding stereo files that originate at 16 bits or above. With these disabled, the encoding remains in true stereo, with all the information from the original left channel going to the left side, and the same for the right channel.

Tips for MP3 Encoding

- Don't hypercompress the source master.

- Cut the high frequencies.

- Use variable bit rate.

- Try not to use a bit rate below 160kbps. (Higher is better.)

- Set the output to –1db less than the source file because encodes are hotter.

STREAMING AUDIO

Streaming audio avoids many of the problems of large audio files. Instead of having to wait for the entire file to download, you can listen to the sound as the data arrives at your computer. This is also a secure method of transmission for the artist and record label because the file is never downloaded.

Streaming audio players store several seconds' worth of data in a buffer before beginning playback. The buffer absorbs the bursts of data as they are delivered by the Internet and releases them at a constant rate for smooth playback.

You can stream many digital audio formats by wrapping them in a streaming format, such as Microsoft ASF (Active Streaming Format), which can stream MS Audio, MP3, and other formats. Table 10.1 shows the 2006 streaming audio formats.

Table 10.1 Streaming Audio Formats

Type	Primary Format	Developer
Windows Media Technologies	Windows Media Audio/Active Streaming Format (ASF)	Microsoft
Icecast (open source)	MP3	The Icecast Team
QuickTime	QuickTime	Apple Computer
RealSystem	RealAudio	RealNetworks
SHOUTcast	MP3	Nullsoft

Alternative Mixes

It's now standard operating procedure to do multiple mixes to avoid having to redo the mix at a later time because an element was mixed too loudly or softly. This means that any element that might later be questioned, such as lead vocal, solo instrument, background vocals, and any other major part, is mixed with that part recorded slightly louder and again slightly softer. This is referred to as the *up mix* and the *down mix*. Usually these increments are small—1/2dB to 1dB, but usually not much more.

With multiple mixes, it's also possible to correct an otherwise perfect mix later by editing in a masked word or a chorus with louder background vocals. Many times an instrumental mix is used to splice out objectionable language.

Although many record companies ask for more or different versions, here's a typical version list for a Rock Band mix. Other types of music will have a similar version list that's appropriate for the genre:

▶ Album version

▶ Album version with vocals up

▶ Contemporary hits radio mix—softer guitars

▶ Album-oriented radio mix—more guitars and more drums

▶ Adult contemporary mix—minimum guitars, maximum keyboards and orchestration

▶ TV mix (minus lead vocal)

The band, producer, or A&R might also ask for an additional version, such as a pass without delays on the vocals in the chorus, more guitars in the vamp, or a version with bass up. There is also a good chance that any singles will need a shortened radio edit.

Thanks to the virtues of the digital audio workstation and modern console automation, many engineers leave the up and down mixes to the assistants because most of the hard work is already done.

Allen Sides: *Invariably, I will do the vocal mix to where I'm totally happy with it, and then I'll probably do a quarter and half dB up and a quarter and half dB down. I really cover myself on mixes these days. I just do not want to have to do a mix again.*

Benny Faccone: *Usually one with the vocal up .8dB and another with the vocal down .4dB. And if there are backgrounds, the same thing. I do not want to come back to remix. Once I'm done with a song, I've heard it so much that I don't want to hear it ever again.*

Don Smith: *I try to just do one mix that everybody likes and then I'll leave and tell the assistant to do a vocal up and vocal down and all the other versions that they might want which usually just sit on a shelf. I'll always have a vocal up and down versions down because I don't feel like remixing a song once it's done.*

Ed Seay: *Generally I like to put down the mix and then I'll put down a safety of the mix in case there was a dropout or something went goofy that no one caught. Once I get the mix, then I'll put the lead vocal up half a dB or 8/10 of a dB, and this becomes the vocal-up mix. Then I'll do a mix with all vocals up. Sometimes I'll recall the mix and just do backgrounds up and leave the lead vocals alone. Then I'll do one with no lead vocal and just the backgrounds. Then I'll do one with track only, just instruments. That's usually all the versions I'll need to do.*

Ed Stasium: *I'll do a vocal up. Sometimes I do guitars up. You get so critical when you're mixing, and when it comes down to it, it's the darn song anyway. As long as the vocal's up there, it will sound pretty good. You won't even notice the little things a month later.*

Joe Chiccarelli: *I'm really bad about that because I'll do a lot of options. I'll always do a vocal up in case someone at the record company complains that they can't hear a line. I'll always do a bass up or even a bass down as well. When I say up, I'm talking about a 1/4 or 1/2dB because I find that if you get your balances good enough, that's the only amount of alteration you can make without throwing everything totally out of whack. A lot of times I'll do a number of other options like more guitar, more backgrounds, or whatever key element that someone might be worried about. And then sometimes if I'm not feeling like I got the overall thing right, I might do one more version that has a little tweak on that as well. Sometimes I'll add like a Massenburg EQ on the stereo buss and add a little 15k and maybe some 50 as well to give the record a little more of a finished master sound.*

Jon Gass: *I'll do the main version, a lead up, just the backgrounds up, and then the lead and backgrounds up. I hardly ever do a vocal down version. Then I'll just go through and pick some instruments that somebody might have questioned, "Is that loud enough?" I'll do those kind of things. It usually comes out to be 10 or 12 versions of each song, believe it or not.*

Lee DeCarlo: *I do a lot. I like to play around with it. I have always thought it would be a wonderful thing to mix your entire album in a day. And instead of doing one song a day for ten days, it would be a really great idea to mix the entire album ten times. Then go back and listen to which ones you like the best.*

Jimmy Douglass: *I used to make just one mix. You put in all the hard work and it would be "the mix." If you had to fix it, we might recall it or we might even go again from scratch because you really didn't like it so let's just start again. Now I'm making vocal up, vocal down, vocal without the backgrounds, etc., etc. Also, with the Rap game, I'm mixing twice because of all the cursing. I have to make both a clean and dirty mix, plus a clean and dirty TV mix, plus an a cappella for the remix market, so you're really making a gazillion passes. And the new thing is to make stems as well.*

Stems

In extreme cases, mixers have resorted to the use of stems to keep everyone (mostly the record company) happy. *Stems* are submixes of mix elements. A stems mix used to be done on an 8-track digital recorder such as a DA-88 or ADAT, but now it's more likely to be a set of stereo submix files if it's done at all. These usually consist of a stereo bed track and individual stereo tracks of the most important elements, complete with effects. This allows for an easy remix later if it's decided that the balance of the lead vocal or the solo is wrong.

Stems are widely used in film mixing because a music mixer usually cannot tell what's going to be too loud or be masked by the additional dialogue or sound effects elements. The stem mix gives the dubbing mixer more control during the final mix if required. It's typical in the dubbing stage to ask for a stereo (or even 5.0—see the next chapter on surround) rhythm submix, a submix of any lead instruments or voices with effects, the bass by itself, and any instruments with a lot of high frequencies isolated on their own submix.

Jimmy Douglass: *So what I do is to record stems of every instrument that I've recorded. Then all you have to do is go back and line up all the instruments in Pro Tools later and you have a mix without the board. Obviously, if you have the whole Pro Tools mix in the box, you don't need stems, but if you still want to use a board, then you need to print stems. Printing stems can take you 3 to 4 hours. This is something that I can live with because I was tired of going back and recalling the mix on the board. That's common practice, by the way.*

CHAPTER 11

Mixing in the Box

Where once upon a time it was assumed that any mix was centered around a mixing console, that's not entirely true any more. Because DAWs have become so central to everyday recording, a new way of mixing has arrived—mixing in the computer without the help of a console, or mixing "in the box" (ITB).

Nathanial Kunkel: *There's nothing different [about] mixing in the box that I didn't do when I was mixing on consoles and tape machines. It just takes me less time. I have to mix in the box. I couldn't afford the infrastructure necessary for the sheer quantity of tracks I have to deal with in the projects that I do.*

Jimmy Douglass: *I mix in the box a lot lately because it's not about the sonics anymore, it's about the convenience. I can mix over the course of a month, and every time I put it up, it comes back right where I left it. That's the benefit.*

Many old-school mixers who grew up using consoles have disliked mixing in the box because they find it's hard to mix with a mouse and they don't like the sound. Although it's true that the sound of the early workstations (or rather their A/D/A converters) didn't sound very good, that is no longer the case today. Indeed, even the least expensive converters have come a long way, so sound quality with converters isn't the issue that it once was. Another objection has been that the sound of the internal mix buss of a DAW degrades the signal. Once again, that isn't quite the case. It's true that each DAW application uses a different algorithm for summing that makes the sound vary from a little to a lot, but a bigger issue is the same one that has faced mixers in the analog world almost from the beginning: It's how you drive it that counts!

Greg Penny: *I did a few tests at home and I thought, "It sounds great to me." I'd invite people over that I respect, and they'd say, "It sounds great. What are you doing?" I'd tell [them] that I'm staying in the box but I'm being real careful with the transfers and just generally being real careful. I'm not doing anything crazy and not using a lot of plug-ins and just trying to proceed real logically. With the amount of files that I need to keep track of, if I go out of the box, it increases the management of the project tenfold, and I don't want to do that.*

Nathanial Kunkel: *I find that I'm having more fun mixing like this, and I find that I'm doing it exactly the way that I used to (on a console). All the things that I thought would change my workflow in the box in fact made me make worse-sounding records. All the things that I find easier to do in the box, like get more level, I find that I'm doing less and less of right now. I find that I use my console (a Digidesign Icon controller) a lot more like an analog console.*

DRIVING THE DESK OR GAIN STAGING

Gain staging is the proper setting of the gain of each section of the signal path so that no one section overloads. On an analog console, this involves making sure that the input gain doesn't overload the equalizer section, which doesn't overload the panning amplifier, which doesn't overload the fader buffer, which doesn't overload the buss, which doesn't overload the master buss. This is why a pre-fader (PFL) and after-fader (AFL) listen and exist: to monitor each gain stage and make sure there's no distortion.

Although all these stages are slightly tweakable, one rule exists in the analog world that aptly applies to the digital, too.

RULE 1:

The level of the channel faders should always stay below the subgroup or master fader.

Rule 1 means that you should always place the level of the master fader higher than each of the channel faders (see Figures 11.1, 11.2, and 11.3). Although one or two channel faders might be okay if they're slightly above the master fader (it's almost inevitable in every mix), just a single channel with big chunks of EQ (like +10dB of a frequency band) or an insert with an effects plug-in that's maxed can destroy any semblance of a good-sounding mix.

Figure 11.1
Channel faders too high; subgroup fader too low.

Figure 11.2
Subgroup too high; master fader
too low.

Figure 11.3
Channel and subgroups faders at
correct levels.

Because many analog consoles have sufficient headroom these days, Rule 1 hasn't been followed religiously, but it has been a golden rule since day 1 of modern consoles. Not following this rule is the main reason why many mixes lose fidelity. The master buss is overloaded!

Speaking of headroom, that brings us to the second rule.

RULE 2:
Leave lots of headroom.

HEADROOM

Recording engineers in the digital world have been taught to increase the level of anything recorded or mixed to as close to 0dB full scale as possible in an effort to "use all the bits." Although this might have been useful back in the days of 16-bit recording, it doesn't apply as much today in the 24-bit and beyond world. The short reason for this is that if we didn't record hot enough in the 16-bit days, we'd get more noise. That's not so much true in our 24-bit world. Today we can record at a level a lot less than 0dB FS and not have to worry about noise. And there's a great advantage in doing so—lots of headroom and less distortion.

Headroom is our friend. We need it to preserve the super-fast transients that make up the first part of just about any instrument (but especially instruments like tambourines, drums, and hand percussion). These transients can typically range as high as 20dB above what a VU meter might be telling you (peak meters are much closer), and recording too hot means cutting them off by going into overload if only for a millisecond or two. This results in a slightly dull recording, but also one that sounds less realistic. The solution? More headroom.

Headroom means that our average level might be −10dB or less on the meter, leaving plenty of room for transients above that. This concept is actually a holdover once again from the analog days where a really good console might have a clipping point of +28dB. Because 0dB VU = +4dB (trust me, it does), you had a full 24dB of headroom before you ran into distortion as long as you kept your mix hovering around 0VU.

Leaving 24dB for headroom might be excessive in the digital world, but leaving 10 or 15dB might not be. It's easy to make up the gain later, you won't increase the noise, and your mix will be cleaner, so why not try it?

Nathanial Kunkel: *I also use tons of headroom. When was the last time you took a console that clipped at +25 and ran it at +24? You just don't do that in analog, so why would you do that in digital? I use at least 10 or 15dB of headroom in my buss. If I'm going to print a loud version, I'll take it out to a t.c. electronics M6000 or something that does a really outstanding job of handling overlevels, and then bring it back into Pro Tools and not change it.*

Rules for Gain Staging

- Keep all channel faders below the subgroup or master fader.

- When using large amounts of EQ or a plug-in with gain, lower the channel fader rather than bringing up the others around it.

- Leave lots of headroom. You can raise the level later.

INTERVIEW WITH GANNON KASHIWA, DIGIDESIGN'S PROFESSIONAL PRODUCTS MARKET MANAGER

We thought it would be a good idea to get some insight into DAW fidelity directly from the source, so we talked to Gannon Kashiwa of Digidesign to provide a manufacturer's perspective.

What are the common things that you see that cause a decrease in fidelity?

Gannon Kashiwa: There's a bunch of things that people do to degrade their sound. One of the things is overcompressing and using way too much processing in order to get that CD sound too early in the process. I see mixes that are totally squashed and maximized up to the top of the digital word, leaving the studio heading to mastering. There's nothing wrong with putting a mastering chain on your master fader so you can check it out, but if you leave it on, you're not giving the mastering engineer any choices to work with dynamically and sonically. If you pack the word up into the final 2 bits of a 24-bit word (that's anything hotter than −12dB FS), there really isn't much left for those guys to do. You can't uncompress something once it's already maximized.

It seems to me that's a holdover from the days of 16 bit where you needed to get as close to 0dB FS to keep the signal from getting noisy. That doesn't seem needed today.

Gannon Kashiwa: Exactly. You've got 24 bits of audio dynamic range to use. That's 144dB of dynamic range that is available to you. There's no reason to record up in that top 2 bits (12dB) and keep the mix there the whole time.

As a matter of fact, if you record everything really hot, then you're going to have to start pulling the channel faders down and the master fader down in order to avoid clipping. I always recommend for people to leave 3 to 6dB of headroom, or even more (depending upon the kind of music) in their recorded files in their mix. Again, if you maximize it out, you don't have the dynamic range later in the game.

Also, if you're always working towards 0dB FS, with highly dynamic material with a lot of fast transients, there's a chance that you're going to have intersample clipping that you wouldn't ordinarily see when the waveform gets reconstructed. If you have a couple of samples that are right at 0dB FS, in between those samples you might have something that's an overage.

I hadn't heard of that. It's really in between the samples?

Gannon Kashiwa: It's what happens with the reconstruction filter. It's only getting its information at the sample points, but it's possible to clip the reconstructed waveform in between those samples.

Coming back to overprocessing, do you have a recommended method for keeping everything as clean as possible?

Gannon Kashiwa: As I said, part of the sound today is to make things compressed and loud, but I think what people do is overcompress. They're listening to a mastered final mix of a CD, which is already mastered, and comparing what they're doing as they go along in the recording process. People try to get to the finished sound too quickly.

What I recommend is to mix in groups (drums in one group, vocals in another, etc.) and try to distribute any EQ and compression across a number of stages so you're not trying to get any one equalizer or any one compressor to do a huge amount of work. If you distribute it across a couple of different compressors or EQs where nothing is used to its extreme, you'll get a much cleaner result.

So use buss compression and compression on the instruments, but don't work any one of them too hard unless you want that real "effect" kind of sound, because the nonlinearities of a compressor are going to become more extreme and more audible as you push it harder. A little bit at a time is the key. Don't work any of the processors or EQs too hard.

One other thing about making a cleaner mix—filtering makes a difference. Being bright is sometimes not your friend because you have all this stuff that's competing for the air in your mix, so using the lo-pass filters and removing some [of] the high-frequency content sometimes cleans things up considerably. Sometimes you have all this high-frequency garbage that you don't need, and you have to make space for the stuff that really belongs up there.

How about the theory that you degrade the sound if you move the faders off of unity gain?

Gannon Kashiwa: Ah, total BS. Pro Tools calculates all volume and pan coefficients as 24-bit coefficients. It doesn't matter where your fader is. Whether your fader is down 5dB or up 5dB, there's no mathematical or sonic consequence.

Does gain staging make a difference? Is it like analog where you can't have the channel or group faders way above the master?

Gannon Kashiwa: Sure. Extremes in any of those cases will affect the output. You still have to observe good gain structure throughout the system, especially when you're doing heavy processing. Good analog engineering practices are still good digital engineering practices.

DAW CONTROLLERS

Although you can mix in the computer with only a mouse, that method takes a lot longer. Faders have been used from the early analog days for a reason: They're easy to see and really easy to use. Because of this, most mixers have made the jump to really serious controllers not only for their ease of use but for their speed.

Figures 11.4 and 11.5 show examples of controller packages at various levels of sophistication and price.

Figure 11.4
Tascam 2400 controller (courtesy of Tascam).

Figure 11.5
Digidesign ICON (courtesy of Digidesign).

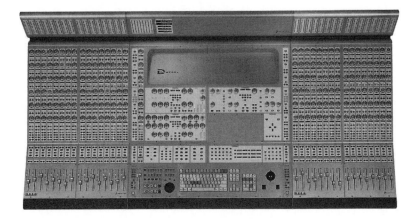

Part Two

Mixing in Surround

CHAPTER 12

Surround Basics

Most of this book applies to mixing in stereo, but music mixers are now faced with a new task: mixing for surround. Surround sound is almost universally claimed to be a more realistic and pleasing experience to the listener than stereo. This applies to just about any type of program, from music to motion pictures to television. People who can't tell the difference between mono and stereo can immediately hear and appreciate the difference between surround and stereo. It is a development so dramatic that many think it will change the way we listen, record, mix, and enjoy music forever.

A Bit of History

Surround sound has actually been with us in one form or another for more than 50 years. Film has used the three-channel "curtain of sound" developed by Bell Labs in the early 1930s since it was discovered that a dedicated center channel provided the significant benefit of anchoring the center by eliminating "phantom" images (in stereo, the center images shift as you move around the room) and better frequency response matching across the soundfield. The addition of a rear effects channel to the front three channels dates as far back as 1941, with the "Fantasound" four-channel system utilized by Disney for the film *Fantasia* and in the 1950s with Fox's Cinemascope, but it didn't come into widespread use until the 1960s when Dolby Stereo became the de facto surround standard. This popular film format uses four channels (left, center, right, and a mono surround, sometimes called *LCRS*) and is encoded onto two tracks. Almost all major shows and films currently produced for theatrical release and broadcast television are presented in Dolby Stereo because it has the added advantage of playing back properly in stereo or mono if no decoder is present.

With the advent in the 1980s of digital delivery formats capable of supplying more channels, the number of rear surround channels was increased to two, and a Low Frequency Effects channel was added to make up the six-channel 5.1, which soon became the modern standard for most films (the Sony SDDS 7.1 system being the exception), music, and DTV.

And, of course, there's always the four-channel Quad from the 1970s, the music industry's attempt at multichannel music that killed itself as a result of two incompatible competing systems (a preview of the Beta versus VHS war soon to come) and a poor psychoacoustic rendering that suffered from an extremely small sweet spot.

Types of Surround Sound

5.1 is the mostly widely used surround format today, being used in motion pictures, music, and digital television. The format consists of six discrete speaker sources; three are across the front (left, center, and right), two are in the rear (left surround, right surround), and a subwoofer (known as the Low Frequency Effects channel, or LFE) is the .1 of the 5.1 name. (See Figure 12.1.) This is the same configuration that you hear in most movie theaters, because 5.1 is the speaker spec used not only by THX but also by popular motion picture release formats such as Dolby Digital and DTS.

Figure 12.1
A 5.1 surround system.

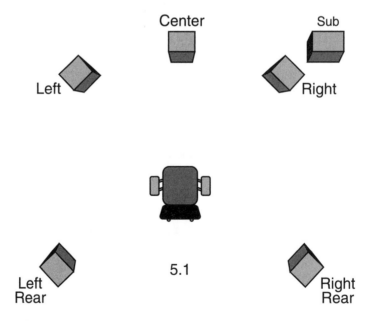

THE LFE CHANNEL

LFE stands for *Low Frequency Effects* and is sometimes referred to in film production circles as the "boom" channel because it's there to enhance the low frequencies of a film, so you get the extra boom out of an earthquake, plane crash, explosion, or other such dramatic scene requiring lots of low frequencies.

The LFE channel, which has a frequency response from about 30Hz to 120Hz, is unique in that it has an additional 10dB of headroom built into it. This is needed to accommodate the extra power required to reproduce the low-frequency content without distortion.

Bass Management

The *bass manager* (sometimes called *bass redirection*) is a circuit that takes all the frequencies below 80Hz from the main channels and the signal from the LFE channel and mixes them together into the subwoofer. This is done to use the subwoofer for more than the occasional low-frequency effect because it's in the system already. This enables the effective response of the system to be lowered to about 30Hz.

Because most consumer surround systems (especially the average low-end ones) contain a bass management circuit, if you don't mix with one, you might not be hearing things the way the people at home are. And, because the bass manager gives a low-frequency extension below that of the vast majority of studio monitors, the people at home might actually be hearing things (like unwanted rumbles) that you can't hear while mixing.

Other Types of Surround

There are many other widely used surround formats. Three-channel (stereo front speakers with a mono surround), four-channel (three front speakers with a mono surround—see Figure 12.2) such as Dolby Prologic, five-channel (three front speakers with a stereo surround but no LFE channel), and eight-channel (the Sony SDDS format with five front speakers, stereo surrounds, and an LFE channel—see Figure 12.3) all abound.

Figure 12.2
Four-channel Dolby Prologic.

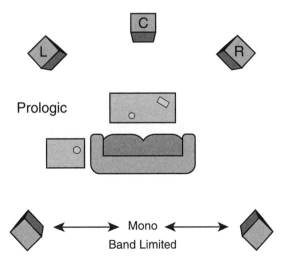

There are other nonstandard formats that use as many as 10 channels for height and extra rear and side channels. (See Figure 12.4.) Many big-budget films and DVD releases now use Dolby Digital Surround EX or DTS-ES 6.1 format, in which a center rear channel is used. (See Figure 12.5.) Many amusement park rides and Las Vegas shows use 20, 30, or even more channels, which are usually played back from a dedicated DAW.

Figure 12.3
Eight-channel (7.1) SDDS.

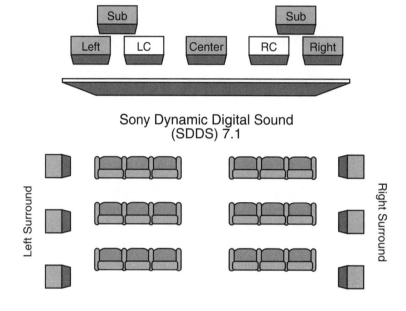

Figure 12.4
Twelve-channel 10.2.

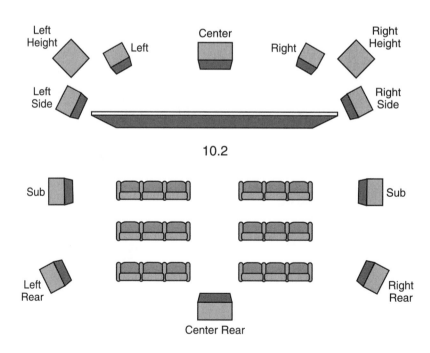

Figure 12.5
Seven-channel 6.1.

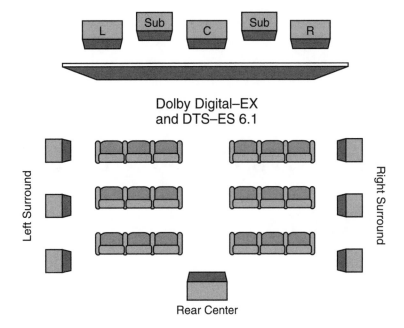

Dolby Digital–EX
and DTS–ES 6.1

Left Surround

Right Surround

Rear Center

CHAPTER 13

Why Is Surround Better Than Stereo?

Surround sound offers quite a few improvements over stereo:

▶ **The sonic clarity is enhanced:** That's because the center channel (depending on how it's used) can anchor the sound and eliminate any "phantom" image shifts that we take for granted in stereo.

▶ **There is no "sweet spot" per se:** Actually, the whole room becomes a sweet spot in that you can move around freely and never lose the sense of clarity, dimension, and spatial continuity. One listener described it perfectly as an "audio sculpture." Just like when you walk around a piece of artwork and get a different perspective of the art, when you walk around the 5.1 room, you get a different perspective of the mix. You might get closer to the guitar player, for instance, if you walk on the left side of the room. Walk on the right, and you're closer to the piano. Indeed, you don't have to even be in the speaker field to get a sense of the depth of the mix. While you're mixing, even people who are sitting on a couch outside of the soundscape often describe an enhanced experience.

▶ **Speaker placement is forgiving:** Yes, there are standards for placement, but these tend to be noncritical. The sense of spaciousness remains the same regardless of how haphazardly the speakers are distributed around the room, as long as the system is calibrated. In fact, stereo is far more critical in terms of placement than surround sound is.

Surround Mixing

Mixing in surround has several surprising advantages:

▶ **Clarity of instruments:** Everything sounds much more distinct as a result of having more places to sit in the mix. This means that you spend a lot less time EQing trying to get each instrument heard.

▶ **Added dimension:** Even mono tracks are big and dimensional in surround. No longer do you need to stereoize a track by adding an effect. Simply spreading a mono source across the speakers with the pan pot makes it sound big.

▶ **Different ambience:** When you mix in stereo, you usually must re-create depth. In surround, depth is almost built-in. Because of the naturally increased clarity and dimension in surround, you no longer have to spend as much time trying to artificially add space with reverb and delays. This is not to say that you won't use these effects, but the approach is different because surround automatically gives you the depth that you must artificially create with stereo.

▶ **Faster mixes:** It takes less time to do a mix in surround because surround sound automatically has a depth of field that you normally have to work hard to create when you're mixing in stereo. Most mixers find that they need less EQ and fewer effects in surround because there's more room in the soundscape to place things.

DIFFERENCES BETWEEN SURROUND FOR PICTURE AND SURROUND FOR MUSIC

Normally in the theater, all the primary sound information comes from the front speakers, and the surround speakers are utilized only for ambience information to keep your attention on the screen. The LFE is intended for special effects like explosions and earthquakes, so it is used infrequently. One of the reasons that the surround speakers don't contain more source information is a phenomenon known as the *exit sign effect*, which means that your attention is drawn away from the screen to the exit sign when the information from the surrounds is too loud.

But music-only surround sound has no screen to focus on and no exit sign effect to worry about. If you take away the screen, you can utilize the surround speakers for more creative purposes.

Surround Mixing Schools of Thought

There are two schools of thought about how to mix surround sound for music: placing you in the audience or placing you in the middle of the band.

"AUDIENCE" VERSUS "MIDDLE OF THE BAND"

The Audience method puts the music in the front speakers and the hall ambience in the surrounds, just as if you were sitting in the audience of a club or concert hall. This method might not utilize the LFE channel, and it's meant to reproduce an audience perspective of the musical experience from what would be arbitrarily called "the best seat in the house."

The second is the Middle of the Band method. In this case, the musical instruments are spread all over the room via the five main speakers, and that puts the listener in the center of the band and envelopes him with sound. This method usually results in a much more dramatic soundstage that sounds far bigger than the stereo that we're used to. Middle of the Band placement may not be as authentic a soundscape as some music (any kind of live music where the listener's perspective is from the audience) might require, however.

What Do I Put in the Center Channel?

In film mixing, the center channel is used primarily for dialogue, so the listener doesn't get distracted by sonic movement. In music, however, the center channel's use prompts debate among mixers.

NO CENTER CHANNEL

Many veteran engineers who have mixed in stereo all their lives have trouble breaking the stereo paradigm to make use of the center channel. These mixers continue to use a phantom center from the left and right front speakers and prefer to use the center speaker as a height channel or not use it at all.

ISOLATED ELEMENTS IN THE CENTER CHANNEL

Many mixers prefer to use the center channel to isolate certain elements such as lead vocals, solos, and instruments with high-frequency information that infrequently appears. Although this might work in some cases, many times the isolated elements seem disconnected from the rest of the soundscape unless they're bled into the other channels.

THE CENTER AS PART OF THE WHOLE

Mixers who use the center channel to its fullest find that it can act to anchor the sound and eliminate drifting phantom images. In this case, all five speakers have equal importance, with the balance changing the sound elements placed in the soundscape.

Nathanial Kunkel: *I guess if I were to encapsulate the rule, the things that I used to put in the middle I put everywhere now. Bass, kick drum, snare drum, lead vocal—all the stuff that has a lot of mono-correlated information goes a bit to every speaker, except maybe the center. If I put something in the front, I will very rarely put it in the center and the left and the right. I will put it in the center and the surrounds if I want to pull it more into the middle of the room. If I want something off to the side of the room, I'll go left, right, and right surround so it leans to that side.*

Elliot Scheiner: *In some regards, yes, but as far as the overall approach, no. I still do a very aggressive mix. I like as much information coming out of the surrounds as I do the front, so I'm still as aggressive as I was when I first started, maybe even more so. The only thing that's really changed for me is how I use the center speaker. I try to use it a little more than I have in the past. I've found that when listening in a car, the center speaker is a little more important that it is in the home. So if I put a vocal in there, it's going to be at least as loud as the phantom center, maybe a little more.*

Greg Penny: *It really started with* [Goodbye] Yellow Brick Road *because I had a few weeks to sit with it and come up with a formula. So I thought, "Here's this incredible record that's got tons of guitar and keyboards on it, so why don't I put the vocal in the center monitor most of the time and the only other things that enter into that monitor are double vocals or harmonies or maybe even a solo instrument? Then I'll bleed out a little bit of the center vocal into the left and right fronts so if Uncle Bob comes over to the house and sits at that end of the couch, he's not missing the lead vocal. Then I'll use divergence and spill a little of that lead vocal into the rear monitors also for that purpose. So why don't we give Elton the front of the room for his piano and Davey the rear of the room for his guitars, or even in quad like in* "Saturday Night's Alright for Fighting": *four guitars, four speakers, with each guitar getting its own speaker.*

What Do I Send to the LFE (Subwoofer) Channel?

Anything that requires some low-frequency bass extension can be put into the subwoofer via the LFE channel. Many mixers put a little kick or bass there if it's used at all. Remember that the frequency response only goes up to 120Hz, so you have to put the instrument into the main channels, too, to gain some definition.

In fact, it might be better not to use the LFE channel unless you're positive that the subwoofer is calibrated correctly. An uncalibrated subwoofer can cause big surprises in the low end when you play back the track later on your typical home theater setup. If you don't use the sub when mixing, the frequencies under 80Hz are naturally folded into the playback sub-woofer, resulting in a smooth and even response.

Elliot Scheiner: *I'm not convinced about the LFE. I run the speakers full range, so I don't have to put all that much in the LFE. I always worry about bass management in people's homes. Every amplifier is different, every DVD player is different; you don't know what's doing what anymore. There doesn't seem to be any way of determining how bass management is being used from manufacturer to manufacturer. They all have their own ideas, and every designer has a different theory about what bass management is, so I just ignore it and use the LFE to put a minimum of stuff in. But generally I like to get things to sound how they should sound on my monitors without the LFE.*

Nathanial Kunkel: *Jeff Levison from DTS told me early on, "Dude, here's what you have to understand. The LFE is a low-frequency effects track. It's used when you have run out of low-frequency headroom in your other channels." That was in the very beginning when I was using tons of LFE, and we'd go into these rooms with an improperly aligned .1 and the low end for the entire track would be wrong. Then I started mixing with bass management, so I only go to the .1 when I cannot put any more level on the main channels and I want more bass.*

Do I Need to Use a Bass Manager?

A debate has raged for some time about the use of a bass manager for monitoring. (See Figure 13.1.) As stated before, the bass manager allows you to use the subwoofer not only for the LFE (the .1) channel, but also for bass extension of the main speakers. (See Figure 13.2.) In recent years, more and more music mixers have stopped using a bass manager, preferring instead to use their main speakers when gauging the balance of the low end in surround just as they did in stereo. Although this provides perfectly acceptable results when mixing music, it's probably a good idea to listen through a bass manager when mixing a typical film. The best of both worlds is to use a bass manager that allows you to insert it as needed.

Figure 13.1
M&K LFE-5 Bass Manager
(courtesy of M&K Professional).

Figure 13.2
Bass management.

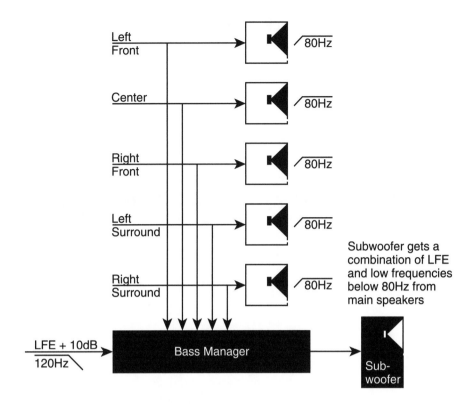

Surround to Stereo Compatibility

Although it's possible to have the surround mix automatically downmixed to stereo via the downmix parameters on the Dolby Digital encoder, the results are often unpredictable and many times unsatisfactory. It's best to prepare a separate dedicated stereo mix whenever possible because sufficient room is usually left on the delivery medium (DVD or one of the advanced optical media formats).

Surround Master Recorders

The majority of mixes are either exported or mixed back to hard disc these days, but sometimes delivery via tape is required. Although you can use any multitrack format as a master recorder, the de facto standard (and the one most often asked for by an authoring house) is the Tascam DA-88 family (DA-98, PCM800, and so on). Other machines occasionally include the Genex GX8500 Magneto Optical recorder and Tascam MMR-8 hard disc recorder. Some engineers even mix to 1- or 2-inch 8-track analog tape if they like the sound and it's within their budget.

Surround Master Track Assignments

Even if you never have to print back to a tape machine, surround track assignments are important to know just from the gear-interfacing aspect. What is the correct track assignment? Actually, there are several generally accepted channel assignment formats for surround, although the first one that follows is considered the de facto standard.

Dolby, SMPTE, and ITU Standard

Channel 1	Channel 2	Channel 3	Channel 4	Channel 5	Channel 6
Left Front	Right Front	Center	LFE	Left Surround	Right Surround

You can record a dedicated stereo mix, Lt/Rt (left total/right total), or encoded AC3 onto Tracks 7 and 8.

This format transfers easily to the corresponding four audio tracks (L, R, C, LFE) of the video formats widely used today, such as DigiBeta or D5. It accommodates the necessary L, C, and R tracks, in addition to the common pairing of channels in Dolby Digital. It's also the SMPTE and ITU standard.

The following two assignment methods are also used, but they're used less and less as the above standard takes hold.

Film Standard

Channel 1	Channel 2	Channel 3	Channel 4	Channel 5	Channel 6
Left Front	Center	Right Front	Left Surround	Right Surround	LFE

and

DTS Standard

Channel 1	Channel 2	Channel 3	Channel 4	Channel 5	Channel 6
Left Front	Right Front	Left Surround	Right Surround	Center	LFE

The previous table shows the channel assignments that DTS prefers. Again, the pairings are logical, but the placement is different from the Dolby standard. Tracks 7 and 8 usually contain the stereo version of the mix, if one is needed.

CHAPTER 14

Data Compression Used in Surround

As stated before, you need data compression with surround sound because the files are so large due to the extra channels and higher sample rate/word length. Such a large file makes the storage and data rate requirements too steep for most media (be it online, DVD, or any other storage medium), especially if accompanied by video, so some sort of data compression is necessary.

Although the exact explanation of each codec is covered in Chapter 10, "The Master Mix," here's a list of how the codecs are normally used with surround-encoded material. Be aware that other codecs (Dolby Prologic, Dolby Stereo, Ambisonics, and so on) are used for surround-sound encoding, but the ones that follow are normally found on consumer products.

Codec	Medium
Dolby Digital	DVD-Video, Cinema, Hi-Definition Broadcast
DTS	DVD-Video, Cinema
Dolby Digital-EX	DVD-Video, Cinema
DTS-ES	DVD-Video, Cinema
SDDS	Cinema
Dolby Digital Plus	Blu-Ray/HD-DVD
DTS-HD	Blu-Ray/HD-DVD
Dolby TruHD	Blu-Ray/HD-DVD
MLP	DVD-Audio
SRS Circle Surround	CD, DVD-Video, Broadcast

Chapter 10 omits a couple of additional codecs that we should mention here.

SRS Circle Surround

Circle Surround encoding allows you to encode up to 6.1 channels of audio for transmission or storage over two output channels or standard two-channel carriers. This represents a substantial improvement over previous Lt-/Rt-based encoding systems, which are not as well suited to handle modern, multichannel media with more than four channels of audio. This means that live television and radio can be delivered for playback and broadcast in surround sound through existing stereo infrastructures. Circle Surround encoding is also backward compatible with mono, stereo, and all matrix decoders.

SDDS (Sony Dynamic Digital Sound)

SDDS is a 7.1 cinema-only format with center left and center right speakers added to the front array. (See Figure 12.3 in Chapter 12.) Most people think that the additional speakers should be on the sides, but SDDS 7.1 was actually designed for large theaters where adequate sound pressure level was a problem. The additional front channels allowed a sufficient level to fill up the theater.

Surround Encoders During Mixing

Although it's not imperative that an encoder be present at the mix, it does help to hear what the codec (the Dolby, DTS, or MLP compressor/decompressor) will do to the final product because codecs can change the sound considerably. There are also quite a few parameters (like Compression and DialNorm) that the mixing engineer might like to tweak rather than leave for someone else down the production chain.

Downmixing automatically folds down the 5.1 surround program to the available number of channels. In other words, if only two speakers are available, the surround mix is folded down to stereo. Although this is less desirable than a separate mix, the Dolby Digital encoder offers you numerous ways to do this.

Dolby Digital Encoding

Many music mixers are dismayed when they find that the Dolby Digital encode of their mix sounds softer and has lost some punch. This is because whoever has done the encode has probably used the default settings in the encoder. These settings might be perfectly fine for a movie, but they frequently leave something to be desired with music. The following are the parameter settings for the best-sounding and loudest Dolby Digital encode. Any parameter not mentioned does not need to be changed from the default setting:

▶ **Audio Coding Mode:** This sets the number of channels to be encoded. For stereo, set this parameter to 2/0 (meaning two speakers in the front and none in the rear). For surround, set this parameter to 3/2.

▶ **Data Rate:** This sets how much data compression is used. Even though you can select as high as 640kbps, many DVD players (especially older ones) do not accept that rate. Therefore, it's recommended that you use either 320 or 448kbps for surround and 192kbps for stereo.

▶ **Dialog Normalization (DialNorm):** One of the most misunderstood parameters, DialNorm is an attempt to make sure that the level of all encodes is relatively the same. This is a noble attempt, but it unfortunately requires an expensive measurement system to set up properly. Contrary to what you might think, the loudest setting is –31. The default is –27, which means that your mix will automatically be 4dB quieter. So, for the loudest possible encode, select –31.

▶ **LFE:** Select this box if you are mixing 5.1.

▶ **Compression Characteristic:** This is actually an audio compression algorithm. It's not a very good one for music. Therefore, the best setting is None.

▶ **RF Overmodulation Protection:** In the earliest days of DVD, a few people connected their player directly to their television using the RF antenna jack. Unfortunately, most DVDs overloaded the TV as a result, so Dolby inserted the RF Overmodulation parameter to eliminate the possibility. But 99.9 percent of people don't need this parameter (they connect their DVD player via the audio/video inputs), and what's worse, selecting it can cause some random distortion and general audio weirdness. Turn this parameter off.

Surround Master Media Prep

Surround sound brings a new level of complexity not normally found in stereo. Therefore, it's imperative that you indicate as much information about your project as possible so that the audio master can be passed along the various production stages without incident. This is especially true when mixing to a tape format, but many of the following also apply to audio files. You can avoid many potential problems as long as you prep the master and note the following items.

SLATE THE MASTER

More than ever before, it's important not only to properly document the master tape or disc but also to prep the master so that you can make sure there's no question as to the actual track assignments. Even an engineer who has mixed the tracks sometimes has a hard time determining which is the center channel and which is the left surround if they're vaguely labeled. It's helpful to take any guesswork out of the process.

The best way to avoid confusion is to go back to the admittedly low-tech but foolproof method of using an audio slate on each channel indicating the channel assignment (that is, Channel One—Left Front, Channel Six—Right Surround).

PRINT A TEST TONE

When you're mixing to tape, print at least 30 seconds of 1kHz tone at −20dBFS, which is the SMPTE standard reference level, across all tracks. A 1kHz tone is a pretty good way to discover if there are any clock discrepancies, because the purity of the signal suffers as a result of clicks and warbles that you might not hear during the actual program material.

Also keep in mind that any program on tape media should start no earlier than 2 minutes into the tape, because that's where most errors and dropouts occur.

OTHER THINGS THAT YOU SHOULD DOCUMENT

▶ Is the LFE channel filtered? At what frequency?

This is important if for no other reason than it's easy to figure out the subwoofer channel if the assignment documentation is lost.

▶ What is the reference level in SPL?

This helps the mastering engineer to better approximate what you were hearing during the mix if there's a problem down the line.

▶ What is the sampling rate?

This helps to avoid any clock or sync issues that might arise during mastering or authoring.

▶ What is the bit resolution?

This is necessary to set dither correctly. *Dither* is a small noise signal of only a decibel or so that's intentionally induced into the digital word to remove unused or unwanted bits at the end of the digital word. (For example, a 24-bit program might need to be converted to a 20-bit program.) Lopping off the bits (truncating) at the end of the word sounds bad, so dither is used instead.

▶ If time code is included, what is the format?

If the audio program is linked to picture, the time code format is necessary to maintain audio/video sync, especially on a long-form program (more than 15 minutes).

▶ Are the surround channels calibrated equal to the front channels or −3dB?

In film-style mixing, the surround channels are calibrated −3dB lower than the front channels. Music-style mixing has the surrounds at an equal level to the front speakers.

▶ What is the media format, and how many pieces are there?

The entire master might be on several pieces of media across several different formats. A warning here can eliminate the confusion of an incomplete mastering or authoring job later.

▶ How long is the program?

This is necessary because it can be a factor in determining the proper data compression settings to fit on the DVD or other optical disc medium.

▶ What is the intended final audio resolution (that is, 96/24 or 48/20)?

Once again, this determines whether data compression is used and how it is set.

▶ Are there glitches, distortion, dropouts, or anything unusual?

These are good things to indicate on a master tape so that the mastering engineer doesn't have to check his own equipment when a defect actually lies in the master.

For more information on surround sound production, delivery methods, and calibration, visit the Surround Sound FAQ at http://www.surroundassociates.com/ssfaq.html.

Part Three

The Interviews

CHAPTER 15

Joe Chiccarelli

Even though he might not have quite as high a profile as some other big-time mixers, engineer/producer Joe Chiccarelli's list of projects is equally as notable as the best of the best. With credits like Tori Amos, Etta James, Beck, U2, Oingo Boingo, Shawn Colvin, Frank Zappa, Bob Seger, Brian Setzer, Hole, and many, many more, chances are you've heard Joe's work more times than you know.

How long does it take you to mix a track?
Joe Chiccarelli: It really depends on the material, the amount of tracks, and the arrangement. I try to work fast because I find that the longer it takes, the more I get into a sort of myopic mindset and get bogged down with the little details. You miss the vibe and the big picture and just suck the soul out of it, so I like to put it to bed in eight hours or so. In three hours, I want it to sound like a record with the basic sounds and feel. In six hours, I should have all the balances, and it should start to sound finished. After that, the artist will come in for a listen.

Having the option to come back the next day is a great thing, though. When you come back fresh, there are always a couple of obvious little things that you've overlooked. I find that towards the end of the day, my ears get a little tired, and I start to put a little too much top or echo on it.

Where do you start your mix from?
Joe Chiccarelli: I have no system. I really work differently for every project and every different type of music. It's a matter of finding out what the center of the song is or what makes the song tick. Sometimes you build it around the rhythm section; sometimes you build it around the vocal.

Usually what I do is put up all the faders first and get a pretty flat balance and try to hear it like a song, then make determinations from there whether to touch up what I have or rip it down and start again from the bottom.

If you're mixing a project, do you vary the sound from song to song or keep it all in the same sonic ballpark?
Joe Chiccarelli: The approach varies from song to song, but I try to keep the same kind of reverbs and treatment for the drums. I try to keep some level of consistency, but again, I'm also treating every song differently as well. I personally like records that take you to 10 or 12 different places.

Do you add effects as you mix?
Joe Chiccarelli: I try to start out with a flat track, then find the tracks that are boring and add some personality to them.

Do you have a standard effects setup?
Joe Chiccarelli: The only thing that I regularly do is to have like an AMS harmonizer on one stereo effects send with one side pitched up and the other side pitched down a little bit. On some projects, I'm not using any reverbs at all, while on some projects, I might be putting all my reverbs through Sansamps or some other kind of cheap stuff. I use a lot of things like Roland Space Echoes or stomp boxes. I feel that those things have a lot more personality than the high-end effects boxes sometimes.

Don't you have a noise problem with them?
Joe Chiccarelli: Yeah [laughs], but I just make it work anyway. I'd rather have the personality with the noise than no personality at all. The cheap boxes have such character. There are a few boxes coming out now that have some color, but a lot of the digital stuff is so bright that it just jumps out of the track too much. The Sony box (the VP55) that I did some presets for is pretty good. I like it because it's kinda dark–sounding, but it finds its home in the track a lot better than the bright, clear digital stuff.

I love to have a real EMT plate or a real live chamber. For me, if I had just one good analog echo or reverb, then I can make the whole record just fine as opposed to four or five digital ones.

When you're using a real plate or chamber, do you go retro with some tape predelay?
Joe Chiccarelli: Usually I'll just use a DDL for that. Sometimes I'll use two sends into it—one that's straight into it and one that's delayed. I'll use the predelayed one for the vocal because of the space between the initial sound and the echo, which really separates the sound and makes it as big as possible.

Do you have an approach to EQ?

Joe Chiccarelli: It's weird. I just use whatever it takes for the particular project. It depends on what's on tape, how well it was recorded, and how much work it needs. Bob Clearmountin is the genius for knowing what to touch and what not to touch, and I think that's really the secret—what to fix and what to leave alone. I find that the more that I do this [mix], the less I actually EQ, but I'm not afraid to put in a Pultec and whack it up to +10 if something needs it.

One thing that I use is a spectrum analyzer that I put across my stereo buss that lets me know when the bottom end is right or the Ss are too sibilant. I know what a lot of records look like in the analyzer, so I can tell when the overall frequency balance is right or might have some obvious little hole in it.

Do you look for a specific curve or something that looks funny?

Joe Chiccarelli: I'm mainly looking at the balance of the octaves on the bottom end, like if there's too much 30 but not enough 50 or 80Hz. When you go into a lot of rooms, that's where the problem areas of the control room are. On certain consoles, depending on how the nearfields sit on them, there's a buildup of the upper [and] lower midrange frequencies. So I look for those kinds of things.

What's your approach to panning?

Joe Chiccarelli: The only thing I do is once I have my sounds and everything is sitting pretty well, I'll move the pans around a tiny bit. If I have something panned at 3 o'clock and it's sitting pretty well, I'll inch it a tiny sliver from where I had it just because I found it can make things clearer that way. When you start moving panning around, it's almost like EQing something because of the way that it conflicts with other instruments. I find that if I nudge it, it might get out of the way of something or even glue it together.

How do you deal with compression then?

Joe Chiccarelli: [Laughs heartily] Compression is like this drug that you can't get enough of. You squish things, and it feels great and it sounds exciting, but the next day you come back, and it's like the morning after, and you're saying, "Oh God, it's too much." So I've been trying to really back it off, especially with stereo buss compression.

What I will do a lot is buss my drums to another stereo compressor, usually a Joe Meek SC2, and blend that in just under the uncompressed signal. Sometimes what I'll do if everything sounds good but the bass and kick drum aren't locked together or big enough to glue the record together, I'll take the kick and bass and buss them together to a separate compressor, squish that a fair amount, and blend it back in. I'll add a little bottom end to that if the record still isn't big enough on the bottom.

This helps fit the bass and kick lower on the record and gets it out of the way of the vocal.

Do you use more delays than reverbs?
Joe Chiccarelli: Depends on the project. If it's a slick Pop thing, then I might use a lot of reverbs, but if it's a Rock band, then I might only use one reverb and maybe a half a dozen delays. I've tried really hard to wean myself from too many effects. I'll try to do different things like put only one instrument in the reverb, or put a reverb in mono and pan it in the same space as the instrument. I like the mono reverb thing because it doesn't wash out the track, especially if you EQ the return of the reverb so that it doesn't conflict frequency-wise with the instrument. I've done some fun stuff like compress the returns of the reverb so that they pump and breathe with the signal that's there. It gives the reverb a cool envelope that comes up after the dry signal and doesn't fight too much with it.

Before I approach a project, I know some basic things like if I want to make this record pretty dry, or I've got an idea of what might work for this guy's voice. The one thing I will do is concentrate on giving the vocal the right character, so I'll fish through a bunch of different limiters to find out which is the right one or a bunch of different effects to try to find which one might complement his voice better—that kind of thing.

There was one record that I did where every time I put reverb on this guy's voice, it just sounded like gratuitous reverb that didn't quite work, but without it, it was still missing something. The voice just wanted a little bit of sparkle. So I searched and searched, and the only thing that sounded right for his voice was the old Ursa Major Space setting on the Cloud setting. I've done things where I've just put an old Eventide 949 on Random and run the input really hot and got this distorted kind of chorus thing that worked great. So you just gotta find that one thing that's like an article of clothing or something.

What are you using for monitors these days?
Joe Chiccarelli: I've fallen in love with these Tannoy AMS10As, and I usually use those in conjunction with the NS10s. Every once in a while, I'll go up on the big speakers if those are good. I might get my sounds at a pretty moderate-to-loud volume, but when I'm getting balances, it's always really soft. I listen in mono an awful lot and find it's great for balances. You can easily tell if something's fighting.

Do you have any listening tricks that you like to use?
Joe Chiccarelli: I'll walk out of the control room and listen to it right outside the door. It's interesting to hear what it sounds like through the crack in the door. Things pop out. Ghetto blasters are good things for sure as well.

What gear do you generally bring with you?

Joe Chiccarelli: I've got tons of gear. Lots of limiters and Pultecs and APIs and a lot of stomp boxes. For me, everything has to have a personality to give something a color so it pokes out of a track.

How many mixes do you do?

Joe Chiccarelli: I'm really bad about that because I'll do a lot of options. I'll always do a vocal up in case someone at the record company complains that they can't hear a line. I'll always do a bass up or even a bass down as well. When I say up, I'm talking about a 1/4 or 1/2dB because I find that if you get your balances good enough, that's the only amount of alteration you can make without throwing everything totally out of whack. A lot of times I'll do a number of other options like more guitar, more backgrounds, or whatever key element that someone might be worried about. And then sometimes if I'm not feeling like I got the overall thing right, I might do one more version that has a little tweak on that as well. Sometimes I'll add like a Massenberg EQ on the stereo buss and add a little 15k and maybe some 50 as well to give the record a little more of a finished master sound.

How much time do you devote just to engineering these days?

Joe Chiccarelli: I work about 30 percent of the year just as an engineer and the other 70 as a producer. I won't take stuff on as a producer unless I truly believe in it. I feel like I have to understand the artist and be able to bring something to the project, whether it's vision, arrangements, sonics, or all of the above. I've been offered a lot of great things, but I haven't felt like I could add anything because it's great the way it is. There's no point in doing it unless I can take it to the next level.

CHAPTER 16

Lee DeCarlo

From his days as chief engineer at LA's Record Plant in the heady 1970s, Lee DeCarlo has put his definitive stamp on hit records from Aerosmith to John Lennon's famous *Double Fantasy* to current releases by Rancid and Zakk Wylde. If you ever wondered where those sounds came from, Lee takes us on a trip to find out.

Before you mix, do you have the final product in mind?
Lee DeCarlo: Before I even start to record something, I've already got the songs in mind—what order they're going to be in, and what style they're going to be recorded in. A lot of times I'll start a record tight and finish it open. Tight, meaning not a lot of leakage, depending upon what the music is going to be doing. Because as the album grows, the music and the ambience grows along with it.

Where do you start to build your mix from?
Lee DeCarlo: The bass and drums. I'll put the bass and the drums up, and I'll get a rough sound on the drums real quick. I don't like to take a long time to do anything. I like to have it up and going. I just get the bass and drums so they just start to pump to where you can actually hear them breathing in and out with the tempo of the song. And as soon as I arrive at that, then I start adding the other stuff in.

How would you do that?
Lee DeCarlo: What I'll do is put the drums and bass in a limiter and just crush the hell out of it. Then I'll play with the release and the attack times until I can actually make that limiter pump in time with the music. So when the drummer hits the snare, it sucks down and you get a good crest on it, and when he lets go of the snare, the ambience of the bass and the drums suck and shoot back up again. You can actually hear a [breathing

sound] going on that was never there before. But it was there—it's just that you're augmenting it by using that limiter.

So are you using individual limiters on each track, or is it just a pair of stereo limiters that you use?
Lee DeCarlo: It's usually a mono limiter, and it's usually something like an 1176 or a Summit or an Audio Design or something like that. It's whatever is handy at that particular point. Usually the best ones for doing this are the old Roger Meyer stereo limiters, but you'll never find one where both sides are working anyway, so you do it in mono and bring it up the center.

Do you have a method for setting levels?
Lee DeCarlo: Yes, I do. I'll have the drums around −5 with the snare drum constantly on the back beat of the tune. From there I'll build everything around it.

A lot of people that really haven't been doing this that long think that what you do is just turn things up and add stuff on top of other stuff. So much of mixing is what you take away, either level-wise or frequency-wise. There are so many things that you have to eliminate in order to make it all sit together and work. Mark Twain once said, "Wagner's music is much better than it sounds." Wagner is a guy that wrote for cellos and French horns doing things in the same register, but it all worked. The only reason that it worked was he kept the other things out of their way. If you have an orchestra and everybody's playing in the same register, it's just going to get away on you. But if you leave holes, then you can fill up the spectrum.

What would be your approach to using EQ?
Lee DeCarlo: When I'm mixing, I use a minimal amount, but when I'm recording, I'm radical when I'm EQing. I do a lot on the recording side, but I'm just redefining what I'm doing on the mixing side.

Do you use gates much?
Lee DeCarlo: Sometimes. I may have a gate augmenting the snare, but it's in such a weird fashion. I always use the original sound of the snare drum, but I may have a gate on it that's so fast and has such a quick release that it sounds like somebody snapping their fingers. I usually mix that in very low with just a ton of EQ on it, or use it just to send to an echo so that the snare drum doesn't have a lot of hi-hat or other things involved with it when it goes to the chamber.

Are you adding effects as you go?
Lee DeCarlo: Oh yeah, I would say 90 percent of the time I record with the effect on. Now, I may take the return of the effect and feed it to a track that's open. I will hold onto it as long as I can until I need a track if I don't want to go to two machines or something like that.

There are some things you obviously don't do, like vocals, for instance. I always have people coming to me and asking me, "How did you make John Lennon sound like that? What is the mojo filter that he puts on his voice?" There is no mojo filter. It's just John Lennon with an U87 and a 15ips delay. That's 133 milliseconds, or however many beats there are in the tune. I always put delays in the tempos of the songs.

Are you timing it to the snare drum?

Lee DeCarlo: Usually I'll take an old UREI click generator and I'll find out what tempo the song is in. If you don't have a delay sheet, what you do is you start a stopwatch when the song is playing, and you count to 25 beats. On the 25th beat, you stop the stopwatch and you multiply that times 41.81, and you'll have how many beats per second there are. Then I'll set the click to that and I'll set up my echoes. I'll just get them so they pump. So when the click happens, you get the back beat or you get a 16th or a 32nd or a triplet or any sort of different returns for your echoes.

Then you're delaying the chambers as well?

Lee DeCarlo: No, I very seldom delay an echo chamber. A lot of guys do, but I don't. I much prefer to use the chamber just as it is, but I do use a lot of different chambers. I use somewhere around four or five different chambers on everything I do.

How many delays would you be using?

Lee DeCarlo: Probably three or four different delays, it all depends. I like little tricks with delays as well. I like to leave out the delay on maybe the last line of a phrase. Then everything has delay on it until the very last word of a sentence, or during an important statement.

How long does it take you to do a mix?

Lee DeCarlo: It all depends. These days it takes me a lot less time than it used to, but I was a lot more messed up in the old days than I am now. I can mix three songs in a day or I can mix one song in a day. But to be really comfortable, I like to take about a day to mix a song and then go away and come back and finish it the next day. If you can't do a song a day, then you've either got problems with the recording or problems with the band or problems with yourself.

Do you use your own monitors?

Lee DeCarlo: I have my own monitors, but I tend to choose the studio for its monitors. I usually use Ocean Way (in Hollywood) because I love their monitors. Dollars to doughnuts, Allen Sides makes the best monitors in the world. There's nothing better.

You're mixing on the big monitors then?

Lee DeCarlo: All the time. Very seldom do I go downstairs. I have to feel my pants move when I'm mixing. I never sit down. I'm always dancing when I'm mixing. I have to feel the bass in my stomach and in my chest.

I do go downstairs (to the nearfields) to check out the relationship between the different instruments. You can't hear shit about the sound with them, but you can check out the relationship between them. But then you run into that trap of when you listen on a pair of NS10s, you get a lot more guitar than you thought you had. Then you bring the guitar down, and when you listen to it on something else, it all goes away. So when I mix, I bring along an old pair of JBL 4311s, and that's what I go down to.

What level do you usually listen at?

Lee DeCarlo: I like it loud. As a matter of fact, I'll start louder and work my way down. I'm always up there, but it's not crushing. People don't come in and bleed from the ears, but I'm over 100.

Do you have any special monitoring tricks?

Lee DeCarlo: Everybody's got those. It depends on how comfortable you are with what you're doing. I find the more insecure you are about it, the more time you spend listening on different systems.

How many versions of a mix do you usually do?

Lee DeCarlo: I do a lot. I like to play around with it. I have always thought it would be a wonderful thing to mix your entire album in a day. And instead of doing one song a day for ten days, it would be a really great idea to mix the entire album ten times. Then go back and listen to which ones you like the best.

What's your approach to panning?

Lee DeCarlo: I have several different approaches. I like to pan stuff around a lot, but I like to have the effects mono. And I like having things wide, but I don't like to have just a guitar on the right and the piano on the left. I've never been a big fan of that.

Do you record stuff in stereo then?

Lee DeCarlo: I record a lot of stuff in stereo. But I would rather do parts and have them mono. In other words, if you've got a guitar part playing in fours, I would have like one track of him playing 2 and 4 and the other track of him playing 1 and 3. Then I could take that and move that around a little bit and then you get that sort of popcorn machine percolating effect. If you have the pump going underneath and that percolation on top, you can make the whole song come alive and fairy dust and sparks and magic will be coming off the whole thing, which is what it's all about. If you don't have the magic coming off of the tape, you might as well hang it up.

So you bring the reverbs up in mono.
Lee DeCarlo: Yeah, I always return them in mono. Just up the middle. See, the very nature of the echo (either a plate or live chamber) changes because they heat up during the day and cool off at night. What happens is if you have them panned left and right, you'll be sitting there and you get the mix of your life, and all of a sudden you realize all your echo on the lead vocal's only coming out of the left side. That's just a terrible disappointment.

Do you have a special approach to treating lead instruments?
Lee DeCarlo: Yeah, sure. Bass and drums are the heartbeat, just like a human body, but the face is what everybody sees. It's kind of like looking at a pretty girl. You see her face and her body, but what makes her run is what's inside. So the pretty girl puts makeup on and gets a boob job. In essence, I give singers and guitar players boob jobs.

What are you trying to accomplish with effects? Are you trying to make everything bigger or to push things back in the mix?
Lee DeCarlo: Bigger, wider, deeper. Everything has to be bigger always. Now, a lot of times I'll do stuff with no effects on it whatsoever, but I don't particularly like it. But, with effects you make a point about your music. Effects are makeup. It's cosmetic surgery. I can take a very great song by a very great band and mix it with no effects on it at all, and it'll sound good, and I can take the same song and mix it with effects and it'll sound fucking fantastic! That's what effects are for. It's just makeup.

You're going for bigness rather than for depth, or both?
Lee DeCarlo: I'm going for pump, always. If the song doesn't breathe, I fucked it up. The better the band, the easier the pump happens. Nothing happens if the band doesn't play it in the pocket to start with. There's not a damn thing I can do to fix it.

Everything has to breathe. Songs have a life, and you have to develop that life within the song. Every single piece of music in the world breathes if it's played properly. A song is about something, and the trick is to capture what it's about and make it live. That's why mixing's an art and not a technology.

What I do, and what the guys that are really good do, is we play a console. It's sort of like the infinite Mellotron, if you will. It's an actual instrument, and the guys that are good at what they do play it like an instrument.

Jimmy Douglass

After learning at the knee of the legendary Tom Dowd during Atlantic Record's glory days, Jimmy Douglass has gone on to become one of the most sought-after engineers/mixers in R&B, Hip-Hop, and Rock. One of the few engineers who can cross genres with both total ease and credibility, Jimmy has done records for artists as varied as Otis Redding, The Rolling Stones, Foreigner, Hall & Oates, Roxy Music, and Rob Thomas to Snoop Dog, Jay-Z, Missy Elliott, Ludicris, Justin Timberlake, Timbaland, The Roots, Destiny's Child, TLC, and Alliyah. But having old-school roots doesn't get in the way of Jimmy working in the modern world, as we'll see.

You were a protégé of the legendary Tom Dowd, right?
Jimmy Douglass: Yes, he was the man that put me on.

That must've been such a terrific experience.
Jimmy Douglass: It was a great experience except that I was a kid that didn't know the difference at the time because I'd never seen anyone else make a record. I didn't even know what making a record was. [Laughs] When I first went into Atlantic studios, it was the first time that I was exposed to the whole concept of recording.

How did you get the gig?
Jimmy Douglass: I was living in a suburban town of Great Neck, New York, and Jerry Wexler (legendary owner and staff producer for Atlantic) lived there. I was a friend and schoolmate of his daughter, so they gave me this little job of tape copying during high school to make some money for college. It started as a summer job, but then I took it into the

school year at night because I really liked it. What's there not to like? [Laughs a bit harder]

How long did it take you to assist?

Jimmy Douglass: They didn't have assistants in those days. What happened was Atlantic Records had the studio attached to the record company. In the front, you had Jerry Wexler and Nesuhi and Ahmet Ertegun (the owners of Atlantic) doing their thing selling records all day, and you had Tom (Dowd) in the back with Adrian Barber engineering and producing, making the records. The first record I saw them make was *Disraeli Gears* (by Cream). The next one was Dusty Springfield's *Breakfast in Bed* album, the one with "Son of a Preacher Man" on it. Tom was working on that album when I came on the scene, doing the overdubs and all that. Then he had nobody in the studio with him. It was just him. So I would just sit there, because when you're doing tape copies, you put a pancake of tape on and you had nothing to do for 20 minutes. It was an easy job, but the idea was for me to be doing my homework. Instead, I'd put the tape on and wander back to the studio and see all of this great stuff happening.

So I would just watch everything he did every night while he was mixing all on his own, sit in the back, and not say a word. We did this for weeks, and then suddenly I got to the point where I knew what he was going to be doing next. I didn't really know what the stuff did, but I knew what he was going to do, so I would help him without any words. I would just give him stuff, and he would go, "Oh, this kid's on it. Let's give him some more responsibility."

What I also did in the summer was to come in the morning before anybody got there. They didn't mind you messing with their old demo tapes (which were incredible in those days—the stuff they turned down was unbelievable), so I started to figure out how to do all the things that I saw Tom do. That's how I learned. I saw it, then I'd go try it myself.

I started getting pretty good, but there was a guy in the maintenance shop who wasn't down with me playing and learning. So he would go in before I got there and sabotage the board by doing things like engaging a solo (there were no solo lights on the boards in those days) or putting a patch cord into the signal path—things that you wouldn't really know because you just don't know yet. There weren't any books on recording in those days, so how would you know? [Laughs] But it made me sit there and figure it out for myself. What he did was make me a very good troubleshooter, and he didn't even realize it.

Was this in the 4- or 8-track days?

Jimmy Douglass: It was all 8-track. I actually did a mix from a 4-track recording that I was very proud of (and they were proud of me). They let me do *The Best of Otis Redding*. They let me remix Tom's mixes, believe it or not.

When did you begin to engineer by yourself?
Jimmy Douglass: The first thing I did for real was with Jimmy Page (of Led Zeppelin). I taught myself how to edit and all this other stuff, but in their heads, I wasn't ready to be an engineer because I was still just a kid in their eyes. One day Jimmy came in, and none of the other engineers were around, and everybody's freaking out because it was Zeppelin's second album and they were hot. So Jimmy wanted to work, but there was nobody around, so they asked me to just sit there with him until somebody showed up to take over.

Jimmy had 10 reels of 1/4-inch tape filled with solos, so we just chopped away at the 10 until we came up with a final solo. I loved Jimmy Hendrix at that point more than anything, so it didn't exactly impress me that Jimmy Page was there to work. I was a kid of 16 or 17 where you do and think stuff totally differently, so I did the work with that attitude. They kept peeking in to see what was going on, and me and Jimmy were having the ball of our lives! I was having a great time, and I was doing a good job, so he was having a great time, too.

This was the solo that goes in *Heartbreaker*. It was the era when a record could come out within a week or two of completion, so the next week that record came out.

So what was your first session as the main engineer?
Jimmy Douglass: Because I worked in a studio, I would meet people that wanted to record. I met a band that sounded like Crosby, Stills and Nash, and I thought they were great, so I asked if I could use the studio to record a demo. I asked, "Who's going to do it for me?" and they said, "You are." That was my first engineering gig. I learned another big lesson from doing that demo when I took it to them and asked what they thought. They weren't that enthused, and I said, "What do you mean? They sound just like Crosby, Stills and Nash," and they said, "But we already have Crosby, Stills and Nash." These are things you don't know as a kid. I did a few more bands, and they said the same thing. Finally they said, "We love the sounds you're getting but don't like the bands." I was trying to be a producer even back then, but my first official released recording that I engineered and mixed was Loudon Wainwright's first album.

How have things changed between then and now in terms of your approach to mixing?
Jimmy Douglass: The urgency factor has definitely disappeared. Back in the day when you were using session musicians, they weren't coming back after you recorded something, so you'd have to get it down correctly and

even mixed together (if on 8-track, for instance) in the right balance. If you erase anything by mistake, you're screwed and probably fired.

Now we don't use a lot of musicians with the stuff that I do. Sometimes we don't use musicians at all; we use machines. Everything is totally replaceable. As a matter of fact, you can erase a part that somebody played, and they'll just replace the part and nobody seems to care about what's not there anymore. Back in the day, it was a major deal to replace anything.

And the rough mix thing is becoming the nemesis of all of us now. Record companies want change, and yet they don't want change. They want it to sound like the rough, but they want it to sound different. Someone will hand in a rough to a record company after taking a lot of time to make it sound good; then they'll hand it to me to do what I do. When I do what I do, they'll say, "Oh, it doesn't sound like the rough," and I'll think, "How am I going to beat a rough that somebody worked on for a month, in 6 or 7 hours?" So lately I've been starting to match the rough. I never used to listen to them because I didn't want to be influenced because then I can't do what I do. Now it's the opposite. If you don't get close to the rough, the mix will probably never be accepted.

How long do you usually take on a mix?
Jimmy Douglass: It's beginning to change a little bit, but I'm a basic 10- or 12-hour man. Back in the day, I could mix four or five songs in a day, but I just don't know how to do that any more. But back then you recorded what you were supposed to hear in the end. Now people want to imagine things they don't hear.

You were telling me that the actual mixing session has changed. Give us an example.
Jimmy Douglass: One of the big things is that we might only actually spend maybe 4 hours of the 12 mixing the record because there are so many visitors and interruptions. People think nothing of stopping your mix and taking the time to play a whole record for a friend. I was in the groove; now I'm not in the groove any more, and it takes some time to get back into it. We used to listen to records to get ideas or emulate, but you were always working the whole time you were there. Now we might end up staying to 5 or 6 a.m. when we could've been done at like 1 in the afternoon. [Laughs]

Also there are so many people hanging around or coming around to listen. Back in the day, the only people hanging around in the studio were part of the band or had a really good reason to be there. Now there are people who aren't connected to the project that are giving their opinion who aren't really qualified to give an opinion.

Is the actual mixing of Rap different from R&B or Rock?

Jimmy Douglass: I mixed the Rob Thomas album, and it was totally old school except that we had three Pro Tools rigs and a Sonoma (DSD workstation used for SACD releases) in the room. Two rigs were running at 96k (there wasn't enough tracks on just one,) and one was used to mix back to at 44.1k. It took a while, but it was fun and came out great. We used a big board and a lot of tracks.

For Rap, I still use a board when I can, but in terms of mixing, the tracking is so generic and sequenced and simple that the tracks have no real harmonics or overtones. There's nothing that's different or blending or making things different, so it's really kind of simple. A lot of times I'll even use a stereo mix that the producer gave me because they can't find the original session to break the individual parts out, so all you're really doing is just putting the vocal on top. You have to try to make something sound really special out of something that's not.

Since you do all sorts of music, from Rock to R&B to Rap, is your approach the same or do you prepare differently depending on the project?

Jimmy Douglass: I've developed an approach to making records today. I approach it like fashion. This week tweed might be in, so even if I'm giving you the best silk in the world, you're not going to be interested. So the one thing that I do is something I call "tuning my ears." I listen to a lot of stuff in that particular genre to get to know what the particular sound of the day is. You want to sound contemporary and current, but you can't know what that is unless you listen to the records that the audience is digging at the moment. I'm not saying to copy it; I just tune my ears to know what the parameters are. So I listen to the genre to go, "Let's see what's considered cool today."

With some old-school guys, they're still making the same kind of records, but I'm making young records, and they're being made totally different. All the things we're talking about I identify with because I was there, but they don't exist any more.

Speaking of which, do you mix in the box at all?

Jimmy Douglass: I mix in the box a lot lately because it's not about the sonics anymore—it's about the convenience. I can mix over the course of a month, and every time I put it up, it comes back right where I left it. That's the benefit. The quality of sound will catch up with you in time, though.

Do you mix with a mouse or use a controller?

Jimmy Douglass: I mix with a mouse basically, but I take along a Tascam 2400 controller because I like to grab faders. If I want to put my fingers on five vocal faders like I used to, it's the only way. Sure, you can group them, but it's so much easier if I just put my five fingers on the faders. That's a dexterity and relationship that I have that people purely in the box don't have. It's like playing an instrument. I can do things with the faders that I just can't do in the box. It's just a feel thing. I'm sure it can be done in the box, but it doesn't feel the same. There's an eye-ear relationship to the distance of a fader throw. That being said, I like to mix with a console as much as I can.

Where do you control your automation from? Do you use faders or draw it in?
Jimmy Douglass: I don't draw it in much. I just don't think like that because to me, once you draw stuff, it's no longer musical. When I work with faders and do punches and things like that, I feel at least like I'm playing a part. I feel more connected. You can quantize things and draw it in and make things exactly perfect, and that's probably what everyone is doing at the end of the day, because when my stuff is sloppy (which used to be really cool), everybody gets bent out of shape. People grew up with everything always being perfect, so when something is just a little off, they don't know how to handle it.

Do you have any tricks to make things sound good in the box?
Jimmy Douglass: I use an outboard summing amp for the warmth factor. I also use inserts with actual analog gear, but I always print it.

Do you use a lot of effects?
Jimmy Douglass: I'm from the old school where if you recorded it right, there's nothing to really add. I don't mix like that now, of course, because people want more bells and whistles and stuff. I always approach it like, "How can I give you what you put in here without changing it?" I know people that are just the opposite, though, who just walk in and start changing things.

How much compression or EQ do you use? Are you old school about it?
Jimmy Douglass: I try to use as little compression as possible because I believe it changes the dynamic of what you've got. Back in the day, compressors were used just so you could get the thing to stay in the grooves of the record. You don't need that anymore! People who are using compression are really making things sound small without realizing it. So I try to use it judiciously.

EQ I use a lot. I like to bring the sound to me. I also add a lot; I don't subtract. I know most of the world doesn't do that, but that's how I learned. Since I didn't know anything, the only way I could tell what an EQ did was to turn it to where it brought something to me. Most engineers try to get something out of the way so they can hear other things. That's really cool, but I don't know how to do that. If I'm listening to a vocal and I don't hear it in my face enough, I bring it out to me. After all, I learned on Atlantic Studios' homemade console with homemade EQs, and they worked real well on the addition side, but they used cut-off filters for subtraction.

Since you're from the Tom Dowd school of recording, I would've expected you to be more subtractive.
Jimmy Douglass: Yeah, but he never really taught me. I just watched the man and learned what I learned.

What monitors do you use?
Jimmy Douglass: I use NS10s for nearfields. For big monitors, I like the Augsburgers (by George Augsburger, the studio designer).

What kind of gear do you bring with you to a session?
Jimmy Douglass: That's in the middle of transition. I have three racks of stuff that I would bring, but lately I'm just using a lot of plug-ins and I'm leaving the gear at home.

How many versions of a mix do you do?
Jimmy Douglass: That's another thing that's changed. You've got to make all these passes now. It takes so much time. It can take up to 2 hours with all the passes.

I used to make just one mix. You put in all the hard work, and it would be "the mix." If you had to fix it, we might recall it, or we might even go again from scratch because you really didn't like it, so let's just start again. Now I'm making vocal up, vocal down, vocal without the backgrounds, etc., etc. Also with the Rap game, I'm mixing twice because of all the cursing. I have to make both a clean and dirty mix, plus a clean and dirty TV mix, plus an a cappella for the remix market, so you're really making a gazillion passes. And the new thing is to make stems as well.

I'll get a call that will say, "I love this mix. Can you just raise the bass in the middle part?" You can't do that if you don't have the Pro Tools session anymore. I say I do things in the box, but I cheat by using a board. I love using the faders. I know just how to dial the EQs in. I have my sweet spots. So once I've taken the Pro Tools away from the board, I'm not going to do a recall of the board for something silly like that.

So what I do is to record stems of every instrument that I've recorded. Then all you have to do is go back and line up all the instruments in Pro Tools later, and you have a mix without the board. Obviously, if you have the whole Pro Tools mix in the box, you don't need stems, but if you still want to use a board, then you need to print stems.

Printing stems can take you 3 to 4 hours. This is something that I can live with because I was tired of going back and recalling the mix on the board. That's common practice, by the way. Once an A&R person knows somebody can do it, if you don't do the same thing, you're not considered a good engineer.

The digital recording revolution is a great triumph for audio. It brings such great flexibility and versatility to the craft. It also brings with it the element of mediocrity in the creativity part of the art. No one has to make any decisions now, and consequentially, nobody really knows or thinks about what they really want. It's digital. You can always change it later.

CHAPTER 18

Benny Faccone

 Engineer Benny Faccone is unique in that he's a Canadian from Montreal, but 99 percent of the things that he works on are in Spanish. From five Luis Miguel records, to Grammy winner Ricky Martin, to the Latin Rock band Mana (also Grammy winners), to the Spanish remixes for Boys II Men, Toni Braxton, and Sting, Benny's work is heard far and wide around the Latin world.

What's the difference between doing a song in Spanish and one in English?
Benny Faccone: First of all, the way they sing in Spanish is totally different than English. The syllables don't fit in the same way. If you notice with English music, it feels like the voice fits right into the music rhythmically. You can't do that with Spanish because it has different accents with harder Ss. You have to treat it a different way on the mixing side by building the rhythm track around it. It's a different flavor with a different kind of emotion.

Are there any other differences between doing an American record and a Latin one?
Benny Faccone: Everything I do is treated like an American record. It may not be exactly what they want, but it's what I do. Even though the language may be Spanish, I try to treat it like I would an English record.

Do you just do Latin Pop, or do you do any traditional Salsa?
Benny Faccone: As a matter of fact, I do everything. The Latin field is not very specific like the American market, where you do one type of thing and that's all you do. In Latin music, you just do it all. I've done a couple of Mariachi records. There were a few records where they wanted some

traditional Salsa, and the only way to get it was to go to Puerto Rico and do it there. I had to get some ideas of how to do it from some engineers down there since they have very specific placement for a lot of the instruments.

And what is that exactly?
Benny Faccone: They've got two or three different ways of doing it, but the things that stay the same are the shaker and the bongos are always in the middle. Usually I do percussion as an overdub. I don't deal with a lot of big orchestras; the biggest is about eight or nine people with a basic rhythm section and a couple of percussion players.

Do you find differences recording in other countries?
Benny Faccone: If you go to Mexico, some of the studios are pretty nice, but the maintenance is bad. I was recording a live concert once on two analog machines at 15ips where you start one and before that machine runs out, you start the next one to overlap. When I brought the tapes back here (LA) to mix, I found out that the second machine was running at a different speed than the first machine, so you really have to be careful.

In Spain, they like everything new. It's really hard to find an analog machine since everything is digital. Whatever's the latest, that's what they want, but you can't find a piece of vintage gear at all. In South America, it's whatever you can get that works. Even in Miami, you have to fly a lot of gear in from New York.

Is the use of effects different?
Benny Faccone: In the Latin market, because you're not just working on one genre like Pop or Rock, everybody's different. One day I could be working with a producer who loves echo (reverb) and wants it real lush, and the next day I could be working with a Rock band that doesn't want to hear any echo. One day I could be working with somebody that wants the vocals up front and loud and the next day with somebody that wants it as tucked in as possible. Rock has become very Americanized in the Latin market where they want it very dry, as is currently the trend.

Do you have a philosophy or an approach to mixing?
Benny Faccone: The only approach is to try to figure out the direction of the song, develop a groove, and build it like a house. It's almost like a musician who picks up a guitar and tries to play. He may have the chart in front of him, but soon he has to go beyond the notes in order to get creative. Same thing with mixing. It's not just a thing of setting levels any more, but more about trying to get the energy of the song across. Anybody can make the bass or the drums even out.

How do you build your mix?
Benny Faccone: It really is like building a house. You've got to get the foundation of bass and drums and then whatever the most important

part of the song is, like the vocalist, and you've got to build around that. I put the bass up first, almost like the foundation part. Then the kick in combination with the bass to get the bottom. Because sometimes you can have a really thin kick by itself, but when you put the bass with it, it seems to have enough bottom because the bass has more bottom end. I build the drums on top of that. After I do the bass and drums, then I get the vocal up and then build everything from there. A lot of mixers just put the music up first, but as soon as you put the vocal up, the levels become totally different. After all the elements are in, I spend maybe a couple of hours just listening to the song like an average listener would, and I keep making improvements.

Do you have a method for setting levels?
Benny Faccone: Yeah, I have a starting point. I usually start with the bass at about −5 and the kick at about −5. The combination of the two, if it's right, should hit about −3 or so. By the time the whole song gets put together and I've used the computer to adjust levels, I've trimmed everything back somewhat. The bass could be hitting −7 if I solo it after it's all done.

Do you put the snare at about the same level as the kick?
Benny Faccone: No. There, it's more a question of feel than level. Because there's so many transients, it could be reading −10 and it could still be too loud.

What's your approach to EQ? Do you have certain frequencies that you always come back to on certain instruments?
Benny Faccone: Yeah, as a starting point. But I'll do whatever it takes, depending on how it was recorded. For bass, I use a combination of a low frequency, usually about 50Hz, with a limiter, so it'll stay tight but still give it the big bottom. Add a little 7k if you want a bit of the string sound, and between 1.5 and 3k to give it some snap.

For the kick, I like to have bottom on that, too. I'll add a little at 100 and take some off at 400, depending on the sound. Sometimes I even take all the 400 out, which makes it very wide. Then add some point at 3 or 5k.

On the snare, I give it some 10k on the top end for some snap. I've been putting 125Hz on the bottom of the snare to fill it out a little more.

For guitars, usually 1.5k gives it that present kind of sound. Pianos and keyboards vary so much that it all depends on how it feels in the track.

For vocals, it really depends if it's male or female. If they sing really low, I don't add as much bottom end. Usually I always take some off at about 20Hz to get rid of rumble. But anything on up, it really all depends on the singer. I might add a little bit in the 4–6k range in there.

What's your approach to compression?

Benny Faccone: Limit the heck out of everything. [Laughs] I like to compress everything just to keep it smooth and controlled, not to get rid of the dynamics. But I don't like a compressor across the stereo buss because then it sounds like it's not breathing right to me. Even for Hard Rock, I don't like to do that. It's easier to do it individually.

Usually I use around a 4:1 ratio on pretty much everything I do. Sometimes on guitars, I go to 8:1. On the kick and the snare, I try not to hit it too hard because the snare really darkens up. It's more for control, to keep it consistent. On the bass, I hit that a little harder, just to push it up front a little more. Everything else for control more than sticking it right up in your face kind of a thing.

Do you have any special effects tricks that you use? Any neat things you like to use all the time?

Benny Faccone: I use a lot of the old PCM42s [see Figure 18.1] on guitars for a very short slap delay. It's mono, but it sounds really big. I use something like 4, 8, 11 milliseconds, so it doesn't sound like a delay. Sometimes I use as much as 28ms on a power guitar. You stereo it out, it'll sound like two guitars on either side of the speakers.

Figure 18.1
Lexicon PCM-42 Digital Delay,
now out of production.

Is there a certain listening level that you always listen at?

Benny Faccone: Yeah, I have my amps set pretty much at a certain level. It's a fairly modest level—not loud, not soft. When I start the mix, I crank it a little bit on the big speakers to kinda get hyped a little bit and check out the bottom end. Then I'll slowly start listening softer and softer.

How many versions do you do of a mix?

Benny Faccone: Usually one with the vocal up .8dB and another with the vocal down .4dB. And if there's backgrounds, the same thing. I do not want to come back to remix. Once I'm done with a song, I've heard it so much that I don't want to hear it ever again.

CHAPTER 19

Jerry Finn

Jerry Finn is one of the industry's new breed of engineers/producers, brought up in the techniques of his successful predecessors yet willing to adapt those methods to fit the music and artists of today. From his mixing debut on Green Day's *Dookie* to producing and mixing Rancid's *Out Come the Wolves* and *Life Won't Wait* to his work with the Presidents of the United States, the Goo Goo Dolls, and Beck, Jerry adds a distinctive edge loved by artists and listeners alike.

I know you still do a lot of records that have relatively small budgets. How much of the money is spent on mixing in those cases?
Jerry Finn: The majority. A lot of times when I get called in at the end to do a record like that, my mix budget ends up being at least twice as much as the budget for the rest of the album. My manager and I always try to work it out with bands that have smaller budgets, though. I've done a lot of Indie stuff with bands that were my friends for anywhere from free to half my rate just because I love the music.

Do you usually have to work fast because of the budget?
Jerry Finn: Not usually. I generally take about 10 to 12 days to mix a record. Some take less; some take more. *Dookie* I think we did in nine days. *Insomniac* took 11 days.

I mixed Beck for a PBS show called *Sessions at West 54th*. We were supposed to only mix four songs in one day, and it went so well that we ended up mixing 7 songs in 10 hours, and it came out great. The stuff was recorded really well, and his band had actually just gotten off a year-and-a-half tour, so they just nailed it so it didn't really require any fixing. And Beck is someone who really trusts his instincts, so he doesn't sit there second-guessing himself. We just went straight for what sounded right and just nailed it.

Before you start a mix, can you hear the final product in your head?
Jerry Finn: Yeah, that's actually one of the requirements for me to feel comfortable going into a record. When I'm sent rough mixes, I really need to hear where I would take it in order to feel comfortable. Sometimes [a] band tells you what they want and the producer tells you what he wants and the A&R guy tells you what he wants, and they're all completely different things. That can be a bit frightening because you end up being the punching bag for their arguments. [Laughs] But I usually can hear the final mastered record from day one, and then it's just trying to get that sound in my head to come out of the speakers.

Where are you starting your mix from? Do you start from the kick drum, the overheads…?
Jerry Finn: Just out of habit, I probably start at the far left of the console with the kick and start working my way across. Lately, I've tried to put the vocal in early in order to create the mix more around that. In a lot of the Punk Rock stuff, you get the track slamming, and then you just sort of drop the vocal on top. But for the more Pop stuff, I've found that approach doesn't work as well because the vocal really needs to sell the song. So I've been trying to discipline myself to put the vocal up early on before I even have the bass and guitars in, and kind of then carve those around the vocals.

One thing that I do with drums, though, is try to get the room mics in early on before I start adding reverbs and stuff like that to the snare. I try to push up the room mics and get the sound right on those, and I try to provide a lot of the drum ambience naturally without going to digital boxes. Unfortunately, recording drums is sort of becoming a lost art. I mean, it is the hardest thing to record. And as engineers have gotten more and more dependent on samples and loops and drum machines, and with more recording being done in home studios, the thing that always suffers is the drums.

Do you get a lot of stuff that's done in garages or homes?
Jerry Finn: Not so much, but I do get stuff where the band thought that going to a good studio would be all they needed, and they didn't really think about the engineer they hired. So I've seen some engineers that get in over their heads. I was actually a drummer myself when I played in bands, so I tend to be real anal about the drum sounds. And I'm a complete phase junkie, so if I think that the drums have been recorded poorly, it doesn't take much for me to criticize the drum recording. [Laughs]

After you put the drums up, where do you usually go from there?

Jerry Finn: I'll get the drums happening to where they have some ambience, then put the vocal up and get that to where that's sitting right. Then I'll start with the bass and make sure that the kick and the bass are occupying their own territory and not fighting each other. Sometimes to my surprise I've nailed it and it all falls together, and then other times when I get the guitars in there, they eat up a lot of the ambience on the drums. Most of the bands I work with tend to have several tracks of very distorted guitars, and they want them all real loud, so then I have to go back to the drums and kind of adjust for that.

How do you deal with that when you get a lot of real big crunchy guitars?

Jerry Finn: When every guy in the band thinks he's the loudest, that's when I know I've nailed the mix. I've always tried to just make it so that you don't have to fight to hear anything. On certain parts of the song, maybe I will bury something a little bit or push something a little louder for tension to kinda pull you into the next part, but overall I try to make it so you can hear everything all the time, and that generally comes through EQ. Like I'll find the bite in the guitar and make sure that the snare isn't also occupying that same range. Then I'll make sure the low end on the guitars doesn't muddy up where the bass is sitting. And I also have to keep the kick and snare really punchy to kind of cut through all the wall of guitars by multing them off and hard-compressing and gating them and sneaking them back in under everything.

Do you find you use compression on a lot of things?

Jerry Finn: Yeah. I'm a big compressor fan. I think that the sound of modern records today is compression. Audio purists talk about how crunchy compression and EQ is, but if you listen to one of those Jazz or Blues records that are done by the audiophile labels, there's no way they could ever compete on modern radio even though they sound amazing. And unfortunately, all the phase shift and pumping and brightening that's imparted by EQ and compression is what modern records sound like. Every time I try to be a purist and go, "You know, I'm not gonna compress that," the band comes in and goes, "Why isn't that compressed?" So yeah, I compress the buss, although I'm very sparing on certain records. *Dookie* for Green Day had no compression on the buss at all, and the Super Drag record that I produced and mixed last year didn't have any either. But if I think it's appropriate for the music, I'll get it on there.

Are you compressing everything else individually as well?

Jerry Finn: Lately what I've gotten into doing more of is multing it off, like I said. The kick and snare I'll put through maybe a 160 and very lightly compress it, maybe pulling down half to 1dB. Then I'll mult them off and go through a new 160S and really compress those and sneak them up underneath so you're basically hearing the character of the drum you recorded rather than this bastardized version of it. Then I also send all of my dry drum tracks—not the rooms or overheads, but the kick, snare, and toms—through another compressor and sneak that in to give the kit an overall sound. Distorted guitars I don't compress as much because when you get a Marshall on 10, it's so compressed already that it doesn't really need it. But cleaner guitars or acoustic guitars, I'll compress. And I actually got into doing the vocals the same way I do the kick and snare; multing it off and compressing it real hard and sneaking that under the original vocal.

When you say "real hard," how much do you mean?
Jerry Finn: I would say 10 or 12dB and at a ratio anywhere from like 4:1 to 8:1. My compression technique is something I actually learned from Ed Cherney. He was telling me about compressing the stereo buss when I was assisting him, but I use the same technique on everything. I set the attack as slow as possible and the release as fast as possible so all the transients are getting through and the initial punch is still there, but it releases instantly when the signal drops below threshold. I think that's a lot of the sound of my mixes. It keeps things kinda popping the whole time. Also, you can compress things a little bit more and not have it be as audible.

Do you have an approach to panning?
Jerry Finn: Yeah, I tend to be a fan of panning things real wide. I think it started from when I was an assistant at Devonshire (North Hollywood). We had a (Neve) V3 (the console that predates the VR) over there that I worked on a lot, and when you engaged the Pan knobs, it changed the sound a little bit. So I tried to avoid using the Pan knob by just assigning it to the left or right buss. Now I'll keep electric guitars, overheads, room mics, and toms hard left and right, and hi-hat all the way to one side. There's not a lot of filling things in between.

The kind of bands I work with want to hit you in the head. For the most part, they're not really worried about having a Pink Floyd- or Steely Dan-style mix where everything has its own spot. It's really supposed to hit you in the forehead, so the panning tends to be really extreme. Also, because radio tends to squash everything back up the middle, I've always found that panning it out like that makes it sound a little bit bigger on radio. If you take the stuff that's panned out wide and make it slightly louder than it should be in stereo, when you listen in mono, it really comes together. I find that helps you avoid that all-snare and vocal-mix thing that you hear a lot of times, and it keeps the guitars up there.

Do you add effects as you go along, or do you get a mix up and then add them?
Jerry Finn: I'm pretty sparing on effects. Actually, over the last year-and-a-half or two years, I've gradually tried to wean myself off of any digital

effects. The last six or so things I mixed, the main vocal effect was a plate reverb and a tape machine or space echo for real tape slap.

Are you delaying the send to the plate?
Jerry Finn: Depending on the song. Sometimes it works, but with a lot of the music I do, the tempos are so fast that you don't really need to do much delaying because you can't really hear it. It's like the reverb needs to speak right away and then go away. I'm a big fan of the EMT250 [see Figure 19.1] on snare. That's probably been a standard since day one on my mixes. Electric guitars tend to stay dry, and bass is always dry.

Figure 19.1
EMT250: World's first digital reverb (long out of production).

What are you using for monitors?
Jerry Finn: When I was an assistant, a lot of the engineers that I liked working with had Tannoy SRM10Bs. When I went independent, I searched high and low and finally found a pair. I carry those around with me wherever I go as well as a Hafler Transnova amp, which gets frowned upon sometimes amongst the guys that are into the more hi-fi kind of thing. But I tried 20 amps, and that just sounded the best.

How much do you use NS10s or Auratones or the main studio monitors?
Jerry Finn: I use the main studio monitors maybe 1 percent of the mixing time, if that. I know a lot of people say, "Well, I like to go to the bigs and listen to the low end and make sure that's in order," but the big monitors are so inconsistent from studio to studio that I can't trust them. Sometimes when the A&R guys come down, the band cranks it up to get them all excited, and that's a fine use for $50,000 speakers.

I like to check my mixes in mono, so I do actually use Auratones a lot. NS10s are sort of a necessary evil. Most producers and bands that I work with are used to them, so that's what they want to hear. But if I'm just listening for myself, I'll try to stay on the Tannoys.

How loud do you listen?

Jerry Finn: Extremely quiet. Like at conversation volume. Probably 85dB or so at the loudest.

Do you usually mix by yourself, or do you have people in the studio with you? Does it matter?

Jerry Finn: It depends. When we did the *Dookie* record, the whole band was so excited by the whole process (they had never made a real record in a real studio before) that they were there the whole time with their elbows up on the console. On the flip side of that, sometimes the band and/or the producer will come in the first day and then I won't see them again. I was doing one record where the producer actually left the country and I didn't even know it. About four days into it, I said to the band when they came by to check the mixes, "Should we have the producer come back?" And they're like, "Oh, he's in England." So I guess he trusted me.

I like to keep the band involved, and I always put their needs before my ego. I think a problem with a lot of mixers is the ego thing where when the band says, "You know that great sound you have? We want it to sound crappy." You have to take yourself out of it and go, "Well, their name's a lot bigger on the record than mine." Like on The Presidents' record, there were decisions they were making that I knew were gonna make the mixes sound weird sometimes, and I would explain that to them. Like, "Do you realize if you do that, it's gonna sound really strange on the radio?", or "It's gonna sound really strange when this chorus comes back in," and they'd be like, "Well, we don't care. That's what we want." So I'll do it and generally the band stays happy.

How many mixes do you do? Vocal up, vocal down?

Jerry Finn: If it's up to me, I'll do the main mix, a vocal up 1dB, a TV mix, and an instrumental, and that's it. I've worked with some producers that want to avoid conflict, so they'll sit there and print mixes all day to please every guy in the band, but all you're doing is prolonging the argument. You end up with a nightmare at mastering as you edit between mixes, so I try to really just get it right the first time. Sometimes the A&R person will want vocal down, but…

Vocal down?

Jerry Finn: Every now and then someone will say, "Do a vocal down just to be safe," but I don't think it's ever been used. [Laughs] I think some people just like to be covered, and it's also probably people who are a little new to the business that think there might be some possible use for a vocal down, but there never is. The instrumental comes in handy sometimes for editing out cuss words and things like that.

Where do you like to work at usually?

Jerry Finn: Conway (in Hollywood) is definitely my favorite studio. Before I went independent, I was an assistant there for about four or five months. When I finally went independent, I was so scared because I had only done the Green Day record, but it was just blowing up so huge and I was getting so many calls that I had to pursue it. Being realistic about the music business, I thought I'd have a red hot career for six months and then be back assisting, so when I left I made them promise that when my career fell apart they'd hire me back as an assistant. [Laughs] I still joke with Charlene, the studio manager, about that whenever I see her. "Are you still gonna hire me back when my career falls apart?"

CHAPTER 20

Jon Gass

Babyface, Whitney Houston, Madonna, Mary J. Blige, N'Sync, Toni Braxton, Mariah Carey, Usher, TLC, Boys II Men, Destiny's Child. Mixer Jon Gass's credit list reads like a Who's Who of R&B greats—and with good reason. Gass's unsurpassed style and technique have elevated him to a most esteemed position among engineers—working with the best of the best on some of the most creative and demanding music around today.

Do you have a philosophy about what you're trying to accomplish?
Jon Gass: Not really. I just go for it. I'm kind of a musical mixer. I grew up playing music, and I'm not a real technical mixer at all. If something breaks, it's like, "Hey, it broke." [Laughs]

I think I try to find the more natural tones of instruments and maybe boost that direction and make everything sound natural as long as it still fits together. I always think of it as a layer cake or something, so I just kind of layer the thing.

Can you hear the final product in your head before you start? Do you know what you're going for?
Jon Gass: Actually, yeah, I can.

What if you come in just to remix something?
Jon Gass: The last five or six years, that's mainly what I've been doing. I know some people push up just the drums and work on them for a while, but I start with everything on and I work on it like that. The reason is, in my opinion, the vocal is going to be there sooner or later anyway. You might as well know where it's sitting and what it's doing. All the

instruments are going to be there sooner or later, so you might as well just get used to it. And I think that's also what helps me see what I need to do within the first passage. That's when I start picturing. So it doesn't take me long.

If you have something with a lot of tracks, let's say you're bouncing back between several vocal tracks, does it bother you that you can't hear everything?
Jon Gass: Yeah, if it's a real car wreck where you need to do a lot of mutes to make it make sense in the first place because there's stuff all over, then I'll actually go through and do a cut pass and get the cuts in it first so I can still kind of listen to everything. I'd rather do that so I can kind of get a grip of where it's supposed to go. If it's going to be one of those kind of songs, I'll have the producer or whoever come down and help with the cuts first, and then send him off so I can get working on it. Most of the stuff I do I really don't have producers or artists hanging out with me too much. It's really great for me. I think they like it, too. I guess I kind of have a style that most people that hire me think, "Okay, he's done this record and that record, so that's kind of what we want." If somebody helps me too much, I can only say, "Gee, you can pay somebody a lot less if you want to mix this. It's your budget." That allows me to be more creative.

And I'm scared to solo stuff a lot in front of the artists because I think individually the tracks that I mix almost have to sound bad. It really doesn't matter what it sounds like by itself, though, because it has to work together. That's where some of the young producers blow it. They go through and solo tracks and make everything sound fat. Then they put it all together and have a big car wreck.

How do you go about building your mix if you have everything up?
Jon Gass: I really start searching out the frequencies that are clashing or rubbing against each other, then I work back towards the drums. But I really try to keep the whole picture in there most of the time as opposed to isolating things too much.

So you don't solo stuff much, then?
Jon Gass: Well, I do, but to solo something and EQ it is insane because it's not relative to anything, unless you're just going to do a mix with just that. [Laughs]

What's your approach to EQ then? Do you just go through and look for things that are clashing?
Jon Gass: Basically, yeah. If there are two or three instruments that are clashing, that's probably where I get more into the solo if I need to hear the whole natural sound of the instrument. I'll try to go more that way with each instrument unless there's a couple that are really clashing, then I'll EQ more aggressively. Otherwise, I'm not scared to EQ quite a bit.

You're doing mostly cuts? You're not adding?

Jon Gass: Yeah, especially on the SSL EQ. I'm definitely into cutting more than adding, and I think that works best with the EQ on that board.

How long do you think it takes you to do a mix?

Jon Gass: A day-and-a-half is perfect. Two days is long.

Do you have an approach to panning?

Jon Gass: Just balanced between left and right. That may differ a lot for different music I like to do. Playing so many years live, my left ear has been trashed by drums and hi-hat because the drummer was always on my left. But for some reason, I always end up putting the hi-hat for the drums from the drummer's perspective as opposed to the audience perspective.

What's your approach to compression?

Jon Gass: I'm pretty light on compression. Individual tracks, pretty light. Just really to add attack on acoustic guitars, electric guitars, stuff like that. Mostly on things I want to poke out of the mix.

What do you mean by light?

Jon Gass: Unlike some of the New York guys that seem to use a lot of compression on a lot of things, I don't use that much. Same with the stereo buss. I barely touch it with maybe a dB or two. Actually I don't even use the SSL buss compressors any more.

Just trying to even things out?

Jon Gass: Yeah. Just even things out, and I think, too, if the stuff's EQed and layered right, you don't really need to do a ton of compression on the stereo buss. If the thing's laying right, at least with R&B, it just kind of sits there.

When you're talking about layering, do you mean frequency-wise or level-wise?

Jon Gass: Frequency-wise. My ears have always been sensitive to frequency clashing, even back when I played in bands. I didn't know why, but frequencies onstage would drive me insane. Too much bottom maybe on the rhythm guitar amp clashing with the bass amp or something.

When you're building your mix, do you look at the meters and go by them? For example, the bass at –5, the kick at –5, etc. Or strictly by feel?

Jon Gass: It's by feel. That's more part of the R&B thing, too. Everything's kind of from feel to me. Sometimes the mix sounds great and somebody says, "The mix feels great, print it." As opposed to a rock record where they might say, "More guitars," or something.

Do you add your effects right from the beginning, or do you wait until you have everything balanced out and then add them?

Jon Gass: As I go. I hardly ever use long halls or long reverbs. I use a lot of gear, but it's usually for tight spaces. Sometimes in the mix it doesn't sound like I'm using anything, but I might use 20 different reverb-type boxes, maybe not set for reverb, though, just to create more spaces. Though you may not *hear* it in the mix, you can *feel* it.

How do you go about getting your sound? What determines what you're going to use?

Jon Gass: I don't have a formula. Whatever feels right. I usually have maybe 24 or 30 'verbs and delays set up almost all the time. Not necessarily set to the same thing, but up. I think I have probably more outboard gear than anybody in the world. I like to use a lot of different 'verbs. Instead of having 20 Yamaha reverbs, I'd rather have one or two Yamahas and one or two Lexicons, because they seem to each have their own sound. The more different ones you use, the easier it is to separate the actual sounds.

Before you start a mix then, do you have the same effects set up all the time?

Jon Gass: Yeah. For instance, on the last song I did, there was a Mini-Moog type sound, and I had this kind of a short, tight room 'verb on it that set it back in the mix really nice. On the next song, I didn't get a chance to change the setting, but I just happened to flip it onto the snare, and it sounded great. So I didn't change it. It's the same effect from the last song, but it's on a completely different instrument. I have certain things set to what they do best; then I'll use them if I'm going to use that particular sound on a song. The next song I might not use it.

Do you use mostly delays or reverbs or a combination?

Jon Gass: A combination. I do like the reverb programs with predelays and delays in them so that you can kind of customize them to the song and the tempo.

So everything's timed to tempo, then, right?

Jon Gass: Depending on the song, yeah. Mainly the 1/8s, 1/4s, or 1/16s. But depending on the tune, I'll add in triplets or whatever feels right.

The other thing I like to do with delays is to diffuse them. I'll put a delay through a bunch of stuff just to make it sound worse. We joke about this guy that mixed a long time ago, and he'd have his delay clearer and brighter and louder than the actual lead vocal. I think that's what kind of got me experimenting with ways to really tone it down.

Sometimes I put a delay through an SPX90 and won't even use the program. I just use it to clip the top and bottom end off and diffuse it off the lead vocal a little bit.

When you're saying you use short spaces, are you trying to move stuff back or just put it in its own space?

Jon Gass: Yeah, put it in its own space. Sometimes it can be just a chorus, even a harmonizer with a really short delay time. What it comes down to is I like short, dry sounds.

How short?

Jon Gass: Like 25ms or less. I use a lot of 10, 12, 15ms on things. For *Waiting to Exhale*, for instance, a lot of that was really different for me because of the big string arrangements. That wasn't something that I'm used to doing, but I sure loved it.

How did you approach the big strings? The traditional way, by putting a big hall on them?

Jon Gass: No, I kind of approached it differently. I didn't think that the stereo pairs were wide enough, so the first thing I did was spread them out about 10 milliseconds or so. Then I took the room tracks and kicked them back maybe 80 or 100 milliseconds, just to really make the room bigger. I was trying to create a bigger room on the room they already had before I started adding verb. And finally I just added a little bit of verb on the delayed room tracks. Once I created that, I thought it worked great. It's still kind of dryish, but it's gigantic. So it's really more of just the delays than 'verbs.

Do you pan it opposite or just put it in back of the source sound?

Jon Gass: Usually stereo. In the R&B stuff, you get a lot of stereo tracks that really aren't stereo. That's one of the first things I do is widen the thing out, even if it's only 3, 5, or 10 milliseconds, and just get that stuff separated out so I can keep my center cleared out. I don't really like that "everything-mono" thing.

With all the effects you're using, it sounds like there's a separate one for each instrument.

Jon Gass: Absolutely. I very rarely use the same effect on more than one thing.

Do you use gates much?

Jon Gass: Lightly, especially on the SSL. I see a lot of the younger cats use them too much along with too much compression.

Lightly meaning the range is set where the level comes down a little bit rather than off?

Jon Gass: Yeah, just a teeny bit. A little hiss is okay. Just the bad hiss is what I'm trying to get out. But also, the SSL gates can sound a little funny. I'll use a lot of outboard gates. Drawmers and stuff are usually around for the hard work if I really need to do something more extreme.

What will you use those on?

Jon Gass: Live drums and for triggers—stuff like that. I don't really use the (Forat) F16 a lot for replacing drums, but what's great about it is I can use the original drums and something from the triggers in combination so that it's maybe not necessary to EQ the original at all. I'll maybe add another kick that already has the frequency I would've added to the original one. It seems like when you try to add a lot of bottom or something to the original kick, it starts to take away from the attack. So if you can leave that sitting the way it is and add another bottom-end kick to it, then you get the best of both worlds.

How about monitoring? Do you carry your own monitors with you?

Jon Gass: No, I don't, but I really only work in about four different rooms. The rooms I work in regularly have stock NS10s with extremely high power on them, and the mains are always TAD Augsburgers tuned by Steve "Coco" Brandon.

And I mix really quiet on the big ones most of the time. That seems strange, but it's something that hit me about 15 years ago when I went to my first mastering session and they were listening quietly on the big ones and it sounded so good. And I was like, "Wow! I could've made that sound better if I could've heard it this way."

When you say quiet, you mean if you have a conversation you drown out what you're listening to?

Jon Gass: Just about, yeah. Like the SSL up on 1 (the Control Room Monitor level control) is what I mix on most of the time. It's really quiet, but I can mix a very long time and not get fatigued. Sure, I do the NS10 thing, and then towards the end of the mix, I'll go really loud on the NS10s and do some adjusting. And I'll go extremely loud on the big ones and do some more adjusting just to fine-tune. But I like it quiet on the big ones, but they have to be the right ones. I always said I could make a great-sounding record on a cassette deck if I just had the right monitors.

Do you ever use headphones?

Jon Gass: No.

Do you have any listening tricks, like going down the hall or out in the car?

Jon Gass: I like to listen outside the room, but one of my favorite tricks is to turn on the vacuum cleaner and lay it up against the wall in the front of the room. Sounds a little strange, but I just kind of want to see if the mix is still cutting through at all. A blender would work, making margaritas or something. [Laughs]

When you're doing a mix, how many versions of the same mix do you do?

Jon Gass: I'll do the main version, a lead vocal up, just the backgrounds up, and then the lead and backgrounds up. I hardly ever do a vocal down version. Then I'll just go through and pick some instruments that some-body might have questioned and put those up. It usually comes out to be 10 or 12 versions of each song, believe it or not.

Covers your bases, though.
Jon Gass: If I don't do that, somebody always says, "It's too bad you didn't do one with this." But if I do that, it never happens. Even though they always pick the main version, I think people just feel better knowing that the alternate versions are printed.

You have an interesting approach, and it certainly does work. You try to make things bigger instead of washing them out...
Jon Gass: I think part of that is probably from my early recording days. I didn't really have any 'verbs, so I had to use more of the ambience that was available. That started adding such a new twist as opposed to everything just miked so close and direct all the time. It adds such a great depth to everything.

That must be the secret then.
Jon Gass: I'm sure that helps. But to me this business is about 95 percent luck, because if people don't call you and you don't have the right stuff to work on with the right gear, then it doesn't really matter. There are so many great, great engineers that are slow (work-wise). It's really luck.

CHAPTER 21

Don Hahn

Although there are a lot of pretty good engineers around these days, not many have the ability to record a 45- to 100-piece orchestra with the ease of someone who's done it a thousand times. Don Hahn can, and that's because he actually *has* done it a thousand times. With an unbelievable list of credits that range from television series like *Star Trek (The Next Generation, Deep Space Nine, and Voyager)*, *Family Ties*, *Cheers*, and *Columbo* to such legends as Count Basie, Barbra Streisand, Chet Atkins, Frank Sinatra, Herb Alpert, Woody Herman, Dionne Warwick, and a host of others (actually 10 pages more), Don has recorded the best of the best. Starting in New York City in 1959 and eventually becoming a VP at the famed A&R studios there and later at Hollywood's A&M studios, Don has seen it all and then some. He was kind enough to let me observe during a recent *Star Trek* session, and then he shared some of his techniques and advice.

How is your approach different from when you do something with a rhythm section?
Don Hahn: The approach is totally different because there's no rhythm section, so you shoot for a nice roomy orchestral sound and get as big a sound as you can get with the amount of musicians you have. You start with violins, then violas if you have them, cellos, then basses. You get all that happening and then add woodwinds, French horns, trombones, trumpets, and then percussion and synthesizers.

What happens when you have a rhythm section?
Don Hahn: Then the rhythm section starts first. Any time I do a rhythm section, it's like building a building. That's your foundation. If you don't build a foundation, the building falls down. I like to shoot for a tight rhythm, not a big roomy rhythm section. I think that comes from all

the big bands that I did: Woody Herman, Count Basie, Thad and Mel, Maynard Ferguson.

Are you building from the drums or the bass first?
Don Hahn: The bass is always first. Everybody relates to the bass. I can remember doing records in New York, and some of the producers would put me on and put paper over the meters. I told them I don't care; just let me get the bass, and I'll balance the whole thing and it'll come out okay. The only time I can get screwed personally on any date with a rhythm section is if the bass player's late. There's nothing to relate to because everybody relates to the bass player. If he's not there, it doesn't work. Now orchestrally, like on *Star Trek*, the bass players can be late and it doesn't matter, because I'm balancing all the other strings and then adding brass and the percussion last. So if the bass player's late, it doesn't matter. But on a record date with a rhythm section, it's the bass player and the drummer that's the foundation, and the colors come from the synthesizer and the guitars.

What's your approach to using effects?
Don Hahn: I'll use effects to enhance what I'm doing, but not to make like a bubble gum record. I don't do those kind of records any more.

A lot of the records that I do are, for lack of a better term, legit records. I've done a zillion Jazz dates. You can't put a room sound on a drummer on a Jazz date. It doesn't work; I've tried it many times. It ends up like a hot Pop record rhythm section, and the music doesn't jive with it.

I saw you using the EMT 250s the other day (at Paramount Studio M during a Star Trek *scoring session). Wasn't the room big enough, or weren't you getting the room sound that you liked?*
Don Hahn: Well, you have to put some echo on it anyway, so when you go to different studios and do the same show, it's got to sound basically the same every week. It doesn't matter what studio I go to, I still rent two 250s to make it sound consistent. Some of the studios have great plates, but I don't have time to fool with them. When you're doing a live television show, there's no mix. You're mixing it as you're doing it.

What would your approach be to adding reverb or echo?
Don Hahn: I mix emotionally until it feels good for me, and hopefully it'll feel good for the producer and the composer and everybody else. I don't use a lot of effects, especially on the television shows. I do on records. Not a lot, but whatever I think is necessary if it's a little dull sounding. I can remember once with Earl Klugh, I had a popping rhythm section, but Earl plays an acoustic guitar and you can't put a lot of effects on it. So I had to tone down the rhythm section a little; otherwise, it sounded like two different entities. You can't use a gimmick on an acoustic guitar like that, so

it's sort of by feel. If the record doesn't make me bounce up and down, I'm doing something wrong.

How about panning? When you're doing a Star Trek *date, I'm curious how you're panning the various sections. Would it be the way the conductor's looking at everybody?*

Don Hahn: No, I do that on movies. When I'm doing *Star Trek*, I do the high strings in stereo, the low strings in stereo, the synth in stereo, the brass and woodwinds in stereo, the percussion in mono, and whatever else mono. That's a stereo room, and I pan it hard left and hard right.

Do you ever worry about what it's going to sound like in mono?

Don Hahn: No, I check it, and it changes a little bit, but it's not like a record because they add dialogue and sound effects. I used to worry about the studio and tape noise until I found out that every time they went into the spaceship on the show, there was a background hum in the ship. So now I get the least amount of noise that I can, but I don't spend a lot of time fixing it because I'm not making a CD. You have to take all those variables into consideration because time is money.

I notice you weren't doing much EQ or compression.

Don Hahn: I used a little bit. I think I had a little on the percussion, maybe a little top end on the cymbal, and take some bottom end off the soft cymbal. But if you use the right microphones, hopefully you don't have to put that much EQ on anything.

You're not doing much compression. Aren't you worried about somebody being out of control?

Don Hahn: Absolutely not. What're you going to compress?

I assume on a record date it'll be a little different?

Don Hahn: Oh, yeah. You might get the French horns to jump right out at you. You might have to put an LA-2A on it and squash them just a little bit, but you shouldn't hear it.

When you were doing the Sinatra dates, I assume it was all live.

Don Hahn: Yeah, I did Sinatra tracking dates in New York, but Frank never showed up, so I've never personally recorded him. He called from his plane and said, "Just do the tracks, I'll overdub them in LA." And then on the *Duets* album, I did some extra vocals with Steve and Edie, and I think Jimmy Buffet and Frank Jr., and I'm not sure who else. Now on the *Broadway* album, I did maybe nine cuts. I'm not sure.

Tell me about that. I'm curious if the vocalists are singing with the orchestra at the same time.

Don Hahn: Sure, that's the best way to make a record, especially with Sinatra, or Tony Bennett, or Streisand, or any major artist. That's the way they're used to doing it, and it's great. I mean you really work your butt off, but you feel like you've accomplished something as opposed to sitting there all day and just overdubbing synth pads.

What problems do you have in a situation like that?
Don Hahn: Headphones are the biggest problem in the studio. You never have enough separate cue systems to keep everybody happy.

Are you worried about leakage?
Don Hahn: No, I try to get the least amount of leakage with as much room as I can. On Streisand, we put the bass player and the drummer in one section of the room with some gobos around. She was in her own booth, three other singers were in another booth, and the whole rest of the studio was filled with great musicians.

How has recording and mixing changed over the years?
Don Hahn: Well, just for some perspective, when I started, there was no Fender bass and one track only—mono with no computers and no click tracks. Everybody played acoustic bass. There was no synthesizer. Bob Moog used to come up to the studio sometimes with his synthesizer that he was working on. It was like 15-feet wide with big old telephone patch cords and tubes. [He'd] have us comment on his sounds.

I think some of the problems you have now is the younger guys don't go into the studio and listen. You must listen to what's going on in the studio. Don't just go into a control room, open faders, and grab EQs. As an engineer, you're supposed to make it sound in the control room like it sounds in the studio, only better. You must listen in the room and hear what it sounds like, especially on acoustic or orchestral dates, and not be afraid to ask composers. Your composers, and especially the musicians, are your best friends, because whatever they do reflects on what you're doing. If they're not happy, you're not happy. Remember: The music comes first.

CHAPTER 22

Ken Hahn

There are few people who know TV sound the way Ken Hahn does. From the beginning of the television post revolution, Hahn's New York-based Sync Sound has led the way in television sound innovation and the industry's entry into the digital world. Along the way, Ken has mixed everything from *Pee-wee's Playhouse* to concerts by Billy Joel and Pearl Jam and a host of others, while picking up a slew of awards in the process (4 Emmys, a CAS award, 13 ITS Monitor awards).

What are the differences between mixing for television and anything else?
Ken Hahn: Right away, the difference is that you have already got a certain restriction presented by the picture. In other words, the picture is only so long, so if you happen to get this great idea to do something that may change the length of what you're working on, it's probably not possible because the picture's already locked. If it's a half-an-hour show, that's how long it's going to be. It's something that most people coming from music can't get over. Like, "Wait a minute. What do you mean I can't fix this?" "Well, no, I'm sorry. The picture's locked." The reason why they can't go back is it's just too darn expensive.

Another major difference is that the deadlines in the TV world are a lot stricter. I always say, if it's in *TV Guide*, it's gonna be on the air. If they say the new so-and-so album's gonna be out the first week in April but it comes out the second week, then it's not as big a deal. But you never hear that *Barbara Walters Presents* will not be seen tonight because we didn't finish the mix. So there is a pressure on everybody to finish stuff, which in TV seems to be bad and getting worse.

How long does it take you to do a typical mix?
Ken Hahn: Well, it depends. We do a couple of series here where we get a couple of days to mix for a half-hour show, which ends up being about 20-something minutes of actual programming. So we need a day to do it and a day for people to see it and to do some changes. It ends up being about 16 to 20 hours, and that's for a show that's "together." You can do it in less, and you can certainly do it in more. News-style shows get less time, and music shows get more, but I guess the answer is never enough.

Video is now getting more like film in that they're doing more post production on live shows. People now actually spend time previewing things, pulling sound effects, looping lines, doing foley. In the last 5 or 10 years, things are much more prepared by the time it comes to the mix. It used to be that you'd start at the beginning of the show and fly through it just to make it digestible. But now it's gotten as sophisticated as film post production, which can be very sophisticated.

So essentially you have a lot of elements that you have to pull together.
Ken Hahn: Yeah, it can be as big as a major film mix: 30, 40, 50, 100 tracks, depending on what's going on. The average viewer now doesn't know the difference between watching *Mission Impossible* on HBO and *Homicide*. They know one's a movie and they know one's a TV show, but when they're watching on a little TV, they expect the same production value for either.

With that amount of elements, where do you start building your mix from?
Ken Hahn: Most television and film is narrative in nature, whether there is a narration voice-over track that's telling the story or the dialogue is. Dialogue is premium, so most people start by making sure you can hear all the words. It's common practice here (Sync Sound) to do a pass mixing the dialogue, making sure that if nothing else played in the scene, the dialogue would still be seamless.

When you turn on the TV, the reality is that you set the level by the volume of the dialogue. You have to make sure all the words are in front, and everything else is sort of window dressing. Music plays a huge role in it, too. What's been nice in the last few years is stereo television, which has only been around since MTV. Stereo music is a nice pad for things.

Do you take advantage of stereo for anything else?
Ken Hahn: Usually stereo ambiences like birds, winds, traffic. You can get into a lot of trouble by panning effects too much. In film mixing, at least you know that it's going to be played in a fairly large room that has pretty good speakers. With TV, the listening areas run the gamut from people laying in bed listening with headsets on up to home theaters, so you have to err on the side of safety, which means put all the dialogue in the middle and spread your music as much as you want left and right. But if you start

panning footsteps and all, it can really get weird, because if you're looking at a 15-inch TV while you mix and you pan footsteps from left to right, then the panning will be all wrong if the viewer happens to be watching on a 30-inch projection TV.

Have you done much with surround?

Ken Hahn: Music concerts, yes. But quite frequently, if it sounds good in stereo, it's just going to sound better in surround. Inevitably, once you kind of get the hang of it, you know what it's going to sound like in surround anyway. The real battle has always been to make it sound good on the lowest common denominator, which is small speakers.

What are you using for monitoring?

Ken Hahn: For a small reference speaker, we use the staple of the industry—the Auratone—but most of our stuff is mixed on bookshelf speakers. We've used the KRKs a lot for the last five years. That's pretty much what we've determined to be like an average stereo speaker, yet it also relates to your average TV. We've done a tremendous amount of listening to various kinds of TVs with built-in speakers and found that the KRKs translate very well from those speakers. That's what it's about—translating from big speakers to small speakers.

What level do you monitor at?

Ken Hahn: I personally monitor about as low as most people would accept. I tend to go that way because inevitably, if you get it sounding good at a low level, it just sounds that much better at higher levels. It sort of forces you to do a lot more manual gain riding at low level, because otherwise stuff just doesn't poke through. I'm sort of doing my own form of manual compression, and I've found that usually works better than the other way around.

Speaking of compression, how much do you use? Do you compress a lot of elements?

Ken Hahn: I've done various things through the years. What's kind of cool about the Logic (AMS/Neve Logic 2 console) that we have, which has an all-digital signal path, is it gives me multiple opportunities to control the gain. I do a little bit at almost each signal path, but I do it a number of times, some limiting, some compression throughout so that it's pretty well controlled by the time it leaves here. Unfortunately, it's really frustrating to pop from ABC to HBO to ESPN and get radically different levels.

Speaking of which, how much does everything change from what you hear in the studio once it finally hits air?

Ken Hahn: It really depends on the network. It's incredible what sometimes happens to stuff on the air. It just flabbergasts me and my clients. We've delivered to anybody and everybody, so we pretty much have an idea what you should do at our place before it gets to them so it will sound like you wanted it to sound like in the first place. You have to sort of put this curve on what you're monitoring so that you know that it'll sound fine on Viacom, for instance. I got a pretty good idea what HBO, NBC, etc. does to our stuff, so you have to process the mix with that in mind.

When you're remixing a live concert, since it's mostly music now, how are you approaching the mix? Where are you starting from?
Ken Hahn: It's usually vocals again. I make sure that those are perfect so that it becomes an element that you can add things around. I always clean up the tracks as much as I can because inevitably you want to get rid of rumble and thumps and noises, creaks, mic hits, etc. Then I always start with bass and rhythm.

It sounds repetitive, but the vocal's where the story is. It's so integral to the music because that's where you're focused, so it has to be as perfect as it can be. It can't be sibilant, tubby, too bright, or too dull. It has to be properly processed so that it becomes another element that you have real complete control over. A guitar track, for instance, will probably be pretty consistent for the most part, but vocals inevitably are less controlled. The person may be on or off mic. They may be sibilant someplace; they may pop in other places. If you don't eliminate all those technical problems so that you can concentrate on the balance, you can really get bogged down.

It becomes even more critical in a production dialogue track where you've got, for instance, three people cut between different scenes and each sounds slightly different with slightly different room tone and different levels. Let's say you have a woman who speaks in a whisper with a guy who mumbles and another guy who yells. Well, if you don't level that out properly, you can't balance sound effects and music against it. I think that's the art of TV mixing. That's what makes the difference between people who really mix television and film for a living and anybody else. If you look at a film mix, there are three mixers, and the dialogue mixer's considered the lead mixer.

And you're cleaning those things up with the automation?
Ken Hahn: Absolutely. Automated filters and just fader moves. That's one of the reasons why we got the console we did. It's completely dynamically automated, so you can roll in a hi-pass filter, zip it in and out, and the pop's gone. You can ride the EQ as you're trying to cover two people with a boom mic. If one is tubby and one is bright, you just literally ride the EQ through the scene until you get it right, so that it plays as close as consistent as possible. It wasn't that I was looking to get a digital console. I was looking to get a dynamically automated console, and it happened that you got one with the other.

Are you staying in the digital domain the whole time?

Ken Hahn: Absolutely. I'll tell you, once you hear it this way, it's hard to go back to analog. What's different about television and film, as opposed to music mixing, is the number of generations that a particular track of audio may travel.

Let's say you recorded a location production soundtrack. It gets transferred to some medium and gets lined up with the picture. It now gets put into a workstation. Then it probably goes back to tape of some kind. That individual track now gets premixed to a dialogue track. So far we're talking like four generations already. Then it gets mixed into probably a final mix. That's five passes. Then it gets laid back to videotape. That's six passes, and that's probably minimal for your average show. Most of them would go even more generations than that. With analog, there's just too many possibilities for phase errors, EQ problems, bias problems, [and] noise reduction units being incompatible, especially noticeable when you mix for stereo. I mean, it gets unbelievable. I've just found that the difference between analog and digital is just like night and day.

Do you sweeten the audience much?

Ken Hahn: Absolutely. I tend to make concerts sound as live as possible. I usually use a lot of the audience mics. I feel like the audience becomes another member of the band. The band is playing off of each other as much as they're playing off of the audience, so let's hear the audience.

How do you deal with effects? Is it at the request of the act?

Ken Hahn: I always try to become familiar with the material before I get to the mix so I know if there are any specific effects that are really important to the songs or to the artist. Also, a lot of people print an effects track that either you can use or get the idea from. But other than that, it's to taste. Luckily for me, people like my tastes.

CHAPTER 23

Andy Johns

 Andy Johns needs no introduction because we've been listening to the music that he's been involved in for most of our lives. With credits like Led Zeppelin, Free, Traffic, Blind Faith, The Rolling Stones, and most recently Van Halen (to name just a few), Andy has set a standard that most mixers are still trying to live up to.

When you're building your mix, where do you start from?
Andy Johns: I don't build mixes. I just go "Here it is!" [Laughs heartily] Actually, I start with everything. Most of the people that listen to and tweak one instrument at a time get crap. You've just got to go through it with the whole thing up because every sound affects every other sound. Suppose you're modifying a 12-string acoustic guitar that's in the rhythm section. If you put it up by itself, you might be tempted to put more bottom on it, but the more bottom you put on it, the more bottom it covers up on something else. The same with echo. If you have the drums playing by themselves, you'll hear the echo on them. You put the other instruments in, and the echo's gone because the holes are covered up.

Do you have a method for setting levels?
Andy Johns: That's all crap. That's rubbish. There was a famous engineer some years ago that said, "I can mix by just looking at the meters." He was obviously an upstart wanker. If you stare at meters long enough, which is what I did for the first 15 years of my career, you find they don't mean anything. It's what's in your soul. You hope that your ears are working with your soul along with your objectivity, but truly you can never be sure.

The only way that you can get a proper mix is if you have a hand in the arrangement, because if you don't, people might play the wrong thing or play in the wrong place. How can you mix that? It's impossible.

The way that I really learned about music is through mixing, because if the bass part is wrong, how can you hold up the bottom end? So you learn how to make the bass player play the right parts so you can actually mix. It's kinda backwards. I've been into other people's control rooms where you see them working on a horn part on its own. And they're playing with the DDLs and echos and I'm thinking, "What are these people doing?" Because when you put the rest of the tracks up, it's totally different, and they think that they can fix it by moving some faders up and down. When that happens, they're screwed. About the only thing that should move is the melody and the occasional other part here and there in support of the melody.

Does the fact that you started on 4-track affect the way you work now?
Andy Johns: Yes, because I learned how to balance things properly to begin with. Nowadays, because you have this luxury of the computer and virtually as many tracks as you want, you don't think that way anymore. But it was a great learning experience having to do it that way.

You know why *Sgt. Pepper's* sounds so good? You know why *Are You Experienced* sounds so good—almost better than what we can do now? Because, when you were doing the 4 to 4 (bouncing down from one four-track machine to another), you mixed as you went. There was a mix on two tracks of the second four-track machine, and you filled up the open tracks and did the same thing again. Listen to "We Love You." Listen to *Sgt. Pepper's*. Listen to "Hole in My Shoe" by Traffic. You mixed as you went along. Therefore, after you got the sounds that would fit with each other, all you had to do [was] adjust the melodies.

What's your approach to using EQ?
Andy Johns: You don't get your sound out of a console. You get your sound from the room. You choose the right instruments and the right amplifiers for the track. If you have a guitar sound that's not working with the track properly, you don't use EQ to make it work. You choose another guitar and/or amplifier so it fits better in the track. It might take a day, and it might take four or five different setups, but in the end you don't have to worry about EQ because you made the right acoustic choices while recording.

With drum sounds, even though where you put the mics is reasonably important, it's the way you make the drums sound in the room. The way you tweak them—that's where the sound comes from. The sounds come from the instrument and not from the mixer. On rare occasion, if you run into real trouble, maybe you can get away with using a bunch of

EQ. But you can fiddle for days making something that was wrong in the first place just different.

How about compression?
Andy Johns: I use compression because it's the only way that you can truly modify a sound. Whatever the most predominate frequency is, the more you compress it, the more predominate that frequency will be. Suppose the predominant frequencies are 1 to 3k. Put a compressor on it, and the bottom end goes away, the top end disappears, and you're left with "Ehhhhh." [Makes a nasal sound] So for me, compressors can modify the sound more than anything else. If it's a bass guitar, you put the compressor before your EQ, because if you do it the other way around, you'll lose the top and mids when the compressor emphasizes the spot that you EQ'ed. If you compress it first, then add bottom, then you're gonna hear it better.

At what level do you listen at?
Andy Johns: If I'm listening on small speakers, I've got to turn them up to where they're at the threshold of breaking up but without any distortion, or I listen very quietly. If you turn it way down low, you can hear everything much better. If you turn it as far as it will go before the speakers freak out, then it pumps. In the middle, I can't do it. It's just not Rock & Roll to me.

Got any listening tricks?
Andy Johns: Obviously, the idea is to make it work on all systems. You listen on the big speakers, the NS10s, out in the car, plus your own speakers; then you go home and listen again. This is a lot of work, but it's the only way to go.

Figure 23.1
JBL 4310 monitor (long out of production).

I tend to bring JBL 4310s, 12s, 13s, and 12As [see Figure 23.1], and I put those out in the actual studio. But you know, I don't care how close you think you've got it that night. You take it home and play it back in the morning, and every time there are two or three things that you must fix. It's never happened to me where I've come home and said, "That's it." You hear it at home and you jump back down to the studio and sure enough, you hear what you hadn't noticed before on all the systems there as well. So every system you listen on, the more information you get. You can even turn up the little speaker in the Studer (2-track tape machine) to hear if your mix will work in mono.

Do you listen in mono much?

Andy Johns: No, but I'll tell you this. If you've got a fantastic stereo mix, it will work in mono as well. For example, "Jumpin' Jack Flash" is a stereo mix released in mono. People don't listen in mono anymore, but that used to be the big test. It was harder to do, and you had to be a bloody expert to make it work. In the old days, we did mono mixes first [and] then did a quick one for stereo. We'd spend 8 hours on the mono mix and half an hour on the stereo.

When do you add effects in the mix?

Andy Johns: I have some standard things that I do that more or less always work. I always need a great plate like an EMT 140 [see Figure 23.2] and a short 25 to 32ms delay just in back of the vocal. If it's kind of a mid-tempo tune, then I'll use a longer delay, which you don't hear because it's subliminal. It doesn't always have to be timed to the track; sometimes it can go in the hole so you can hear it. I've been talked out of putting reverb on electric guitars, but "Start Me Up" has a gorgeous EMT 140 plate on it. Most studios you go into don't even have one anymore.

Figure 23.2
EMT 140 plate reverb.

So you usually predelay the plate?

Andy Johns: Usually but not always. In the old days like on the Zeppelin stuff, you'll hear very long predelays on vocals. You know what that was? That was a 3M tape machine which was originally designed to do video, so it had about a 9-inch gap between the heads as opposed to the 2-1/4-inch gap on a Studer or Ampex. Sometimes I'd even put it at 7 1/2ips. Another thing we used was the old Binson Echorec. [See Figure 23.3.] Listen to "When the Levee Breaks." That was me putting two M160s on the second floor with no other microphones at all because I wanted to get John Bonham the way he actually sounded. And it worked! Page would say that he made me do it, but he was down at the pub. He did bring me his Binson Echorec for the track, though.

Figure 23.3
Binson Echorec used an electrostatic drum for delay.

Do you prefer analog or digital?

Andy Johns: What I like is the sound that's coming into the mixer. I don't want it modified by some tape machine. I've always fought with analog. I've always fought with vinyl. With digital, the sound that's coming in, you get it back. It's much truer than any analog machine ever was. If you've got to smooth out your sound with some analog machine, then you're in trouble to start with. With analog, the noise factor is like a security blanket in that the hiss can cover up some weasely things.

Which automation do you use, or do you prefer to mix manually?

Andy Johns: They're all shitty because you're fighting a machine. I suppose the GML is the easiest, but I still have to have somebody there with me to help. That's the part of the job that pisses me off. You've now got to be a bloody scientist. Sometimes it makes you too clever for your own good. If you just learn the tune, then you're in tune with the tune. You let it flow through you. Now you might listen to it years later and say, "I think I missed that one." Or, you might go, "Fucking hell, I wish I was that guy again. That could not be any better. Who was that man?"

CHAPTER 24

Kevin Killen

In a prime example of how people interact today via high technology, I bumped into engineer/producer/mixer extraordinaire Kevin Killen via an Internet newsgroup. It seemed that a popular thread turned to how the bass sound on Peter Gabriel's "Sledgehammer" was recorded, and all manner of know-it-alls replied with the wildest of supposed methods and equipment, all of which were wrong. Eventually the real answer (Tony Levin's Musicman bass straight into the desk with a little compression) emerged from the real voice of authority, Kevin Killen, who not only recorded and mixed Gabriel's seminal *So*, but also recorded U2, Elvis Costello, Stevie Nicks, Bryan Ferry, and Patti Smith to name just a few.

Can you hear the finished product in your head?
Kevin Killen: In certain instances I can. If I'm hired just to mix a project and I'm not intimately familiar with the material, I have just a general overview as to what I'd like it to sound like. As soon as I get in the studio, that's where I really start thinking about pushing or pulling a track one way or the other. For stuff that I've recorded, I usually have a pretty clear vision of what I want and actually try to start mixing as I'm recording. I like to work 24-track (rather than 48), so I try to make decisions based upon that. I'm always kind of mixing in advance.

Where do you start your mix from?
Kevin Killen: Usually the vocal. Maybe some of the rhythm section. I listen to what the strengths or weaknesses are and then build the track up around that. At some point maybe I'll just pop the vocal out and work on some of the rhythm stuff. I found that if I start with the vocal first, I finish a lot more quickly rather than if I start from the ground up. If you're dealing with an artist who's a strong storyteller, that's going to be the main focus anyway.

Do you have a method for setting levels?

Kevin Killen: I've never subscribed to the point of view that there is a method. I just go with the flow. I had an experience about three years ago on a Stevie Nicks record with Glyn Johns, who's been making records since the 50s. We were mixing without automation, and he would just push the faders up and within a minute or two he would have this great mix. Then he would just say that he didn't like it and pull it back down again and push it back up. I relearned that the great art of mixing is the fact that the track will gel almost by itself if it was well performed and reasonably well recorded. I find that the stuff that you really have to work a lot harder on is the stuff that has been isolated and really worked on. The tracks all end up sounding like disparate elements, and you have to find a way to make them bleed together.

What's your approach to EQ?

Kevin Killen: I would imagine that I apply EQ based on my own hearing curves, whatever that is. I definitely hear a lot more high end than other people, maybe because my ears stick out and aren't pinned back flat to the head like other people. Because of that, I tend not to over-exaggerate EQ. I try to get it sounding smooth. Most people mix in a much more aggressive fashion. I don't have individual instrument curves that I keep coming back to because every bass drum is different and every player is different, so I don't have particular settings or sounds that I go for except to make it sound as musical and pleasurable as possible.

Do you have an approach to panning?

Kevin Killen: That's one of the things that I actually spend a lot of time on. I will get a balance that I like; then I'll just try moving the panning around. I might spend a couple of hours experimenting, because for me, that is the kind of detail that can create a lot of space in a mix. I love to explore and create holes for instruments to sit in, but I'm not into gimmicks such as spatializers to make the panning seem wider than the speakers.

How about compression?

Kevin Killen: When I can get it to work, sometimes I really like it. It's one of those things. I listen to other people's mixes and go, "That sounds amazing," but when I try it, I can never get it to sound the same way. I tend to be quite modest on compression because my rationale is that you can always add more but you can never take it off. Since it will probably be applied at a later point during mastering and broadcast, I tend to err on the side of caution.

Since SSLs hit the marketplace, I know what a temptation it is to set up the quad buss compressor even before you start your mix. I tried that for a while, but I found out that I didn't like the way it sounded. What I came up with instead was almost like sidechain compression where you take a couple of groups on the console and you assign various instruments to them and use a couple of compressors across the buss and mix it in, almost as an effect, instead of using compressors across the inserts. You actually get a sense that there is some compression, yet you can ride the compression throughout the song, so if there's a section where you really want to hear it, like in the chorus, you can ride the faders up.

How about adding effects?
Kevin Killen: If they're tracks that I haven't recorded, I get a quick balance with the vocal and the basic instrumentation to get a sense of the space around each instrument. If they've been recorded with a lot of ambience, I'll shy away from it, but if the artist wants it to sound lush, then I'll add some. Each situation is unique.

Do you have a standard effects setup?
Kevin Killen: I have some effects that I'll definitely go to, but I won't necessarily have them set up beforehand. I really want to hear what's on tape before I start jumping in. What I normally request is a tape slap machine with varispeed because it's still such a great sound.

Do you bring your own monitors?
Kevin Killen: I actually bring a set of English Proac Studio 100s and a Cello amplifier and my own cabling. Bob Ludwig at Gateway Mastering hooked me up with them, and I've been using them almost exclusively for about 3 years. I find that when I take my stuff to mastering that it translates really well.

Is there a difference between the way English engineers approach mixing from American engineers?
Kevin Killen: I believe that the trend in the UK is to enhance the mixes with the appropriate effects, and there seems to be less resistance to the notion of effects in general. In the U.S., it seems a little more contrived, i.e., if you want to be a cool alternative band, you cannot use any reverb on the vocals, etc., etc. Personally I'm bored with that philosophy. Every recorded instrument including the voice will have an ambience associated in the room in which it was recorded. Therefore, I believe it's important to highlight the inherent musical quality of the performance. Of course, an artist such as Elvis Costello likes his material to be slightly less reverberant, but I used more than he ever knew because it was mixed appropriately. I try to show reverence to the artist and the producer because when they recorded the track they had a particular philosophy in mind. I'm just a person to help them realize that vision.

CHAPTER 25

Bernie Kirsh

Bernie Kirsh has certainly made his mark as one of the top engineers in the world of Jazz. From virtually all of Chick Corea's records to working on Quincy Jones' *Back on the Block* (which won a Grammy for Best Engineering), Bernie's recordings have consistently maintained a level of excellence that few can match. Although technical know-how is all important for an engineer these days, Bernie tells us that there are other, more human requirements involved in mixing, too.

Can you hear the final result before you start?
Bernie Kirsh: It depends on whether I've tracked it and I've been into it. If it's not something that I've tracked and overdubbed, then I'm discovering it as I'm mixing. But often, especially in the Jazz world, it's much more simple because I start out with wanting each individual instrument to have a pleasing quality. There's a preconceived notion I have of what that is. If you're talking about straight-ahead Jazz, there's a balance that's been accepted as part of the form. In that world, the cymbals are important, the position of the bass, piano, where the horns sit—all that kind of stuff has been listened to for decades. It's kind of a traditional form, so that's somewhat predefined. If you move away or want to make a variation of that, then you're on your own. If it's something more in the electric vein, and something that I've worked on, then I'll come up with a notion of where I want it to go.

How do you start to build a mix? Where do you start from?
Bernie Kirsh: The first thing that I actually look for is the melody. After that, I'll go for the bottom of the mix.

The bottom being the bass?

Bernie Kirsh: The bass usually. I don't necessarily go for the drums first. Before I hit the rhythm, I usually try to get the melody and some sort of harmonic setup first because I want that to be clear, and I'll often shape the rhythm to accommodate that. So that's the simplicity of it. If it's something that's more hard hitting, I'll spend more time with the rhythm to get those guys pumping together.

Do you have certain frequencies that you seem to come back to that need attention on certain instruments?

Bernie Kirsh: Let's say for piano (which I've dealt with a lot), typically what happens is that in the analog domain it loses definition and openness if it's mixed some time after it's been recorded, so I'll usually boost in a couple of areas. First, up around 15k (sometimes that gets lowered down to 10 or 12, depending on the instrument), and maybe a little midrange at 3k or 5k. It depends on the instrument and setting, but that's pretty typical. I'll do the same thing usually with cymbals. I'll add between 12 and 15k on cymbals pretty typically. Those are the normal areas of EQ that I find that I'm constantly using.

The frequencies that you adjust seem to be a little different than R&B or Metal.

Bernie Kirsh: With this kind of music, it's all about trying to go for more of a natural sound, for lack of better phrase. So, if there's going to be any hype at all, it's going to be with the loudness button, where you get the larger bottom and accentuate the top. Normally, if you're going to add anything else to a piano, for instance, you're in the 500Hz range adding some warmth. But I find sometimes that when I finally get to mastering, the mastering engineer wants to take some of the warmth out for clarity purposes with just a little notch around 200 or 300. So, my tendency is to go for the warmth and then sometimes wind up taking some of that back out to achieve a little more definition or clarity later, if needed.

Do you have an approach to panning?

Bernie Kirsh: No, I normally keep things wide. Drums in stereo; piano open. I personally like a wide piano. I like it so that it feels like you're sitting at the instrument.

You do it wide, left to right?

Bernie Kirsh: Yeah, wide left to right. I position everything as the player is seeing it rather than the audience. So the drums are from the drummer's perspective, piano's from the pianist's perspective, etc., unless there's a leakage situation where I have to worry about the phase. If, for instance, the piano and the drums are in the same room, I have to make sure that the cymbal is appearing in the right place and isn't smearing because of the leakage into the piano.

What projects are you the most proud of?
Bernie Kirsh: What I'd like to do is delineate between the musical experience and the audio experience because they're two different things. There are albums that I did early on which musically I enjoy and I think at the time were sonically enjoyable. One was an album called *The Leprechaun* by Chick Corea. That was 20 years ago. The reason it was a lot of fun was because we just did live recordings in those days. You had the horns and the strings, if strings were there, and the rhythm section playing all at once.

It was the most fun because you became part of the creative process. It's actually not a process at all; it's a different kind of craft. A different type of musical creation. So I do enjoy that.

Although I didn't do the mixing, I did do some recording on Quincy Jones' *Back on the Block* record a few years ago. That was a great experience, and it won the Best Engineering Grammy Award. I actually learned a lot doing the record because it was so different than the Jazz world, flying parts in and around, and using all these techniques that people use that may not be used in straight-ahead Jazz.

There was such a cross-pollination of different types of music on that.
Bernie Kirsh: On that record, I was recording Rap, R&B, straight synth parts. It was a playground in there. It was so much fun. Working with a guy like Quincy was just a fantastic experience in itself because this guy is a genius. He's a superb musician, and he knows how to work with creative people. He understands it, and he gets people to do what they do best.

Is there a certain psychology that you use when recording?
Bernie Kirsh: I wouldn't call it psychology, but it's in the realm of human interaction. I've had people approach me and say, "Why don't you tell people how you deal with others," meaning that they felt good during this creative process, whereas in some instances, they haven't.

So what's the difference between how I was treating them as opposed to how they've been treated by other engineers? I think there are certain basic things that occur in that little microcosm called a studio which a lot of guys don't recognize. You're getting into some basic human sensibilities that may not be apparent as you look at it. For instance, you have artistic creation going on. You have a guy who has come into the room who has done something that's very, very close to who he is. It's not PR. It's not show. It's something that he holds very, very dear to himself. Now he's, for lack of better word, open and vulnerable, and he's not being social.

So now you've got an engineer in the room whose attention isn't on that. Often you get engineers who, through various different bits of behavior, will invalidate the artist, evaluate for the artist, and not respect the frame of mind that the artist is in when wanting to make his musical statements—in other words, not looking at what the artist is doing at the moment. I think you'll find that the best engineers, the ones that the artists want to work with, have a notion that what the artist is doing is important and is something that needs to be treated with attention and respect. When I say that, I mean not to hold it up on a pedestal, but to understand that the action is something that's very close to the artist and not just a commodity.

For some reason, the creative process is different in the Jazz world. Guys are coming in, not necessarily to just lay down just a rhythm track, but with the idea of making music. So I put a lot of attention on making the players happy with what they're hearing and make it comfortable for them. I don't work with a lot of engineers, so I don't see it, but from the feedback I get, a lot of the younger guys don't recognize that element is really important. It seems like the job is really 10 percent technical. The rest of it's how you work with people and help them get what they want.

CHAPTER 26

Nathanial Kunkel

 It can be said that Nathanial Kunkel was always meant to be an engineer. The son of session drummer extraordinaire Russ Kunkel, he grew up literally at the feet of the best that the LA music scene had to offer. But patronage doesn't mean much in this business, and Nathanial had to work hard and pay his dues just like thousands of others. All that has paid off handsomely, because Nate is now one of the most in-demand mixers in the business, with credits that range from James Taylor, Lionel Ritchie, and Sting to Good Charlotte, Fuel, and Insane Clown Posse.

How did you get into the business? You were a protégé of George Massenburg, right?
Nathanial Kunkel: I loved audio. I wanted to be a drummer, but I saw Jeff Porcaro (the late drummer for Toto and countless studio sessions) play, and I thought to myself, "I'll never be able to play like that. I've got to find something else to do."

Yes, but you have such good genes. You probably would've been a great drummer.
Nathanial Kunkel: Yeah, I know, but between my dad and Jeff, I thought, "Why would I want to get into this?", so I ended up meeting George when I was 13 or 14. My dad was doing a movie with Billy Payne (keyboardist from Little Feat) and George at The Complex (George's former LA studio). I saw George sitting behind his (custom-built) console with an Ampex ATR-124 and an ECO synchronizer furiously typing, and I thought, "I so want to do this." And that's how I kinda got into it.

Once I did get into it, I sort of pursued George vigorously. At that time, George and Greg Ladanyi owned The Complex. I had known Greg from when my dad was doing *Running On Empty* (Jackson Browne's break-through 1977 release). So in my sophomore year in high school, Greg gave me a job as a runner at The Complex. I didn't have a driver's license, so I just stayed at the studio and cleaned up and learned how to solder and all that kind of stuff. I did that for the summers when I was in high school and right after I graduated from high school.

Did you start to assist for George right away?
Nathanial Kunkel: No. I wanted to be an assistant engineer righ t away, but when you're young and in the recording studio, you make lots of mistakes, so while I was in high school, they told me that I had to be 18 before they'd let me assist. At that time, it was all analog tape machines, so there was no such thing as a backup and no margin for error.

George had stopped working there, and I was a little bored, but soon I got an offer from Ed Wong at Jackson Browne's GrooveMaster's studio to go there as an assistant and a tech. So I was there for about a year and a half working for Jackson, which was fantastic. Ed Wong is one of the greatest human beings that I've ever known in my entire life. He taught me so much about the technical side of audio, but also how best to interface with clients regarding technical issues. He taught me how to give the client just enough information that shows that you respect their opinion without overloading them with too much technical information.

Then I got a call from George, who was at Skywalker Ranch about to start a Little Feat record, offering me a job as his assistant. George and I were always excellent friends. This was something that I had always hoped would happen but sort of moved on from it until it did. So it fell into place really quickly from there.

How long did you assist for him?
Nathanial Kunkel: For about 2 or 3 years. At that point, he was working with Peter Asher (producer for James Taylor and Linda Ronstadt, among many others) a lot. Midway through that relationship, I became integral to the way Peter worked as well. When Peter didn't have access to George as an engineer, I would always be there. I was also in charge of taking care of his instruments and sequencers and computers and would always be the person that would assist George when he was mixing.

When it became apparent that I would be working with Peter just as much as George, I became an employee of PG Technologies, which was a company that Peter and George had for a while, and I would bounce between the two of them. It was really great because at that time it was when everyone was going to London to do strings and stuff like that, so I got to go to Air Lyndhurst and Abbey Road, which was really fun.

You don't work in a traditional studio much these days, do you?
Nathanial Kunkel: As much as I can. I miss working in studios. I especially miss meeting other engineers to talk to during lunch when we'd all be working in different rooms of a facility. That's why I love AES shows so much. It's the only time I get to hang out with my peers these days.

Do you do much tracking anymore?
Nathanial Kunkel: No, but only because people don't ask me to anymore. I love to track, but people call me when they think they want a certain kind of a sound, like a pristine Lyle Lovett kind of thing or something that I'm known for cutting. I work with (producer) Michael Beinhorn a bunch, so I've gotten to do some cool Rock stuff. I worked on the last Fuel record, and that was good fun. But I just do tons of mixing these days.

Do you start a mix with a particular approach?
Nathanial Kunkel: I think I learned the best approach on how to begin a mix from Ed Cherney. Ed just sort of pushes up the faders and listens to the song. Maybe he'll just pull the guitar down and listen to the song. Maybe he'll just push up the bass and drums and vocal and listen to it. He really just spends a lot of time listening, and he really gets a feeling for where the gems of the track lie. In listening to all the stripped-down versions, he finds the little moments that can be brought to fruition in every one of the tracks. Then he does it like everyone else where he pushes up the kick drum and checks the phase with the overheads, then puts the bass in, and so forth. Everyone kind of does it the same way, but it's really what you are looking for out of the individual instruments.

Can you hear the finished product in your head before you start?
Nathanial Kunkel: Absolutely. I could hear the final mix in my head for a lot longer than I had the skill to get it there. What happens is that when your skill lets you down, you run out of time, which doesn't really mean that you have to leave the studio but that you no longer have the same perspective when you had it fresh in your head. So to me, the secret combo is for you to come in, have a really great idea about what you want the song to be, then have the skill set to get the tracks to that point before you lose perspective because you're fatigued.

So how long does it take you usually?
Nathanial Kunkel: I usually lose perspective in about an hour and a half or two hours. I can mix solid for about eight, but I find that I can't do really vigorous knob twisting after about an hour and a half into it. Then I just start to chase my tail a little bit.

What do you do after an hour and a half? Do you switch to another song?
Nathanial Kunkel: Yeah, unless I can do something else to break the concentration for a half hour or so.

When you start a mix, where do you start from?
Nathanial Kunkel: If the song is a consistent dynamic all the way through like a Rock song, I really don't have a method. I just sort of push it up. If I've gotten a great balance on the guitars and vocals before the drums, I'll just mute them (the guitars) and get my drum balance a bit better, then just group it and balance it against the guitars and vocals. If I've gotten something really great going on like a background blend, I'm certainly not going to whack it in order to get a better kick drum sound, because if it's something consistent like a Rock song, you certainly don't get into much trouble because you can push stuff up or down as you go along and sort of end up in the right place.

In situations where there's an intro where things are quieter, like an acoustic and electric guitar and a vocal before the drums kick in maybe in the chorus, when the drums kick in during that chorus, you don't want the level of the vocal to change very much, but you want what's happening between the vocal and the drums to be right. And that balance is very difficult to build after you've built an introduction. So often I'll go and get a drum sound and push up a vocal and get a rough blend with the band, and then I'll go back to the intro and I'll push up the other instruments around that admittedly loud vocal. But I'll build it so my automation brings it back to the balance that I had before. So if I have a song that will dip down dynamically once or many times, I'll go and get the core instruments to sit exactly where I want them in the loudest place because I'd rather have the automation return it to the up part rather than the down part.

What's the difference between mixing on a console and mixing in the box for you?
Nathanial Kunkel: There's nothing different mixing in the box that I didn't do when I was mixing on consoles and tape machines. It just takes me less time. I have to mix in the box. I couldn't afford the infrastructure necessary for the sheer quantity of tracks I have to deal with in the projects that I do.

Did you have to change your approach when you decided to mix in the box?
Nathanial Kunkel: [Laughs] I had to unlearn the lies (about mixing in the box). I find that I'm having more fun mixing like this, and I find that I'm doing it exactly the way that I used to (on a console). All the things that I thought would change my workflow in the box in fact made me make worse-sounding records. All the things that I find easier to do in the box, like get more level, I find that I'm doing less and less of right now. I find

that I use my console (a Digidesign Icon controller) a lot more like an analog console. I put the same EQ and the same compressor on every channel, so I never have to go to the plug-in menu. I use all outboard reverbs and effects. I still use all outboard vocal compressors—my distressors, GMLs and Alan Smarts.

I also use tons of headroom. When was the last time you took a console that clipped at +25 and ran it at +24? You just don't do that in analog, so why would you do that in digital? I use at least 10 or 15dB of headroom in my buss. If I'm going to print a loud version, I'll take it out to an M6000 or something that does a really outstanding job of handling overlevels, and then bring it back into Pro Tools and not change it.

When you used to sit down at a console with a tape machine that was overbiased, you would play it and say, "Something doesn't sound right," and then you'd turn around and address it. How many times have we sat down behind a Pro Tools rig and said, "Uuugg, something's wrong?" That's the same thing as with a tape machine; it's just a different toolbox. It may be the headroom or clock distribution or a variety of things, but you have to pay attention and then fix the things that are wrong. If it sounds digital, then try something different. So it's a new toolbox, but it's really the same auditory skill set.

Do you have any tricks that you use when mixing in a DAW?
Nathanial Kunkel: No. That's frightening to say, I know. Maybe it's because I was taught by fantastic analog engineers. When I started engineering, we were doing anything anyone asked for no matter how hard it seemed at the time. Fly that here, tune that, etc., etc. It might take us 3 days to tune a vocal, but we'd tune them.

So what can you really do with audio? You can store it, you can change its level, you can delay it, or you can EQ it. That's really it. Reverbs are combinations of two. Those four things have never, ever changed. Give me 25 PCM42s (old Lexicon rack mount delay) and a patch bay, and I'll do any type of multitap delay that you can do inside Pro Tools. It might take me longer, but I can do it.

So mixing inside the box—what in the world is different about that? It's still the same problem that we've been having forever: making good artistic decisions, then following through with the right toolset. It's all the same; you take your ideas [and] then make them something, so if you have shit for ideas, it doesn't matter what you have access to. We could make a Buddy Holly record now, and if we apply all these new methodologies to them, it would probably suck.

Another case in point. Look at the records that Al Schmitt is making. He's making these Diana Krall records that are equally comparable to anything he's done in his entire life. And what is he doing with Pro Tools? He's recording into it, then he's playing it back. He's using that tool for how it will perform best for him, which is as a reliable high-resolution 192kHz audio recorder. There's no reason for it to do anything else for him.

So for me, there's nothing that I do within a digital workstation that I didn't do in the analog domain before. I can do it better in some cases, but it's not a different task.

Do you have an approach to EQing?
Nathanial Kunkel: Take out the stuff that's bad, then make the things that are good louder if they're not loud enough.

Do you have an effect that you keep on coming back to?
Nathanial Kunkel: My M6000 (t.c. electronic) is my effects processor of choice. It's the single-best effects processor that I have ever seen or used.

But never underestimate the power of a good delay. Delays are really wonderful ways to open up mixes. Maybe it's just a simple ping-pong or a guitar on one side with a delay on the other; they don't have to be loud and obvious. They can be subliminal and add some groove.

Effects in general don't have to be obvious. The best effect to me is when you're not really aware of it. I often have Rock songs that have all kinds of things going on, but when everything is raging, you don't even hear it. All you'll know is that it has a little more swing that it did before. That to me is the win of using effects—when you can just enhance the emotional response that people have to the music without drawing their attention to some kind of trickery.

Also, the GML Series 3 limiter circuit in my GML 2020 [see Figure 26.1] is the best vocal limiter that has ever been made, and I cannot do what I do without it.

Figure 26.1
GML 2020 Input Channel (courtesy George Massenburg Labs).

Do you use it just on vocals or on other instruments as well?
Nathanial Kunkel: Almost exclusively on vocals, mainly because I don't have 40 of them. I've only got two, so they end up on things where I can't get enough extreme RMS compression out of anything else.

How much compression do you use then?

Nathanial Kunkel: I don't want to say [sheepishly]. More than 10dB—I mean, not all the time. There are times when there's singing when they're not in compression at all, but if my limiter hits 15 or 20dB of compression and I don't hear it, I don't think about it for an instant more.

Do you put a compressor across the stereo buss?

Nathanial Kunkel: I use very little. I find I'm using more multiband compression on my buss as nothing more than a way to elevate my level so I have something that's competitive for approvals. But I print almost all of my mixes without limiting. Even though it eventually goes out with limiting, I do my best to make sure that it sounds as timbrely accurate as the mix sounds without it.

The truth is that I compress things enough instrument-wise. I don't really need to compress more on the buss. When I do compress the buss, it's maybe 2 or 3dB. The multiband lets me take it up there and hold good level on the disc. I find that it allows me to get more competitive level with less compression.

Is this onboard the DAW?

Nathanial Kunkel: No, it's with my 6k (tc M6000).

How about your monitors?

Nathanial Kunkel: I'm using these new JBLs (LSR 4300s). I really love them. They're dynamite. They translate so well.

Do you have any special listening tricks?

Nathanial Kunkel: I listen quietly as much as I can. It's hard to check kick drum level when it's quiet, so certainly you have to push it up every once in a while, but I fatigue pretty quickly when listening at loud levels. I can make better emotional and timbre decisions before I fatigue.

What are you printing to these days? 1/2 inch or back to disc?

Nathanial Kunkel: I don't think the tape today sounds too good. It doesn't come back with the same snap for me, and I can't find an alignment that I like. I own an ATR-102, but I can't seem to use it. I'm looking forward to listening to Mike Spitz's (from ATR Services) tape. But in general, it costs too much, I do too many different versions, I do a lot of multichannel (surround) stuff, and I don't like the new tape.

Let's go there for a moment. What's your approach to mixing surround?

Nathanial Kunkel: I guess if I were to encapsulate the rule, the things that I used to put in the middle I put everywhere now. Bass, kick drum, snare drum, lead vocal—all the stuff that has a lot of mono-correlated information goes a bit to every speaker, except maybe the center. If I put something in the front, I will very rarely put it in the center and the left and the right. I will put it in the center and the surrounds if I want to pull it more into the middle of the room. If I want something off to the side of the room, I'll go left, right, and right surround so it leans to that side.

The Sony DMX1000 (digital console) is really what got me into this because, unlike the Pro Tools buss, you can just turn off one of the speaker outputs. In Pro Tools, you can't pan it in the middle and then turn off just the left surround so it's going equally to the left front, right front, and right surround, but that's a really cool thing. So now I make that happen with sort of unique bussing architecture, like aux sends that feed back into a buss or something.

But I find that the more speakers, the better, as long as it's not the center and the left and the right because I don't like comb filtering that way. I know that sometimes when I've had to do that for a TV thing, I'll filter the center channel so I don't have so much of the high frequency to prevent the comb filtering because that really bothers me when I move around the listening space.

And it's so funny—you never know what people are going to like or dislike. I did this James Taylor reissue where I put him in the center speaker and the left and right surrounds and I put the duet vocal quad but mainly in the front speakers so there was still the same amount of pull-back into the center of the room for both of them. James was in the very hard center middle, and the duet was phantom imaged in the center. I thought it was so cool because I could finally bring that duet vocal up, but yet it didn't step on James because it held a completely different space in the room. But the first review I read said, "I don't know what he was thinking. The duet vocal is not even in the center channel at all. Thank God he didn't do this on more than one song." I'm reading this thinking, "You just have no idea."

Was it in an audiophile magazine?
Nathanial Kunkel: [Laughing] Of course.

What do you usually put in the center?
Nathanial Kunkel: That changes. I always put something in the center. Mostly vocal.

How about the LFE?
Nathanial Kunkel: Jeff Levison from DTS told me early on, "Dude, here's what you have to understand. The LFE is a low-frequency effects track. It's used when you have run out of low frequency headroom in your other channels." That was in the very beginning when I was using tons of LFE and we'd go into these rooms with an improperly aligned .1 and the low

end for the entire track would be wrong. Then I started mixing with bass management, so I only go to the .1 when I cannot put any more level on the main channels and I want more bass.

One last thing. What was the most important thing that George taught you?
Nathanial Kunkel: After about 5 months working for him he said, "You know Nathanial, the hard part about this gig is not getting good sounds or getting along with the artist. It's about paying attention to every little thing that's done every moment of the day and knowing exactly what it means." And the really great engineers know what will happen with every button in the room, and that's why we all go so bananas when people change things.

CHAPTER 27

George Massenburg

From designing the industry's most heralded audio tools to engineering classics by Little Feat; Earth, Wind & Fire; and Linda Ronstadt (to name only a few), George Massenburg needs no introduction to anyone even remotely connected to the music or audio business.

Can you hear the final mix in your head before you start?
George Massenburg: No. I generally look for a trace of feeling and I diddle things until I get a response. Whether it's EQing or changing arrangements, it's got to work as a feeling. And as such, I feel that what I do is significantly different from anybody else. I don't go into a studio to make money. [Laughs] I go in to experiment.

Is that a collective feeling, or is it singular?
George Massenburg: Just about any successful piece of music is not something that can be performed by one person. It's almost always a collaboration. I can't think of anything that only one person has done in Pop music.

What I go after in mixing is a collaboration. Let me describe what I do with Linda (Ronstadt). I go after what I need, and she tells me what she needs, and then I try to steer a middle course between the two.

When you begin to build your mix, where do you build it from?
George Massenburg: I always start Rock and Roll with drums, but very quickly I'll get a voice in there so that the instruments are crafted to work to the texture and the dynamics of the voice. I don't have any real rule. I actually can start just about anywhere.

When you start with your drums, are you starting with the overheads first and building around that?
George Massenburg: Yeah, I generally will start with overheads.

Room mics or overheads?
George Massenburg: Well, first and foremost I'm listening to the music, so I'll start with whatever gives me the best picture of what's going on in the room. I'll get a fast, overall mix, and while I'm figuring out the tune, I'll start listening for problems or things to improve. Problems might range from a less-than-effective instrument amp or a mic placement to some big, funny boink somewhere that's sticking out. I like to tune things—line up overtones. I feel that equalizers are best used when used the least. I use them most to get rid of tones that are somehow not flattering. I'll most often use parametrics, sharp and subtractive, to look for the two or three biggest out-of-sorts characteristics. A snare drum, for instance, has any number of boinks that I'll locate. I'll just have them ready to go on an equalizer. I may take them out or bring them up as I'm listening to the whole presentation, but I'll already know what and where they are.

How about effects? Do you add effects as you go along, or balance everything and then add them?
George Massenburg: I think of engineering as an art. I think that anything we do, we do for emotional reasons. So, the more we can keep what we do, the better. I start saving a mix on the very first monitor mix of the track. I'll save a snapshot and sometimes save the automation. What I'd really like to do is save everything—every reverb, every delay. So if you think of what happens with a painter and a canvas, he picks up where he left off, and he may erase things or add things. If you X-ray a Rembrandt, there's all kinds of other ideas under the surface, but they start where they left off.

Well, we're not able to do that yet. We can't start where we left off because there's not the facility to do it yet. You get to a point in the track where everybody's really excited, but then you come back and it's completely different. "You know, it really sounded good the other night. Let's do that." But you can't get it back. Everything is subtly different, and it throws you off. Have you ever tried to match a mix to a cassette that the artist brought in? It's impossible.

You're pretty much staying with all the effects that you start with and just building on that then, right?
George Massenburg: Well, I may or may not stay with them. I have to see if they still count. Often delays and things that are musically related or effects the guys play to, especially like long reverbs, I'll print them. Delays, choruses—print them. Anything that's sonically significant to musical performance, I'll print.

Do you have an approach to using effects?

George Massenburg: I don't have an approach. This is probably my biggest strength and my biggest weakness at the same time. I really try to invent everything from scratch every time I walk in. But yeah, I have basic things that I keep going to.

When you're beginning to set up for a mix, are there certain boxes that you automatically put up?

George Massenburg: Yeah, there's probably eight different starting points, and two or three of them will stay. The starting point is a plate, a delay, a (AMS) DMX, a (Roland) 3000 or 3500, a (t.c. electronic) 5000 for different kind of reverb, and a (Eventide) 2016 [see Figure 27.1]. I'll use the 5000 for short stuff. I'll sometimes have a second 2016 for chorus. An (AMS) RMX is standard.

Figure 27.1
A reissue Eventide 2016 Reverb
(courtesy Eventide).

I'll have about eight delays set up. If I can send something into a delay, I'll do that because it takes up a lot less room. If I can make it sound like a reverb, I'll use it. I'll always go with the delay instead of a reverb if I can hide it.

Hide it meaning time it to the track?

George Massenburg: Yeah, timing it so you don't really hear it as blatantly. You hear richness and warmth.

And the timing is what? 1/8 notes or dotted or triplets?

George Massenburg: No, it's musical. The timing will change. Often it's just by feel. I just put it up and try to get something that rocks.

What's your approach to panning?

George Massenburg: I've got two or three different approaches, and I'm always changing it. I used to be impressed by a drummer liking what I did, so I pretty much only got a drum perspective. But I've gone wide and I've gone narrow.

I've been working with Glyn Johns, and Glyn is a master of the accidental big airy drums, of course with Led Zeppelin. It's a great story. I was having dinner with Glyn and Doug Sax (mastering engineer extraordinaire) one night, and he was telling us about the first Led Zeppelin record and how they set up the drums in mono. They had one 67 right over the snare, but they always needed a little bit more floor tom, so he stuck a mic at elbow level, kind of off by the floor tom, pointing into the snare. After he finished the track, he grabbed the mic and put it on the guitar and panned it. When he put it back on drums, he forgot to pan it back. "Oh, that sounds great. I wonder what happens if I take the overhead and pan it right?" And Doug and I looked at each other and said, "You got stereo drum miking by accident?" And in that case he became well known for that big airy Led Zeppelin and The Who sound. It was a different sound than what was being done in New York, which was almost all mono, or California, which was a spaced-pairs kind of thing. The earliest stereo that I knew didn't even include stereo drums.

Is there a general mixing approach that you have?

George Massenburg: I want to hear something authentic. I want to hear an authentic room or an authentic performance. I want to hear authentic instruments. It's not necessarily a sophisticated or elegant thing. It's just authentic. In stereo, I try to paint a picture that makes sense—that your brain doesn't say, "Hey, what are you trying to put across on me?"

How are you applying compression during the mix?

George Massenburg: The big difference between engineers today is the use of the compressor. At one time or another I tried to compress everything, because I was building a compressor and I wanted to see how it did on every instrument. I'm a little off on compression now because there are so many people that overuse it. Everything is squeezed to death. As a result, I'm backing off. When anybody goes that far out, I'll go the opposite way as hard as I can. But generally I will pretty much always have an option to compress the mix. I'll use my EQ, my compressor, then my converter and an M5000 to do three band. Then I can dial it up from extremely subtle to pressed ham under glass.

I'll always compress vocals. I may recompress vocals again during the mix. I'll almost always have a bunch of compressors if I have to bring an element or a group of elements together like a background vocal, level them, then drop them into a pocket. Then I'll do some extreme stuff like compressing a room, then gating it. Maybe I'll compress a drum room and then gate it with the snare drum to get a real rectangular reverb. I do that a lot. Maybe I'll add reverb to a guitar and then gate the result of that. I do that some. Boy, I wish I could give you a rule.

What are you trying to accomplish?

George Massenburg: Trying to get a thrill. [Laughs] I'm almost always trying to get, as Lowell George used to call it, "decibel excursion," which is a bullshit term, but I love it. I try to make an instrument denser or give it some weight. Half of it's reverb or ambience, and the other half is bringing that ambience right up in your face, which is compression.

How about monitoring? What's your typical monitoring setup?

George Massenburg: I started using Tannoys in '79 and '80. They do one thing. I love Genelec 1032s; they do another thing. We used KRKs for the Journey record because they were little rockin' monitors. Light them up, and it's a completely different mix than what lights up Tannoys. And Yamahas, except that whatever lights those up makes for boring mixes. For rocking monitors, I'm just looking for something with that impossible-to-describe, lively factor. I don't know what it is.

I monitor on a lot of different things. I might go up to the wall monitors to try to hear subsonics. I'll go to Yamahas to hear what the idiots at the record companies are listening to. Tannoys for fun. KRKs for fun. Earphones.

You listen on headphones?
George Massenburg: I listen on headphones because you can hear if you're making a mistake.

I always put up a set of headphones myself, and when I don't do it, I'm sorry.
George Massenburg: Yeah. You know who taught me that was Jimmy Johnson. He would always find that snap in bar 30 of the sax solo, and you'd listen to it and sure enough, a tiny little snap to get rid of. And for the kind of music he was doing, that was appropriate.

What levels do you usually monitor at?
George Massenburg: Everything. I'll monitor way loud to see what rocks. I'll monitor at a nominal level to get sounds together. Then I'll monitor about 5dB over background noise to hear all the elements into focus. If a mix works at 30dB SPL, 25dB SPL, it'll almost always work a lot louder.

What are you listening for down that low?
George Massenburg: That the instruments work together. That you don't lose anything. If you can hear everything at that low a level, then when you turn it up, you'll have a very even balance. That's the way to get everything in the same plane—by listening extremely low.

Do you have any playback tricks? Do you go outside in the lounge and listen through the walls sometimes?
George Massenburg: All the time. I'm a big one for hallway. I hate cars. Through the control room doors is always an important thing for me, because I almost never do loud playbacks. I like listening around the corner and on a blaster.

How many versions of a mix do you normally do?
George Massenburg: Well, I prefer to have one version of a mix. It's the same theory as a horse race. You never bet against yourself. You never bet on two horses to win. I believe in one mix, and I believe either it's right or it's not right. I will walk out of the control room with only one mix. It's possible these days to do up and down in 1/2dB steps, but I don't really do it. At around that point, it's important for you to let go of a mix. It doesn't belong to you anymore.

Do you go back often and do any touchups or remixes?

George Massenburg: Yeah, all the time. But I think usually we go from scratch again. Some of the best mixes I've done have been the fourth or fifth or sixth passes. I remember on "Shinin' Star" (Earth, Wind & Fire's hit) we kept going back in the studio and tracking, and I think the more we went back in, the more we found what didn't work.

It seems like it's so much easier to refine things as you go back like that.

George Massenburg: Oh yeah, because you know what your priorities are. You know what doesn't work, because the first couple times you go in, you're trying exotic EQing and delays. You go back in, and it doesn't make any difference except for the stuff that's right. The thing that makes a difference is vocals. I've spent more time than anything else trying to find how to do vocals and how they tell the story.

What do you look for in a studio? Is there anything special that you have to have?

George Massenburg: Good food! [Laughs] It has to have that vibe. You have to take the studio seriously. You have to walk into a studio knowing that great music has been made there. Yeah, I need that in a studio because then I rise to the challenge. If you go in and record strings at Abbey Road Studio 1 and they sound bad, you know that you messed up. [Laughs] When Linda Ronstadt opened Skywalker with her record, we (including Peter Asher, the producer) intended to make a fairly large record. We used every aspect of that big room; it won two Grammys and sold three million copies right away and had two substantial hits. Well, the next guys that came into Skywalker could say that they didn't like our record or our music if they wished, but they certainly couldn't say that the room didn't work. So I look for that vibe. I look for whether really successful music—preferably music that I love—has been made there. If I went to Rudy Van Gelder's to record jazz, I would be really motivated to get it right.

If he would let you in. That's the problem.

George Massenburg: He wouldn't. We know that. Herbie Hancock said Rudy Van Gelder yelled at him once, and it's the first and last time he ever tried to lift the lid on the piano. Rudy came shooting out yelling, "Don't touch!"

What you bring to the table in the control room seems to come through. I've been gifted to work with great musicians, and any of the sounds that we get, any of the sounds that any of the really good cats get, it's because of great musicians.

CHAPTER 28

Greg Penny

Born into a music business family to bandleader/producer Hank Penny and hit recording artist Sue Thompson, Surround Music Award winner Greg Penny seemed destined for a life in the studio. Indeed, Greg's production aspirations resulted in hits with k.d. lang, Cher, and Paul Young, among others, but a meeting with Elton John while in his teens turned into an award-winning mixing journey with the legend many years down the road. Greg gives us an inside look at his long relationship with Sir Elton, and some insight into his sensational surround remixes.

How did you get into being an engineer/producer?
Greg Penny: I was born into a music business family. My father, Hank Penny, was a bandleader and a producer, a great guitar player, and an entrepreneur. My mother, Sue Thompson, had a lot of hit records in the early '60s. As a young boy, I would go with her to Nashville when she recorded, and I always thought that the producer's gig was the greatest. They got to make the rounds between the artist and great session players on the floor, talk to the engineer, pick the songs, and in the case of my mom's producer, who was a very multitalented guy, rehearse my mom before the session.

I think it had a lasting effect on me. I was really into the idea that I could move around all the different jobs and stay in the studio and make numerous records, while the artist could only make one every year or 18 months. I thought that this was really the thing for me.

I loved George Martin, and I loved Chris Thomas. Those guys were my icons as I was growing up. I admired them and wanted to be like them, and that's sort of how producing came about. Engineering came as a secondary thing. I would ask questions and often wouldn't be able to get my ideas across, so I just began grabbing faders and knobs and twisting things and eventually sort of found my way.

How long have you been engineering then?
Greg Penny: Probably just a few years after I started producing, so it probably was in my late teens or early 20s when I started engineering. I had a home studio, and I started recording bands and started to write songs of my own. You know, a 4-track-in-a-bedroom kind of situation.

I grew up in Las Vegas, and when I first came to LA when I was 17, I would beg for midnight studio time at studios in Hollywood and learn about the board and tape machines and things like that. I was never that great technically and would always get stumped when I tried to align things or do the really deep tech stuff, but I knew what all of the buttons did, so that was all that mattered to me.

Did you apprentice with anybody?
Greg Penny: I took a brief course from a guy named Bill Lazerus, who was a very famous engineer. He recorded *Sweet Baby James* (James Taylor's first hit album) and the Stone's *Let It Bleed* album. He's a great engineer and really great guy, real down to earth and sort of a "hip cat" who talked in kind of Jazz nomenclature. I took a course with him that taught me things like editing and the sort of day-to-day things that you run into as an engineer, like how to place mics and handle tape and what the signal path on the board was. That was very helpful to me, but I kind of tended to stay away from formal education. I didn't go to college or anything like that. I tried to get on to the street and learn as much as I could as fast as I could. I don't know if that would work for everybody, but it worked for me.

How did you get hooked up with Elton?
Greg Penny: When I was a teenager—14-, 15-, 16-years-old—I was like that kid in the movie *Almost Famous*. I was the guy that would go to all the gigs, and because my folks were in the music business, I knew everybody. I met Elton backstage at his first Vegas gig, and then the second time he came through, I brought my Mom down to see him. He was a fan of hers, so he was very happy to see us. After that, I stayed in pretty close contact with him, and I'd go to the gigs when he'd come through town, so he knew that I was a real sincere fan and that I wanted to be in the record-making business.

When I was 17, I decided to go to Europe on my own to find a music school that I could attend, and Elton told me that my trip was going to tie in with their recording at The Chateau in France. He invited me to stop by if I came through to check it out, so I went down to watch them record the back end of [*Goodbye*] *Yellow Brick Road*. I got there on the day when

Dee (Murray—Elton's longtime bass player) was fixing up the bass track to "Saturday Night's Alright for Fighting." They cut the track the night before, and he was just patching some things up.

Forget going to school. That's an awesome education right there.
Greg Penny: It also had a lot to do with me inheriting Gus Dudgeon's (Elton's producer) projects because I had so much respect for him, and he was one of my heroes. Gus let me sit in on stuff and never shooed me away. He never had an attitude with me and was always encouraging because he knew that this was what I wanted to do, so he sort of gave me the space to hang out and be a fly on the wall. I didn't go to London to the mix sessions for the record, but I stayed pretty up to the minute on everything they were doing. Of course, when I came back to the States and announced to my friends where I had been, everyone was like "Yeah, sure, dude."

But over time, we've remained friends. Then in the early '90s, I produced these records with k.d. lang that were real successful, and it turned out that Elton was a fan of the records. So he rang me one day and said, "I want to do this album of duets. Would you do a track with me and KD?" At the tracking session, he asked me if I'd do more songs on the duets album, which I did, and then he asked me to do his next studio album. We then made the *Made in England* album, which was really successful.

That kind of got me started to where for about 3 years all I did was Elton stuff, from studio to live stuff to remixing other things to following up on B sides and things for charity albums. There was just a lot of work, and I gladly fell into it and kept on going.

A couple of years ago, I went back to him with the idea of doing his catalog in surround, and he was really open to the idea. So I started doing a surround mix of *Made in England* as a demo to play him. He was on the road, so I took it to London to play it for his management and the record label. They loved it but stopped me in the middle and said that they needed a 30th anniversary release of [*Goodbye*] *Yellow Brick Road* instead. That sort of started the current set of things that I've been doing for the last couple of years. I'm on my 12th album right now.

What's it like finding the masters? Are they all in the same place?
Greg Penny: It was a difficult task to find the master tapes of all the songs associated with the album because they had not been appropriated in some time, so finding the tapes has been lengthy and frustrating. Very often, tapes had been mislabeled or put in a different box, so we've really had to struggle to find things. Plus the masters were spread out in a number of different places within this storage facility, so it took a long time to put it back together. The current album that I'm working on, *Blue Moves*, has always been kept in Elton's locker and hasn't been moved much, so they're in pretty good shape.

You once told me that it was extremely necessary to always refer back to the original stereo mix because Gus Dudgeon used a dynamic curve in his mixes. How did that work?

Greg Penny: We transferred the 2-track and the multitrack mixes at the same time and then imported any subsequent mastered or remastered CDs as well. These are brought into the system at 24-bit/96kHz, which is the environment that I'm working in now.

Then I use all of those as a reference as I'm mixing because there really isn't any one person across Elton's whole camp that knows all of these records. There's been a lot of engineers that have worked across 10 or 12 albums, and it would be difficult to involve them all, so I just have to sleuth it out, and the best way to start is with the original mix.

In the '90s, Gus Dudgeon and Tony Cousins at Metropolis Mastering in London remastered most of Elton's catalog for CD because the first time they came out, they didn't really optimize it for the medium. So when they remastered, Gus felt it was his chance to pull a George Lucas and fix some things that have always bothered him, so he ran the 1/4-inch tape mixes through a small digital mixing desk and added EQ and level changes and reverb in some cases while it was going into the digital workstation. That lent another set of variables to the mixes, so when I listen to the original 1/4-inch master mix and then listen to the mix from the remastered CD, it'll have a completely different tone color and maybe a different level.

Gus would often remaster the way that he mixed, where he'd work on it section by section and cut it together. On the first 10 albums that I've mixed, they didn't have automation. There were maybe four guys manning faders with Gus conducting the mix, and they would do it as a performance basically until they got it or got a big enough section where they could go back to pick it up. So when I'm remixing for surround, I'm really chasing the movements of eight hands, and the moves are incredibly subtle at any given moment.

If there was a part that I discovered in the multitracks that wasn't apparent in the 2-track mixes, I would try to incorporate it into the surround mix so that it could be more audible rather than the way it was during the original stereo where Gus would have to make a priority decision because he had to favor another part. I've got six places to put it now, so I've been able to incorporate things that might not have been heard in the original masters.

When Elton heard the mixes, he caught all those things right away and loved them. There were background voices on [*Goodbye*] *Yellow Brick Road*, little added stuff that (vocalist) Kiki Dee did and (guitarist) Davey (Johnstone) did and keyboard parts that Elton did that are very subtle in the stereo soundfield that can now poke out in the surround mix that sound pretty cool.

It's pretty amazing when even the players have never heard the parts that they played.
Greg Penny: I know. Because of the sheer pace that they had to move at in the '70s when Elton was so popular, they would only have 2 or 3 weeks to track a whole album and then they'd have to get on a plane to tour for a week, so they'd never get a chance to look back over their shoulders. I played [*Goodbye*] *Yellow Brick Road* back for both Davey and Elton in Atlanta when I finished it, and they sat together and high-fived each other for about 2 hours about how good the band was because they'd forgotten. When they were in the moment, they didn't have time to think about it.

Do you incorporate the mixing tricks you learned from Gus now on your more recent stuff?
Greg Penny: Yeah, more often than not I do because I find that when I listen to mixes where I've been subtle or timid about the level of a part, I tend to later feel that more dramatic colors or more dramatic mix rides had to be done. So more often than not in the last 2 years I've gotten more radical with things, and when it's time for them to be featured, crank 'em up.

Let's talk a little about your general mixing philosophy, Elton aside.
Greg Penny: If I stand back and try to look at things objectively, I've been told that one of the things that I do well is work with singers. KD, Elton, Paul Young, Cher. The comment I always hear is that I always have the singer foremost in my mind, and I would agree with that.

I usually start from the vocal. Obviously, there are instrumental things that you have to be concerned with, but my thought is how the vocal is going to work with the elements that are supporting them, so I guess I mix from the vocal out.

Is that where you start your mix from?
Greg Penny: No, not always. I'll poke around on drums and bass to get a good floor, and then I'll take them out and put the vocal in to try to get a really good sound on the vocal, then put all that together and put all the other elements around it, always bearing in mind that the vocal has to be the thing that pulls people in. Because for me, that's really the most important thing, although that's not necessarily true for everyone that mixes or all artists. There are grooves from each of those artists that are special to them but they're nothing without their vocals.

It's been fun to do the surround thing because I've been able to highlight things just by virtue of the fact that in stereo, things get crowded. In surround, I've been able to pull out instrument passages around the vocals.

What's your approach to mixing surround?

Greg Penny: It really started with [*Goodbye*] *Yellow Brick Road* because I had a few weeks to sit with it and come up with a formula. So I thought, "Here's this incredible record that's got tons of guitar and keyboards on it, so why don't I put the vocal in the center monitor most of the time and the only other things that enter into that monitor are double vocals or harmonies or maybe even a solo instrument? Then I'll bleed out a little bit of the center vocal into the left and right fronts so if Uncle Bob comes over to the house and sits at that end of the couch, he's not missing the lead vocal. Then I'll use divergence and spill a little of that lead vocal into the rear monitors also for that purpose. So why don't we give Elton the front of the room for his piano and Davey the rear of the room for his guitars, or even in quad like in "Saturday Night's Alright for Fighting"—four guitars, four speakers, with each guitar getting its own speaker?" And that started me moving in that direction, and then it got more radical as I went through the album. By the time I got to *Madman Across the Water* with those incredible string arrangements that Paul Buckmaster did, it was amazing to put the whole string section in the back and the band in the front so it was like you were sitting there when they were cutting the live orchestra.

And you know those songs were cut live. Elton didn't cut the basic tracks to *Madman* and then 3 weeks later put some strings on it. They recorded everything at the same time, so when you listen to it, it's like you're sitting midway between the band and the string players just like on the original date.

It sounds like the fact that everything was cut live greatly influenced your surround mixing philosophy.

Greg Penny: As Nate Kunkel says, you've got to make records for the guys that have the right system, because if you back off from that and try to dilute the vision down to the most common denominator, we'll never get anywhere. You have to somehow set the benchmark. More often than not on these blogs on the Internet about Elton's mixes, I either get slammed for being sacrilegious or lauded as a genius. They always talk about how the use of the surrounds is extreme on Elton's records, but then a lot of guys say, "Finally I'm able to figure out my system. I've got some stuff that puts something through all of my speakers." So my objective is to use the system entirely and not to be too timid, but there are some songs where you just don't have enough data to put in all the speakers and have it make sense without it seeming lopsided.

I have a new thing I call a "D Mix," where you select songs that you can remove a lot of the extraneous musical material, boil it down, and come up with sort of a distilled version of the song. In the case of "Candle in the Wind," I soloed the acoustic guitars, background vocals, and lead vocal to try to hear what the reverbs were doing without the drums and the bass and the piano and electric guitars, and it was so compelling to just hear it stripped down that I just left it like that and did a mix of it. When I played it for Davey, he started crying, it was so moving to him. Elton had gotten wind that I had done something to "Candle in the Wind," but he didn't know what, so when I played him [*Goodbye*] *Yellow Brick Road*, he asked to hear the D mix of "Candle in the Wind." He was totally blown away. He went "Yeah, do that more."

So I've tried to apply that on other songs, although it doesn't apply often because there's just not enough musical information to hold things together. But in the cases when you can distill things down, ambience then works in your favor. Like on the Diana Krall records where you achieve this space by virtue of the fact that there's nothing there. You can feel the air around you rather than the air being filled up with sound.

What kind of gear are you using?
Greg Penny: I use a Pro Tools HD system. All of Elton's stuff is at 24/96. It seemed that the jump up to 96k was much more noticeable than up to 192. I have a very simple single interface with a (t.c. electronic) System 6000. I mix in the box. On occasion, I'll go out to a little TL Audio tube desk to try to get analog warmth out of some things if I can't get it within the box, so I have that set up as a pull-down plug-in.

For speakers, I use Dynaudio Air 6s. [See Figure 28.1.] I come right out of the back of the HD interface into the back of the speakers with nothing in the way because the controller that comes with it is sufficient for me. I'm not doing any downmixes with the mixes that I'm doing, and if I need that, I can test it with a Waves plug-in across the buss rather than having something like a StudioComm box (monitor controller). Then you have an analog path, and I found that all the analog paths that I previewed in my room were off by some degree. If I was listening loud and then I wanted to listen quietly, it would shift the center. They just weren't as accurate as I wanted them to be, whereas the Dynaudios are incredibly accurate right down to a whisper level and then can also get incredibly loud. The system also translates very well when my mixes are played back in other rooms.

Figure 28.1
Dynaudio Air 6 monitor.

What was the transition to mixing in Pro Tools like?
Greg Penny: Initially it was a little frightening because of the magnitude of the record that I was starting with. The first surround record that I ever did in its entirety was [*Goodbye*] *Yellow Brick Road*, so it was scary. Because I had the authority to take it wherever I wanted to, I probably could've stayed at Air London when we finished the transfers. After several days there, we sort of approximated a surround mix on a beautiful old Neve that they had, and it sounded incredible. But I realized that if I was going to take the time that I needed for it to have all the impact that the original album had, I needed time. And in order to get the time, I needed to do it in my own environment, which didn't have a big board or an analog situation. So I took the step to mixing in the box.

I did a few tests at home, and I thought, "It sounds great to me." I'd invite people over that I respect, and they'd say, "It sounds great. What are you doing?" I'd tell that that I'm staying in the box but I'm being real careful with the transfers and just generally being real careful. I'm not doing anything crazy and not using a lot of plug-ins and just trying to proceed real logically. And after the first album, it made sense to do it that way.

With the amount of files that I need to keep track of, if I go out of the box, it increases the management of the project tenfold, and I don't want to do that.

Are there any tricks you've found to make mixing in the box work or sound better for you?
Greg Penny: I use a pretty simple set of tools inside. I don't use a lot of onboard plug-in reverbs. I have a couple of short things that I use, but predominantly I use the System 6000 surround reverbs. If I don't have enough firepower with the one unit that I have, I'll print back the reverbs and then I'll go back and do it again.

I use the Waves 360 suite a lot. I use their panner. I find it's easier to automate because I can just grab the toggle thing and fly it around. I like the L360 limiter. It's pretty straight ahead. It's actually a very simple set of tools that I use. I don't believe for the albums I'm doing that I need to get complicated, because when these albums were originally mixed, they only had a couple of plates available—maybe one that was a second or so long and then maybe another one maybe about two-and-a-half seconds. Over time, they got a digital delay, and that's how they did the handclaps on "Benny and the Jets," but most of it was tape slap. They used very, very basic things, so I try to stay with very basic stuff. If I do use anything high-tech, I try to make it sound transparent.

Has the Elton stuff influenced how you work on other things?
Greg Penny: Yeah, it has. It's influenced me to stay simpler, because I think I can get better imagery. I remember hearing Elliot Scheiner talk a

couple years ago at the Surround Conference. I remember him saying, "More often than not these days, if I want something to be in a speaker, I put it there. I don't often try to occupy the space between monitors (phantom image) because I find I get a lot of phasing and strange clarity issues." I've adopted my own version of that. It depends on the instruments that I'm using, but I have a fairly formalized way of placing things now, and it seems to work. I know where I like to put drums, I know where I like to put the bass guitar, all the way down to background vocals and strings and things like that. You tend to kind of set those things up, although I never start a song with a prepared template. I always start a song from the ground up. Then depending on what the song dictates, I'll change the placement.

I'm lucky in that the emotional impact of these songs has already been established. The production techniques of the '70s had things start fairly simply. Then they built to choruses that had more instruments, and then back up again and back down again and back up again. So they had sort of a dynamic to them that's very effective for surround stuff.

The dynamics are built into the arrangements.
Greg Penny: Yeah, dynamics [are] built into the musical arrangements where you have background vocals and guitars and things like that coming in at the chorus, for example. It's great to throw those into the surrounds and then just pull them back down to just the vocal in the center monitor after that. So you have some really good ways to play with the musical dynamics in surround.

You were telling me once before that you tried to get the sound of the early Elton records by first going back to the original MCI gear that was used, but that it didn't work for you.
Greg Penny: I know that [*Goodbye*] *Yellow Brick Road* was done on the MCI console at The Chateau in France. They had a very simple setup—I think it was called the "producers package" at that time. I think it was an MCI JH-24 (24-track 2" tape machine) and a 28-channel desk. [See Figure 28.2.] There was a certain sound to that board. The prevailing wisdom these days is to go back [and] mix it on an MCI or Trident or Neve or SSL board, but when I put the clean transferred tracks back through the board, it really colored the sound again. To me, mixing in the box just didn't color the sound as much as putting it through a desk (console), so I figured if I went out of the box through a desk, it wouldn't sound enough like the original. I did try to run things through various desks, but they just didn't work for me.

In the future when you do projects aside from Elton, will you still stay in the box?
Greg Penny: You're always influenced by what your peers do, and I listen to things that Al (Schmidt) or Elliot (Scheiner) do over at Capitol (Records

Studios) and the stuff sounds so good, but once I finish this set of Elton things, I would like to do some things that are initiated in surround and are repurposed later into stereo, which is sort of the reverse of the way things are done these days. So I'll probably stay in the box for that not only for simplicity but because that's where the project started and it will probably organically take shape that way.

Figure 28.2
MCI JH-528 console circa 1975.

I think it would be different if I had a different budget structure to work within, but there just isn't a lot of support financially for it (mixing in surround), so you have to find a way to be clever if you want to do it, and that makes me stay in the box. And I like it. I actually really enjoy the atmosphere that I work in. My studio is a really pleasant room to work in. It's not professionally constructed or anything. It's the bedroom of a large guest house, and it's about 16 feet long by about 14 feet wide. I've put some deadening material on the walls and some bass traps on the front of the room. It sounds very good, and it's a comfortable atmosphere for me to work in. So it depends upon the project and the budget, but I would probably stay within my own environment because I know it so well now.

I went kicking and screaming into mixing in the DAW, but I'm a convert now.
Greg Penny: I can hear it in your voice that you're saying that you almost have to resign yourself to it, but it's really not so bad. In the end, you wind up saying to yourself, "Well, this is working, and it's faster and it's probably better." I can understand that we don't want to abandon something that's been so wonderful, and I agree that when I put the analog tapes up to [*Goodbye*] *Yellow Brick Road* or even something new, it sounds incredible. But it has to be practical, and if you do the math, there is so much to keep track of out of the box that I can't keep track of it that easily. Oftentimes now I'll work on something for a half an hour, and if it's not coming, I can just put another track up, so you can work on three or four songs a day. Nothing ever gets boring, and nothing ever suffers because you're trying too hard, and I think that's really the beauty of it.

CHAPTER 29

David Pensado

Of all the genres of music, R&B may be the toughest to mix thanks to the almost constant change in the state-of-the-art and the penchant by the participants to experiment with new sounds. Mixer David Pensado, with projects by Christina Aguilera, Justin Timberlake, Kelly Clarkson, Pink, Mya, Destiny's Child, Bell Biv DeVoe, Coolio, Take 6, Brian McKnight, Diana Ross, Tony Toni Tone, Atlantic Starr, and many more, has consistently supplied mixes that have not only filled the airwaves, but also rank among the most artful.

What's harder to mix: an R&B or a Rock track?
David Pensado: I mix both, and R&B is infinitely harder to mix than Rock. Think of it this way. Let's say you're painting a portrait. Rock is like having the person you're painting sitting in front of you, and you look at them and paint, you look at them and paint. So you have a reference. In R&B, there is no reference. It's like trying to do a portrait from memory, but because you don't have the person there, you can paint something that transcends what he is. You can make him prettier, you can make him uglier, or you can make him abstract if you want. Doing R&B, you've got less limitation and a lot more freedom. We don't have to have the snare drum sound a particular way. It can sound like anything from an 808 to a hand clap to a little spitty sound to a Rock sound. But you put certain snare sounds in a Rock song, and it's just not a Rock song anymore.

Do you hear the finished product in your head before you start?
David Pensado: Yeah. I really can. I might not have 100 percent of the final product in my mind when I start, but I pretty much have it outlined. Then as I start filling in the outline, sometimes things change a little bit. Every once in a while, maybe out of two or three hundred, I might just

pull the faders down and say, "I don't like any of this" and start again from scratch.

What's your approach to using EQ?
David Pensado: Well, I think of EQ as an effect much the same way you would add chorus or reverb to a particular instrument or vocal. Like, I might have a vocal where I think it's really EQed nicely, and then I'll add a little more 3k just to get it to bite a little more. Then it just makes me feel like the singer was trying harder, and it brings out a little bit of passion in his or her voice. So I tend to be most effective when I do the standard equalizing, then take it to the next level, thinking of it as an effect. Some of my favorites for this are the NTI EQ3, API 550 [see Figure 29.1] and 560s, the old "Motown EQs" at Larrabee (studios in Hollywood), and the Avalons.

Figure 29.1
API 550b equalizer (courtesy ATI, Inc.).

Are there certain frequencies that you keep on coming back to?
David Pensado: I notice that in a broad sense there are. In other words, the frequencies from say 120 down to 20 cycles, I'm always having to add. It seems like the frequencies from say 10k up, I'm always having to add those. A lot of the music I do has samples in it, and that gives the producer the luxury of pretty much getting the sound he wanted from the start. In the old days, you always pulled out a little 400 on the kick drum. You always added a little 3 and 6 to the toms. That just doesn't happen as much anymore because when I get the tape, even with live bands, the producer's already triggered the sound he wanted off the live performance, and the drums are closer. It frees me up because now I have the luxury to really get inside the tracks within the time frame I'm given, whereas before, I would have to spend that time just getting it up to a certain level. Now, in most of the stuff you're given, it's really starting out a lot better than it started 10 or 15 years ago.

How about panning?

David Pensado: I think that there are three sacred territories in a mix that if you put something there, you've got to have an incredibly good reason. That's extreme left, center, and extreme right. I've noticed that some mixers will get stereo tracks from synthesizers and effects, and they just instinctively pan them hard left and hard right. What they end up with is these big train wrecks out on the ends of the stereo spectrum. Then they pan their kick, snare, bass, and vocals center, and you've got all this stuff stacked on top of each other. If it were a visual, you wouldn't be able to see the things behind the things in front. So what I do is take a stereo synthesizer track, and I'll just toss one side because I don't need it. I'll create my own stereo by either adding a delay or a chorus or a predelayed reverb or something like that to give it a stereo image. I'll pan maybe the dry signal to 10:00, and then I'll pan the effects just inside the extreme left side. I would never put it hard left, because then there's too many things on top of it. I would pan it at 9:00 and then pan the dry signal to say 10:30, something like that.

Do you use a lot of compression?

David Pensado: There again, I look at compression as having two functions. One as an effect, and when you want to keep a particular sound right up front in your face in the mix. I use quite an array of compressors, because each one seems to give a little different characteristic as a result.

Do you compress individually or on the stereo buss, or both?

David Pensado: Well, I do both. There's a trick that some of my favorite New York mixers do to get the drums really fat and in your face. They would feed a couple of busses to a compressor and EQ the compressor output. Then they feed kicks and snares and things like that to that compressor and just squeeze the heck out of the sound source. It literally is thought of and treated just as if it were a reverb or a chorus. In other words, just treat it as an effect that's mixed in with the original signal. More often than not, you're compressing the individual sounds as well.

I recently read an interview with a well-known engineer where he was praising a particular compressor for its ability to take the dynamics out of a drum performance because the drummer would get happy on the first downbeat of every chorus and play a little louder. I thought, "I spent my whole career trying to add those dynamics and trying to make the drummer sound like he got happy going into the chorus." I very rarely use a compressor to even out dynamics. Dynamics are something that I just can't get enough of. The compressors I like the most tend to be the ones that actually help me get dynamics. That might be a contradictory statement, but if you're careful with the attack and release times, you can actually get a compressor to help you with it.

Most mixers I've talked to don't think of their compressors that way. What do you use in particular to do that?

David Pensado: Well, for kick and snare, I'll use a 160X and I'll set the ratio at 2 or 3 to 1, depending on how much transient response is already there. The Over Easy button will not be in. It ends up where I'm knocking off sometimes 20dB and no less than 15. There's a point at which you get an amazing attack in the range from about 400 to 3k. Then I'll take the output of that compressor and I'll feed it to a Pultec or a Lang or an API 550 and I'll add back sometimes 15, 20 dB of 100–200Hz and a little 10k, and sometimes even 3–5k. Then I'll get my original sound where I like it, and I'll add in that compressed sound. Man, it just puts the drum right in your face and makes it huge and fat. Basically what I'm doing is trying to take the frequencies that I want and add those back into the original sound in such a way that I can't do with EQ.

A lot of times what I'll do is put the effects only on the compressed sound. In other words, an effect I use a lot would be "Locker Room" or "Tile Room" on a PCM70, and I'll add that effect only to the compressed sound. As a result, the reverb actually has a snap and aggressiveness to it. Every once in a while I'll make it stereo, where I'll take two 160s and I'll set them up identically, but on the insert of one, I'll put like anywhere from a 9- to 15-millisecond delay so the tight compressed sound is out on the edges of my stereo spectrum, but the original sound's in the center. That creates an incredibly nice image, particularly for ballads and slow tunes where you have a lot of space between the downbeats. That setup works great for snares, kicks, and hi-hat. Every once in a while, it'll make a guitar come alive, too.

So what you're doing is you're controlling the dynamics, but you're actually increasing the dynamics. It's the strangest thing because psycho-acoustically, it's not getting louder, but your mind is thinking it is. On the radio, it just jumps out of the speakers.

Do you have a philosophy about adding effects?

David Pensado: The way I think of it is the Pan knob places you left to right, while the effects tend to place you front to rear. That's a general statement, but it's a good starting point. In other words, if you want the singer to sound like she's standing behind the snare drum, leave the snare drum dry and wet down the singer, and it'll sound like the singer is standing that far behind the snare drum. If you want the singer in front of the snare drum, leave him dry and wet down the snare drum.

That said, I like a vocal mostly dry, but then it usually doesn't sound big enough. You want the vocalist to sound like they're really powerful and dynamic and just giving it everything, so I'll put an 1/8-note delay on the vocal but subtract a 1/16, a 1/32, or 1/64-note value from that 1/8 note. What it does is gives a movement to the delay and makes the singer have an urgency that's kind of neat. So put the 1/8 minus 1/64 on the left side, and put the 1/8 note straight on the right side. You can experiment with putting the pitch up a little bit on one side and down on another. If your singer's a little pitchy, that usually makes them sound a little more in tune. Sometimes putting the 1/8 note triplet on one side and the 1/8 note straight on the other, if you've got any kind of swing elements of the track, [it] will make the vocal big, but it doesn't make the singer sound like he's taken a step back.

Another thing I like to do is to take the output of my effects and run them straight into another effect. I'll take an exciter and just dump the output straight to a chorus so it's only chorusing the high frequencies. I think that's more pleasing than having low notes chorusing all over the place. Another thing I'll do is set up an SPX1000, or SPX90 both on chorus. I'll put one where I'll pan it hard left, and then I'll pan the right return at 2:00. Then I'll take another SPX90 and I'll pan it hard right, and then the left return from that one I'll pan at 10:00, so now the left and rights are kind of overlapping. On one I'll have the chorus depth just a little less than the other, and I'll have the other modulating one-third faster. When you add a vocal to that, you get this real nice spectrum that just widens because you're sending the both of them an equal amount, but yet one of them is chorusing deeper and slower than the other one. If that's not wide enough for you, add a delay in front of both of them that's different on each side, and then add that to your background vocals. They don't take any steps back in the mix, but they just get fat.

A lot of times I'll take two PCM70s, and instead of running them stereo, I'll run them mono in and mono out and pan one just inside the left and one just inside the right. I'll use the same program on both, but I'll slightly alter the values. Even if you don't use two PCM70s, just return the darn thing mono, and you'll be surprised at how much better it sounds.

What monitors do you like to work on?
David Pensado: For the main monitors, I like the Augsburgers with TAD components, and for small monitors, I use NS10s with the old tweeters. I also use Auratones, but in an odd way. A lot of times I'll start EQing my kick drum on the Auratones, which is kinda strange because you're adding a lot of frequencies that you can't hear, but you can see your meters going up. It forces you to EQ higher, because if you're sitting there listening to dual 15-inch speakers and you're adding 20dB of 40Hz, you think you're killing the world. You go to the Auratones, [and] you can't hear any of it, so it's useless. So a lot of times I'll use the Auratones to EQ my extreme low and top end. You think you're adding high end when you're adding 10, 12, 14k, but really what you need to be adding is 5k, and you'll put it on the Auratones, and then it'll make it more honest and work within what is the real range. Then I'll go up to the big ones and I'll watch my meters and

make sure that I'm not getting too crazy, and then I'll add the super-low stuff and the super-high stuff.

What level do you usually listen at?
David Pensado: I usually listen to NS10s kind of medium, and Auratones I listen at the same volume you would listen to TV. I found that on the NS10s, in order for them to really work, it's best to have them stay at one level for most of the mix. Then near the end of the mix, check your levels and your EQ with the NS10s about 20 percent lower and again about 20 percent higher, and you'll make adjustments that you'll really be pleased with when you hear it on the radio. The big speakers I use mostly to show off for clients and to just have fun. I like to turn it up, and if my body is vibrating properly, then I'm happy with the low end. A lot of engineers use them to hype the client, but I also use them to hype myself! If I'm cranking and I'm not getting excited, then I just keep on working.

CHAPTER 30

Elliot Scheiner

 With his work having achieved tremendous commercial success, Elliot Scheiner has also attained something far more elusive in the music business—the unanimous respect of his peers. Indeed, if you want a mix that's not only a work of art, but a piece of soul that exactly translates an artist's intentions, then Elliot's your man. With a shelf full of industry awards (five Grammys, four Surround Music Awards, the Surround Pioneer Award, the Tech Awards Hall of Fame, and too many total award nominations to count) from The Eagles, Beck, Steely Dan, Fleetwood Mac, Sting, John Fogerty, Van Morrison, Toto, Queen, Faith Hill, Lenny Kravitz, Natalie Cole, the Doobie Brothers, Aerosmith, Phil Collins, Aretha Franklin, Barbra Streisand, and many, many others, Elliot has long been recognized for his pristine mixes.

Elliot's recent pioneering work in 5.1 surround sound has made him perhaps the most in-demand mixer in the genre. Besides his superb work on the surround mixes for the Eagles' *Hell Freezes Over*, he's done 5.1 remix projects for, among others, Faith Hill, Sting, Beck, Steely Dan, Donald Fagan, Flaming Lips, Phish, and REM, besides that surround pièce de résistance, Queen's *A Night at the Opera*. His expertise in the field of surround sound led him to work with Panasonic Automotive Systems to develop the first 5.1 channel DVD-Audio system for the car available in North America. The result was dubbed ELS Surround to signify his involvement and debuted in Acura's 2004 TL.

How did you get started in the business?
Elliot Scheiner: I was a drummer, and I hacked around in a bunch of different bands until I just didn't want to do it anymore. My uncle was a

trombone player who was a studio musician in New York City and really good friends with Phil Ramone (legendary producer of Billy Joel, Ray Charles, Rod Stewart, Paul Simon, Elton John, and many more). He knew that I wanted to get into this business, so one day he brought me up to meet Phil. Phil hired me on the spot, and I never looked back.

You started at a great place (A&R Studios in NYC, which Phil owned).
Elliot Scheiner: Oh, it was the best. It was maybe the best studio in the country back in 1967 and one of the better ones in the world.

You started as an assistant, right?
Elliot Scheiner: Yeah, they would generally start you as an assistant, and I was basically like an assistant to an assistant until I learned what was going on. Obviously, the technology was minimal then, so you really had to know what mics to use on what occasions and where to place them, and the rest would come at a later date. But the main thing was just how to set up the room for each engineer.

Was this in the days of 8-track?
Elliot Scheiner: 8-track had just come in, and I remember them talking about how wonderful it was, but most people were still primarily using 4-track at the time. The majority of dates done at A&R were 4-track dates. I remember Phil making records with Burt Bacharach and Dionnne Warwick, and all of those were 4-track dates.

How were the tracks usually split out?
Elliot Scheiner: Track 1 would contain horns and strings, track 2 would be the lead vocal, 3 would be the rhythm section, and 4 would be background vocals. If there were no background vocals, they would put the strings on 1 and the horns on 4.

When did you start to engineer on your own?
Elliot Scheiner: I don't remember exactly how long, but it was definitely within a year. I was assisting Phil, and he was doing a Jimmy Smith date at night. I don't remember how many nights we were working on this record, but he called me and said, "I'm going to be late. You're going to have to start this date."

That was my first shot at engineering, but I think it was pretty much that way for most guys. You ended up being thrown right into the fire because someone was going to be late or couldn't make it or was sick. That's how I started, and that's how pretty much all of the guys I know started.

So did they trust you to be a first engineer after that?
Elliot Scheiner: I went back and forth, but at that point the office knew that I could do some small dates, so they started throwing me voice-overs

for radio and TV commercials. Eventually I ended up doing advertising, and then it moved on like that. Something would develop into another thing.

The way it worked back then was that everybody was a staff engineer, so the only way that you really made money was when you left one position and moved to another. The theory behind it was that if you left one studio, you'd carry the clientele over to another studio. I would say that in most cases it worked that way, but most clients at A&R weren't interested in following an engineer. They were [interested] in staying at that studio because it was such a great-sounding place, and it was so service oriented that they were willing to work with someone else that they hadn't worked with before just to remain there.

It was a different philosophy back then.
Elliot Scheiner: Yeah, it was. Here all of a sudden I would inherit somebody's clients that had moved onto another studio just because he'd gone, so that's how you ended up becoming an engineer. There were a lot of staff engineers that would just float around from studio to studio. It was a lot easier to do it back then obviously.

What was your first hit?
Elliot Scheiner: *Moondance* (Van Morrison's seminal hit album). I don't even know if there were any singles off the record because in those days it was just about getting FM radio play. Pop music got the singles airplay, the Frankie Valle and the Four Seasons, and all the Motown stuff. Artists like Van Morrison were more album oriented, so what they did was more oriented towards album radio, so it would be hard for me to determine what was a huge hit singles-wise.

Let's talk about mixing. Isn't that mostly what you do these days?
Elliot Scheiner: Oddly enough, I've been tracking lately, but I'd have to say that overall, the majority of my work is mixing.

Do you have a philosophy about mixing?
Elliot Scheiner: I've always believed that if someone has recorded all this information, then they want it to be heard, so my philosophy is to be able to hear everything that was recorded. It's not about burying everything in there and getting a wall of sound. I've never been into that whole concept. It was more about whatever part was played, if it was the subtleties of a drummer playing off-beats on the snare drum next to the backbeat, obviously he wants that heard. So I always want to make sure that everything that's in that record gets heard.

If you were able to accomplish hearing every single instrument in the mix, that was a huge achievement. Granted, maybe there wasn't as much information when I started as there is now. I myself have come across files that have been a hundred and some odd tracks, so it's not as easy to do that today.

I have to admit that the way some people record things today is a bit peculiar. All of a sudden you'll be dealing with seven or eight different mics on the same instrument. Like, for example, an acoustic guitar will all of a sudden have seven different viewpoints of where this guitar's being recorded. It's mind-boggling that you have to go and make a determination and listen to every single channel to decide which one you want to use. And if you pick the wrong ones, they come back at you and say, "Oh, we had a different combination," or "It doesn't sound quite right to us," but they don't tell you what they did! So granted, it is a little more difficult to deal with those issues today, but I still take the same approach with every mix.

If you have a hundred tracks, will you try to have them all heard? Or do you go in and do some subtractive mixing?
Elliot Scheiner: Well, it depends if that's necessary. I don't usually get those kind of calls where they say, "Here's a hundred tracks. Delete what you want." It's usually not about that. And I have to say that I'll usually get between 24 and 48 tracks in most cases, and hardly ever am I given the liberty to take some of them out. I mean, if something is glaringly bad I'll do that, but to make a judgment call as to whether background vocals should be in here or there, I generally don't do that. I just assume that whatever an artist and producer sends me is kind of written in stone. They've recorded it, and unless they tell me otherwise, I usually don't do subtractive mixing.

Do you usually work on your own?
Elliot Scheiner: If I'm working at home, I'm usually working on my own.

How often do you work at home?
Elliot Scheiner: It happens quite a bit because a lot of people don't want to pay to mix in a commercial studio for financial reasons. I just finished a project last week that was very low budget. The artist and producer live in California, and they sent me the files. I was able to do it at a low figure because I could do it when I wanted to, and I wasn't spending anybody's money except my own.

How long does it take you to do a mix on average?
Elliot Scheiner: Depending on how complicated it is, it usually takes anywhere from 3 hours to a day.

Three hours is really fast!
Elliot Scheiner: Yeah, well a lot of time you just get a vibe and a feel for something, and it just comes together. Then you look at it and say, "How much am I actually going to improve this mix?" I mean, if it feels great and sounds great, I'm a little reluctant to beat it into the ground.

For me, it's still about a vibe, and if I can get things to sound good and have a vibe, that's all I really care about. I still put Al Schmitt on a pedestal. Look at how quickly he gets things done. He can do three songs in a day, and they'll be perfect and amazing-sounding and have the right vibe. So it's not like it can't be done. Some people say that you can't get a mix in a short time, and that's just not true. Al's my proof.

Where do you usually start your mix from?
Elliot Scheiner: Out of force of habit, if there's a rhythm section, I'll usually start with the drums and then move to the bass and just work it up. Once the rhythm section is set, I'll move on to everything else and end with vocals.

How much EQ do you use?
Elliot Scheiner: I can't say that there are any rules for that. I can't say that I've ever mixed anything that Al has recorded, but if I did, I probably wouldn't have any on it. With some of the stuff done by some of the younger kids, I get it and go, "What were they listening to when they recorded this?" So in some cases I use drastic amounts, where I'll be double-compressing and double-EQing—all kinds of stuff in order to get something to sound good. I never did that until maybe the last 5 years. Obviously, those mixes are the ones that take a day or more.

When you're setting up a mix, do you always have a certain set of outboard gear—like a couple of reverbs and delays—ready to use, or do you patch it as you go?
Elliot Scheiner: Usually I don't start out with any reverbs. I'm not one for processing. I'd like to believe that music can survive without reverbs and without delays and without effects. Obviously, when it's called for I'll use it, but the stuff I do is pretty dry. The '70s were a pretty dry time, and then the '80s effects became overused. There was just tons of reverb on everything.

Most of your Steely Dan stuff is pretty dry, isn't it?
Elliot Scheiner: It's pretty much dry. What we used were plates usually.

Real short ones?
Elliot Scheiner: Not necessarily. In the days when I was working at A&R, we had no remotes on any of our plates there. Phil wanted to make changing them difficult because he tuned them himself, and he really didn't want anybody to screw with them. There would be at least four plates in every room. Some of them might be a little shorter than another, but generally they were in the 2- to 2 1/2-second area. There was always an analog tape predelay, usually at 15ips, going into the plates. The plates were tuned so brilliantly that it didn't become a noticeable effect. It was just a part of the instrument or part of the music. You could actually have a fair amount on an instrument, and you just wouldn't notice it.

Is the sound of the A&R plates something that you try to get today?
Elliot Scheiner: Oh, I'm always trying to get that reverb sound. If I'm using plates either at Right Track or Capital, I'll still use an analog tape delay going into it.

You're not mixing in the box at home, are you?
Elliot Scheiner: No. I've got a Yamaha DM2000, and I have a bunch of outboard gear as well. [See Figure 30.1.]

Figure 30.1
Yamaha DM2000 digital console (courtesy of Yamaha Professional Audio).

Have you ever mixed in the box?
Elliot Scheiner: Once when I first got it. All I remember is that I sat there for 8 hours with a mouse in my hand and never really moved. I don't even remember going to the bathroom for 8 hours. When I finally did get up, I took a look at my watch and realized that I had been there all day and hadn't accomplished very much. And when I got up, I couldn't move. My neck was stiff and my back hurt. As an engineer, you're always moving. You move from one end of the console to another. You stretch to get to an EQ, which you don't do working in the box. I just don't like doing it. I'm not saying that you shouldn't do it, because everybody's got their method, and some guys make great records in the box.

How much compression do you use?
Elliot Scheiner: Very, very little. Growing up at A&R, there were only four pieces of outboard gear in every room: a pair of Fairchild 670 compressors and two Pultecs, and that was it. There was no inboard EQ because we used broadcast consoles, so you were very selective about what you put that outboard gear on. It was usually something where you had trouble. If you had trouble getting a sound, you would either move or change a mic, or move the guy to a different place in the room. It was more about moving the mic or the musician or having them play differently rather than EQing or compressing.

Most of the compression I did was hand compression, where you rode a fader and you learned how to ride it smoothly so you didn't screw up. So I never got into the habit of relying on compressors for anything. I probably do a little more now than I did in the past. I'm doing a Walter Becker date today where I have a Fairchild on the bass, which is primarily what I used to do back in the '70s. I used the Fairchild for the bass and the kick drum. I use a stereo compressor across the buss usually when I'm mixing, but it's not for compression as much as it is for the sound of the compressor.

What do you use?
Elliot Scheiner: I use a Neve 33609. There's very little of it going on. It's a safety net, I guess. Sometimes I'll put a GML EQ across it as well just to add a little air on the very top.

What do you use for monitors, and how loud do you listen?
Elliot Scheiner: I'm still using NS10s for stereo and five of them for surround, and generally when I'm mixing I monitor at about 40dB.

Wow, that's quiet.
Elliot Scheiner: Yeah, I just find that I can definitely hear the balances better at a lower level, so I can hear if I've got a little too much or not enough of something. That comes from wanting to hear every instrument. If I can hear it when it's soft, then it's probably going to be there at any level. You don't beat yourself up, and I'd like to believe that I can still hear a little bit because I've monitored so softly for so long.

Do you go up on bigger speakers to get your low end?
Elliot Scheiner: No, I go a tiny bit louder initially. I might go to 80 or 85 when I'm putting the kick and the bass in just to hear where they're sitting comparatively, but once I establish that, I'll go right down to 40 or so.

Do you have any listening tricks like going outside the control room or anything like that?
Elliot Scheiner: Yeah, at A&R I used to take a disc (record) home. Back in those days, you had to actually cut your own disc, which I was very bad at. But I would go in and cut a reference disc for myself, which used to take me longer than it would to record the thing. Then I'd take it home to listen on my speakers.

Then I found out that I was getting better results by listening in whatever car I was driving. Sometimes I would buy a car based on what the system sounded like. Like I bought a Chevy pickup once because it seemed to have a really, really flat system in it back in the early '90s. I could go in there and actually hear what was wrong with a mix and come back and fix it based on what I heard in the car. I know a lot of guys that used to do that. At A&M back in the late '70s/early '80s, they had their own low-power radio transmitter with a 56 Chevy parked out back rigged to receive it so you could hear what it would sound like on a broadcast. So a lot of guys used to base their mixes on what it sounded like in a car because a lot of the times the car was the lowest common denominator.

Now it's an iPod.
Elliot Scheiner: Yeah, but it's no longer the lowest common denominator because you listen on headphones, and everything always sounds a little better on headphones than on speakers.

How many versions of a mix do you do?
Elliot Scheiner: Usually just two or three. Pretty much vocal up and vocal down unless there's something so weird that I'm worried about it. I might do an alternate version with something lowered or out. I've got to say that with most engineers, your initially instinct is usually correct.

Do you draw your automation in on the workstation, or do you only use fader automation?
Elliot Scheiner: I use a combination. I have a DM2000 at home, so I use the console automation as my primary. But occasionally you get more tracks than I have outputs on the DAW, so I'll combine tracks inside the box and use the automation inside the computer to do whatever needs to be done.

Do you have any special tricks that you use when you're mixing?
Elliot Scheiner: That type of stuff is so dependent on what's in the recording. Like I just finished mixing this project, and there was a lot of stereo percussion stuff where there'd be two close-up mics and two that were more roomy, so what I do in that case sometimes is employ a delay on one side or the other. And not a big delay—maybe only a couple of milliseconds or so and in some cases as much as 10 or 11 milliseconds. Once you add room mics in there, it's almost like anything can go because who knows what the placement was, so there's a little more freedom to use delays.

But I've never relied on any trick stuff. I wish I could say that I've been using something all these years that's some kind of secret, but I don't do anything that's of a secret nature. I'm more than willing to tell anyone that asks me what I did because I don't have any problems because I've never had any tricks. I've always felt that the trick is in how you hear it. It's not what you employ to get the mix but how you hear the mix.

What would you tell someone about honing their hearing?
Elliot Scheiner: My common practice has always been before I would get a sound on an instrument—especially acoustic guitars—I would go out in the room and get down to where the guy was playing and listen to what that guitar sounds like 12 inches away and see how he's playing it and how he wants it to sound. I would mainly just try to duplicate what I'm hearing

right there in front of the guitar. To me, you've got to duplicate what's being played, so having the ability to go out in the room and hear what it sounds like is still a very important issue to me.

Of course, that's assuming that it sounds good to begin with.
Elliot Scheiner: That's so subjective. I'd go out into the room like at Phil's place, and you'd hear one guitar player like an Eric Gale, who's the most phenomenal player, yet his amp never really sounded good. You'd go out and hear somebody else's amp, like Steve Kahn—his amp always sounded phenomenal. Some guys like a trashy-sounding guitar amp, but you have to go out and sort of duplicate it.

Let's talk about surround. Has your approach changed over the years since you've done so many surround mixes?
Elliot Scheiner: In some regards, yes, but as far as the overall approach, no. I still do a very aggressive mix. I like as much information coming out of the surrounds as I do the front, so I'm still as aggressive as I was when I first started, maybe even more so. The only thing that's really changed for me is how I use the center speaker. I try to use it a little more than I have in the past. I've found that when listening in a car, the center speaker is a little more important than it is in the home. So if I put a vocal in there, it's going to be at least as loud as the phantom center, maybe a little more.

Do you only put the lead vocal in the center?
Elliot Scheiner: No, I put the snare, bass, kick drum, sometimes an instrument that's a mono track like a tambourine or bells, or something that I can just put in one speaker.

Do you still keep the mix fairly dry?
Elliot Scheiner: Yeah, pretty much.

Do you use the LFE much?
Elliot Scheiner: I'm not convinced about the LFE. I run the speakers full range, so I don't have to put all that much in the LFE. I always worry about bass management in people's homes. Every amplifier is different, every DVD player is different; you don't know what's doing what anymore. There doesn't seem to be any way of determining how bass management is being used from manufacturer to manufacturer. They all have their own ideas, and every designer has a different theory about what bass management is, so I just ignore it and use the LFE to put a minimum of stuff in. But generally I like to get things to sound how they should sound on my monitors without the LFE.

What's your approach to doing a live concert as compared to a studio record in surround?
Elliot Scheiner: I'm probably the only guy that does it, but I don't believe in setting an arena perspective in surround. I don't like the idea of having

just some ambience and room mics in the back. I still want to hear the music coming from everywhere. I still try to be as aggressive with live stuff as with a studio record, so I take the creative license to move to the stage and put instruments in the rear.

I did a bunch of Phish stuff, and it's only guitar, bass, drums, and keyboards, so I had to figure something out. It was taking a chance because it's only four pieces, but I had bass and drums basically front-loaded coming to the surrounds just the tiniest bit, and the same with the guitar, then I had all the keyboards dedicated to the surrounds. You either liked it or hated it. The good thing was that they loved it, so I couldn't be all that wrong. As long as the band likes it, I'm going to continue to do what I do until somebody says, "This is bullshit."

I think if the rear speakers aren't lit up, the listener feels cheated.
Elliot Scheiner: Yeah, I agree with you. What really gets me off is hearing information coming from the rears because that's what's unusual about surround. We've been listening to the front side for as long as we've had recordings. Now that we have other speakers, that's where a good deal of the information should be coming from.

How much surround do you do these days? What's your ratio of stereo to surround?
Elliot Scheiner: I would have to say it's about 50/50 right now. A few years ago I was about 80/20 in favor of surround. It's dropped off a little bit, but I'm anticipating that it's going to return.

With the new formats coming that will support 7.1 and beyond, it seems like there might be some new opportunities to remix some things with the additional speakers.
Elliot Scheiner: I'm going to ignore that only because it's been so difficult to get people to put in 5.1 systems. To ask someone's old lady to now put speakers on the side? They're not going to do it unless you have a dedicated room. If you have people walking through your living room, you can't have speakers on the sides.

As far as I can tell, it's the manufacturers that want you to buy more speakers, new amps, etc. I don't see the need for it. It's difficult to hear the sides unless you turn to it. You really can't get a perfect perspective. So I don't know that I would employ those speakers, and I don't know that I would force the consumer to buy them. I know in the car it's just not going to happen because there's no room.

Would you have any advice for someone that's just starting to mix?
Elliot Scheiner: I would say that you have to believe in yourself. You can't second-guess what you're doing. I've always been of the mind that if I can

make myself happy listening to a mix, then hopefully the people that are employing me will be just as happy.

I don't try to guess what someone might want. If there's someone there in the room with me when I start a mix, I know that sooner or later I'm going to hear whether they hate it or they love it.

But generally I try to mix for myself. At this point in my career, I know that if people are calling me, they like what I do. Just remember that what we do is to convey the artist's feelings and make it as musical as possible without harming it.

CHAPTER 31

Ed Seay

Getting his start in Atlanta in the '70s by engineering and producing hits for Paul Davis, Peabo Bryson, and Melissa Manchester, Ed Seay has since become one of the most respected engineers in Nashville since moving there in 1984. With hit-making clients such as Pam Tillis, Highway 101, Collin Raye, Martina McBride, Ricky Skaggs, and a host of others, Ed has led the charge in changing the recording approach in Nashville. Here, in addition to his insightful observations about mixing, Ed describes the evolution of the sound of Country music to what it is today.

Do you hear the final product in your head before you begin to mix?
Ed Seay: To some extent I can. I think one of the things that helps me as a mixer, and one thing that helps all of the ones that have made a mark, is what I call "having the vision." I always try to have a vision of the mix when I start. Rather than just randomly pushing up faders and saying, "Well, a little of this EQ or effect might be nice," I like to have a vision as far as where we're going and what's the perspective. Definitely, I try to grasp that early on.

Is there a difference between mixing Country music and what you did before?
Ed Seay: Country music is definitely lyric driven. One of the mistakes that some people make when they try to work on the stuff is they tend to downplay the lyric or downplay the lead vocal. And at first, I think some people begrudgingly push up the lead vocal and just say, "Listen to how loud it is." But there's actually an appreciation for having a really great vocal out there with a great emotion-selling lyric. In Pop and in Rock, sometimes you don't always hear every word, and it's kind of okay if it's buried just a little bit, but Country is usually not that way. People definitely sing along with Country songs, so that's the biggest thing. The vocal rules. But at the same time, it's pretty boring if it's all vocals. It sounds like

a Country record from the '60s where you don't have any power in there. There's an art to keeping the vocal on top without making it dominate.

What changed, and how does that affect what you do?
Ed Seay: Back when I used to listen to my dad's old Ray Price and Jim Reeves Country records, they weren't very far from what Pop was in the early '60s. Very mellow, big vocals, very subdued band, very little drums, strings, horns, lush. Mix-wise, there wasn't really too much difference in an Andy Williams record and one of the old Jim Reeves records.

What happened was that Country got too soft sounding. You'd cut your track and then do some sweetening with some horns and strings. At one time, strings were on all the Country records, and then it kind of transformed into where it's at today, with almost no strings on Country records except for big ballads. For the most part, horns are completely dead. They're almost taboo. Basically it's rhythm track driven and not really very far off from where Pop was in the mid to later '70s. The Ronstadt "It's So Easy to Fall in Love" and "You're No Good" where you hear guitar, bass, drums, keyboards, a slide or steel, and then a vocal background—that's pretty much the format now, although fiddle is used also. Ironically enough, a lot of those guys that were making those records have moved here because at this point, this is one of the last bastions of live recording.

Let's talk about your mixing. When you start to mix, how do you build it?
Ed Seay: Well, I'll usually go through and push up instruments to see if there are any trouble spots. All this is dependent upon whether it's something that I've recorded or if I'm hearing it fresh and have no idea what it is. If that's the case, then what I'll do is kind of rough-mix it out real quick. I'll push it up and see where it's going before I start diving in.

If it's something that I know what's on the tape, then I'll go through and mold the sounds in a minor way to fit the modern profile that it needs to be. In other words, if it's a real flabby, dull kick drum, it doesn't matter what the vision is. This kick drum's never going to get there. So I'll pop it into a Vocal Stressor or I'll do whatever I have to do. I'll work through my mix like that and try to get it up into the acceptable range, or the exceptional range, or at least somewhere that can be worked with. It takes a couple of hours to get good sounds on everything and then another couple of hours to get real good balances, or something that plays itself as if it makes sense. Then I'll do some frequency juggling so that everybody is out of everybody else's way.

The tough part, and the last stage of the mix, is the several hours it takes for me to make it sound emotional and urgent and exciting so that it's just not a song, it's a record. It's not making it just sound good, it's making it sound like an event. Sometimes that means juggling the instruments or the balances or adding some dynamics help. That's the last stage of when I mix, and that's the part that makes it different or special.

So how do you go about doing that?
Ed Seay: I try to find what's important in the mix. I try to find out if the lead vocal is incredibly passionate, then make sure that the spotlight shines on that. Or if the acoustics are sitting there but they're not really driving the thing and they need to. If, for instance, the mix needs eighth notes, but they're going [Sound effect] and it's not really pushing the mix, sometimes playing with compression on the acoustics or auditioning different kinds of compression to make it sound like, "Boy this guy was into it." Maybe pushing and pulling different instruments. Somebody's got to be back, and sometimes it's better when things are back and other things are further up front. It's just basically playing with it and trying to put into it that indefinable thing that makes it exciting. Sometimes it means making sure your cymbals or your room mics are where you can actually feel the guy, or sometimes adding compression can be the answer to making the thing come alive. Sometimes hearing the guy breathe like the old Steve Miller records did. They had that [Breathing]. With a little of that, you might say, "Man, he's working. I believe it." It's a little subconscious thing, but sometimes that can help.

When you're building your mix, are you starting with bass first, or starting with the kick drum?
Ed Seay: I start with the kick drum sound. But then I put up the drum kit and put the bass in. Then I'll push up all the static channels that aren't going to have giant moves like the acoustic stuff, keyboard pads, maybe a synth or Rhodes or piano that doesn't have a whole bunch of stepping-out licks. Early on, I'll try to make sure that there's room for the lead vocal. I think one of the big mistakes is to work on your track for eight hours and get it blistering hot and barking, but there's no way that this baritone vocal can cut through. So then you're forced with the choice of turning this baritone vocal into steel wool with ridiculous EQ or just turning him up so loud that he sounds inappropriate. It's cool to have a bright record as long as everything kind of comes up together, but if you've got an incredibly bright snare drum and the vocal's not so bright, then it makes the vocal sound even duller. If you are thinking all the way to the end to when you add EQ when you master the record, it'll brighten the vocal, but it's also going to bring up the snare worse. So you have to have everything in perspective.

But eventually, I get the vocals in and get the backgrounds around them. Then put up the solos and the signature stuff. Then I get an overall rough balance of everything that sits there pretty well and then juggle the pieces. Once again, it helps if I know what the music is. Then I know exactly where I'm going. If I don't, sometimes I have to listen to a rough mix or create a rough mix on the board to get a feel for what their intent is.

Do you have a method for setting levels?

Ed Seay: Usually a good place to start is the kick drum at –6 or –7 or so. I'll try to get a bass level that is comparable to that. If it's not exactly comparable on the meter because one's peaking and one's sustaining, I get them to at least sound comparable. Because later in mastering, if you affect one, you're going to affect the other. So as long as the ratio is pretty correct between the two, then if you go to adjust the kick, at least it's not going to whack the bass way out as long as they relate together. That's kind of a good starting place for me.

I used to let the snare dominate real hard and heavy, but now I'm pulling back just a little bit instead of bludgeoning the audience. I'm letting them get into some of the other midrange things.

Do you have a special approach to EQ?

Ed Seay: I don't know if I have a special approach. I just try to get stuff to sound natural but at the same time be very vivid. I break it down into roughly three areas: mids and the top and the bottom. Then there's low mids and high mids. Generally, except for a very few instruments or a few microphones, cutting flat doesn't sound good to most people's ears. So I'll say, "Well, if this is a state-of-the-art preamp and a great mic and it doesn't sound that great to me, why?" Well, the midrange is not quite vivid enough. Okay, we'll look at the 3k, 4k range, maybe 2500. Why don't we make it kind of come to life like a shot of cappuccino and open it up a little bit? But then I'm not hearing the air around things, so let's go up to 10k or 15k and just bump it up a little bit and see if we can kind of perk it up. Now all that sounds good, but our bottom is kind of undefined. We don't have any meat down there. Well, let's sweep through and see what helps the low end. Sometimes, depending on different instruments, a hundred cycles can do wonders for some instruments. Sometimes you need to dip out at 400 cycles, because that's the area that sometimes just clouds up and takes the clarity away. But a lot of times adding a little 400 can fatten things up.

On a vocal, sometimes I think, "Does this vocal need a diet plan? Does he need to lose some flab down there? Or sometimes we need some weight on this guy, so let's add some 300 cycles and make him sound a little more important." So it's kind of contouring.

Also, frequency juggling is important. One of the biggest compliments people give me is that they say, "You know, Ed, on your mixes, I can hear everything." There are two reasons for that. One is, I've pushed things up at the right time or the right things up that they want to hear or need to hear. But the other thing is, you don't EQ everything in the same place. You don't EQ 3k on the vocal and the guitar and the bass and the synth and the piano, because then you have such a buildup there that you have a frequency war going on. So sometimes you can say, "Well, the piano doesn't need 3k, so let's go lower, or let's go higher." Or, "This vocal will pop through if we shine the light not in his nose, but maybe towards his forehead." In so doing, you can make things audible and everybody can get some camera time.

Do you have a specific approach to panning?

Ed Seay: Yeah, I do. The most significant approach is I pan as if I were sitting in the audience, especially with the drums. The reason is, I don't play the drums; therefore, I sit in the audience and listen, and that means with most drummers, unless they're left handed, put their hi-hat to the right. To me, I can get away with anything except the drums being backwards because it just strikes me funny. So I do the drums that way. However, I thrash a bit at piano, so I always put the low end on the left-hand side and the high end on the right-hand side.

Hard left and hard right?

Ed Seay: Usually, but not always. With a piano, it depends on who recorded it and how phase coherent it is. If it's not dramatic stereo, I'll try to make it more dramatic. Also, if whoever recorded it didn't pay real good attention to the phasing on the mics and the thing is way wide and it falls apart in mono, I'll be panning it in so that in mono it doesn't go away. Sometimes flipping the phase on one side can fix that because a lot of people don't check. Of course, stereo is more important now than ever before, but on a lot of the video channels, you're listening in mono. So I check for that.

I always put the electric guitar on the left and steel on the right. I try to make stereo records, and I'm not afraid to pan something extremely wide. I like my mixes to have a few things that stick out and get some attention and not just blend in with the crowd. That way, there can be all kinds of contrast—not only volume dynamics, but panning dynamics as well.

One of the things I don't like is what I call "big mono" where there's no difference in the left and the right other than a little warble. If you pan that left and right wide, and then here comes another keyboard and you pan that left and right wide, and then there's the two guitars and you pan them left and right wide, by the time you get all this stuff left and right wide, there's really no stereo in the sound. It's like having a big mono record, and it's just not really aurally gratifying. So to me, it's better to have some segregation, and that's one of the ways I try to make everything heard in the mixes. Give everybody a place on the stage.

How about compression? Do you use it as an effect, or just to even things out, or both?

Ed Seay: Both. I have a lot of different compressors, and one of the reasons I have a lot of outboard gear is because they're all different colors on the palette. A DBX 165 is basically working all the time, but you can't really hear it working and you can't really get it to suck and blow. If you want the suck and blowish thing, there's several other ways to go. An 1176 or one of several VCA compressors can really do something dramatic. It also depends if it was cut with compression. Sometimes it doesn't need any or as much, and sometimes you need it to give it life.

To me, the key to compression is that it makes the instrument sound like it's being turned up, not being turned down. If you choose the wrong compressor or you use it the wrong way, then your stuff can sound like it's always going away from you. If you use the correct compressor for the job, you can make it sound like, "Man, these guys are coming at you." It's very active and aggressive. Quite often, I'll use it on the stereo buss, but I try not to be too crazy with it.

But if you remove all dynamics or if you really lean on it in an improper way during mixing, when it goes to mastering, there's not much for the guy to do there. If he does, it'll only compound the problem. Then by the time it gets on the radio, there's nothing left that'll pump the radio compressors, so then it just kind of lays there. It's loud, but nothing ever really jumps out of your mix. So nothing ever gets real loud.

But yeah, lead vocals almost always. Bass, certainly when I'm tracking it, and quite often when I'm mixing it. I time the release to the tempo of the song or to the end of the note release, especially if the guy's using flat wound strings for more of a retro bass that has a lot of attack and less hang time. Sometimes if you use the wrong compressor on a snare drum, all you'll get is the initial [Sound effect] and then it'll turn it down, but if you use the right kind of compression, slow the attack down, speed up the release maybe, you'll get a different effect; there's more length to the snare type of a sound. It'll come sucking back at you. Compression's important, but it's gotta be the right kind, and I think that's the key.

How about gates? Do you use them often?
Ed Seay: Well, I do, but I'm not fanatical about gates. There's two reasons to use gates. One is to get rid of amp hiss or something that's not attractive to the music. Or if the hi-hat's wiping out your snare sound that leaked in on your snare mic because you added a bunch of EQ, then the gate can help you. But generally we're on digital tape, and the sounds are done in different rooms, so it's not as important to me. Now one exception is if I'm doing my room mics that I was talking about. To have the room mic hang up there with all that kick drum—that can wipe out your kick drum sound per se, and it also makes it lean towards Led Zeppelin, which might be the red flag. "Ooh, what are we doing here? Sounds like a Rock song and it shouldn't." If it should, great. But if it shouldn't, then a lot of times what I'll do is time the gate to the tempo so that the kick drum's out of the way. Open/close, open/close, and then play with the ramp so that it doesn't just sound trendy.

How about setting up effects? Do you add effects as you go along, or do you get the balance up and then add the effects?

Ed Seay: Well, I kind of come and go with this. I'm in a drier phase now than I used to be. What I'll do is try to make things sound as good as I can dry. If I hear something that just sounds too iso'ed and too unrelated to the mix, then I'll add some effects as I go, but I don't go too crazy with it until I get the whole picture. Then once it's all sitting there, you can easily tell if it's just not gluing together. My general setup for a mix is I'll have one send setup for long verb and another setup for a short, kind of a room simulation.

Long being what, 2.5, 3 seconds?

Ed Seay: Yeah, 2.5, 2.3. For a ballad, sometimes 2.6. Then I'll usually have a delay send with something, whether it's eighth note or sixteenth note or dotted eighth triplets, that kind of works with the music. Then sometimes I'll have a little pitch change, like a Publison or an AMS harmonizer kind of sound. I may have a gated reverb or something that can kind of pull sounds together. Sometimes an isolated guitar sounds great dry and in your face by itself, but other times it seems like, "Wow, they had an over-dub party, and look who showed up." Sometimes a little of that gate can kind of smear it together and make it sound like he was actually on the floor with them.

So what are you trying to accomplish with the effects? Are you trying to make everything bigger or give it depth?

Ed Seay: Sometimes depth and sometimes you just want it to sound a little bit more glamorous. Other times you just want it to sound appropriate. Well, appropriate to what? If it's an arena Rock band, then all this room stuff is going to make it sound like they flunked out of the arena circuit and they're now doing small clubs. But if you got a band where that's more of an in-your-face, hard-driving thing, you want to hear the room sound.

I've done records where I didn't use any effects or any verb, but quite often just a little can make a difference. You don't even have to hear it, but you can sense it when it goes away. It's just not quite as friendly sounding, not quite as warm. Obviously, an effect is an ear catcher or something that can just kind of slap somebody and wake them up a little bit in case they're dozing off there.

Let's talk about monitoring. How loud do you usually listen when you're mixing?

Ed Seay: I mix at different levels. I try not to mix too loud because it'll wear you down and fool your perspective. I don't find it extremely valuable to listen loud on big wall monitors very often. The only reason I'll go up there is to check bottom end. That's the best way to do it, but most of the time I work off my nearfields and I try not to get too loud.

In fact, what I like to do is use the studio bigs 1 percent of the time, my nearfields 70 percent of the time, and then use a third reference that's not straight on me, but off to the side in a different place. My philosophy is that most people don't sit right in between the speakers when they listen to music. They're in the kitchen and the music's in the living room. Even in the car, you're off to one side a little bit. So to me, that's a valid place to arrive at kind of an average.

Sometimes it's very valuable to turn things down, but there's an up and down side to both. If you listen too soft, you'll add too much bass. If you listen too loud, you'll turn the lead vocals down too much. What I like to do is make it sound good on all three unrelated systems; then it's got to relate to the rest of the world.

Do you ever go out and listen in the car or go in the lounge and listen through the door or anything like that?
Ed Seay: Yeah, although I don't go to the car as much as I used to. What I'll do about an hour before printing the mix is prop open the control room door and walk down the hall or into the lounge where the music has to wind its way out the door. I find that very valuable because it's not like hitting mono on the console—it's like a true acoustic mono. It's real valuable to see if you hear all the parts, and it's real easy to be objective when you're not staring at the speakers and looking at the meters.

How many versions of a mix do you do?
Ed Seay: Generally I like to put down the mix and then I'll put down a safety of the mix in case there was a dropout or something went goofy that no one caught. Once I get the mix, then I'll put the lead vocal up half a dB or 8/10 of a dB, and this becomes the vocal-up mix. Then I'll do a mix with all vocals up. Sometimes I'll recall the mix and just do backgrounds up and leave the lead vocals alone. Then I'll do one with no lead vocal and just the backgrounds. Then I'll do one with track only, just instruments. That's usually all the versions I'll need to do. There are some people that get so crazy about it because they don't want to make a decision. At some point, you burn up $400 worth of tape or whatever you're using just to print all these mixes. Generally, those cover about all of them.

CHAPTER 32

Allen Sides

 Although well known as the owner of the premier Oceanway studio complexes in Los Angeles, Allen Sides is also one of the most respected engineers in the business, with credits that include the film scores to *Dead Man Walking*, *Phenomenon*, *Last Man Standing*, *Sunchaser*, the Goo Goo Doll's *Iris*, and Alanis Morissette's "Uninvited" for the *City of Angels* soundtrack. He's also done records with the Brian Setzer Big Band, Joni Mitchell, Phil Collins, Barry Manilow, and a host of others.

Even though he remains on the cutting edge of the latest that recording technology has to offer, Allen continually finds modern uses for many long-forgotten audio relics, proving that sound technique, good ears, and an interesting piece of gear never go out of fashion.

Do you know what you're going for before you get there? Can you hear the finished product in your head?
Allen Sides: It depends. I would say that if it's a project that I've been working on, I've already put it up dozens of times, I have a pretty good idea of what I'm doing. If it's something I'm mixing for someone else, then I listen to their roughs and get a concept of what they have in mind. I really want to understand what they want so I can make that a part of the picture that I draw. How many times have you had a mix that you thought was killer, and they come in and change a few things and it becomes perfectly acceptable, but no longer great?

Do you have a special approach to mixing or a philosophy about what you're trying to accomplish?

Allen Sides: First, I like it to be fun to listen to. I'll do whatever it takes to make it satisfying. I tend to like a little more lows or extreme highs and a lot of definition, and I like it to sound as punchy as I can make it. So much involves the arrangement. When the arrangement is great, then the music comes together in a very nice way. If it fights, then it becomes very difficult to fit together. Getting the arrangement right is an art in itself.

How do you go about building a mix? Where do you normally start from?

Allen Sides: I would say that it really varies. Sometimes I'll throw up everything and then after I hear how the vocal sits, then I'll look at a section and refine it. But before I do, it's really nice to hear how it relates to the vocals, because you can spend time making the whole thing sound great, but it might not relate to the vocal in any way. So I'd say that I listen to the whole thing, then go back and work on each section separately, then put it all together.

Do you have a method for setting levels?

Allen Sides: Yeah. When I set up my track, I'll set the monitor level to where I'm comfortable, and I will make it sound as impressive as I can at maybe –2 on the VU meters because I know I'm going to come up from there. I want to make it as impressive as I possibly can at a fairly modest setting.

This is the whole mix now.

Allen Sides: Yeah. I get it to where it's really kicking. Then I do my vocal track and get it all happening. Even when I do that, I probably will end up trimming the individual faders here and there. The problem, of course, is that when you trim the individual faders, the way that they drive the individual effects changes slightly. All the plates and effects sound different when they're driven differently. That's why I try to get everything happening in that lower level so I have to do as little trimming as possible. And I like to keep my buss masters all the way up. This, of course, depends on the console.

So you're putting the whole mix up first and then you're adding the vocals later.

Allen Sides: Yeah, but as I say, I will probably put the whole mix up, put the vocals in, and listen to how it all fits together before anything. Based on that, I think it's a decision of how I'm going to make the rhythm section sound.

And another thing I'd say is that I'm definitely a fan of your first impression being your best impression. I like to move very quickly so no matter how complex it is, within two to three hours, it's kind of where it should be. Some of the mixes are so complex these days that you have three and four 24-tracks locked together, or two 48s and a 24. It's insane. So a lot of times the music is so complex that you can't actually hear the mix until you put all the mutes in with all the parts playing in the right place. If you just put all the faders up, then you'd have one big mess. So there's a tremendous amount of busy work just to get it prepped so that you can play it back.

Do you have an approach to the rhythm section in particular?
Allen Sides: Believe it or not, I typically bring in the overheads first because my overheads are overall drum mics. So I bring in the overheads to a good level, then I fit the snare into that. Then I get the kick happening. Then I take a look at the toms and see if they're really adding a lot of good stuff to the drum sound. I'll just keep them on and set them where I want and then push them for fills. If they tend to muddy things up, then I'll do a whole set of mutes so they're only on for the tom fills. Obviously, you can set certain ambience and effects on the toms that you don't want on the rest of the kit, and you can make them as big as you want that way. I hate gates. I'd much rather control every fill myself. But usually overheads first, then snare, then kick, and then the toms; see how it fits, then tuck in the hat.

Do you have an approach to EQ?
Allen Sides: What I would say is that I tend to like things to sound sort of natural, but I don't care what it takes to make it sound like that. Some people get a very preconceived set of notions that you can't do this or you can't do that. Like Bruce Swedien said to me, he doesn't care if you have to turn the knob around backwards; if it *sounds* good, it *is* good—assuming that you have a reference point that you can trust, of course.

Here's a good example of that. Do you know what UA500 EQs are? It's a passive EQ with a great-sounding 15k. I remember one time I was doing a record, and I had a really great-sounding Steinway B but it was very, very soft. I think I boosted 10dB at 15k on the left and right channels, which sounds exorbitant, but it sounded completely natural. A tastefully EQed piano played softer can sound better than a bright piano.

When I'm recording digitally—particularly when I'm printing things that are fairly quiet and fairly soft—I want to make sure that my harmonic structure above 12kHz has sufficient energy to be in a higher bit range. Because if you have to boost when it comes back, there's nothing there but noise and grit. So I think that I tend to do most of my EQing when I record. That's often the opposite of what many people do, but I'm very careful and everything is to taste so that it sounds good. I really hate mixes where they've taken various center points of the band and boosted the crap out of them. The harmonics are gone, and all you end up with is just harsh unpleasantness.

Do you add effects as you go along, or do you put the mix up and balance it and then add the effects?

Allen Sides: No, the effects are usually added as I go along because a lot of times I'll work on multiple image effects on kicks and snares and stuff and tie that in to overheads so you can hear all the sounds as a single entity. Obviously, that can change again when the vocals come in. Invariably, what works by itself is not going to be exactly the same when you put the vocals in. You may have to increase or decrease those effects to get your overall picture to happen.

The other important thing is that when I'm using effects, I hate it to sound generic. I'd much prefer it almost to sound like we're going for a room sound. You have a great natural kick and snare, plenty of attack and punch, and the ambience surrounds it in such a way that it doesn't sound like an absolute tin can cheeseball effect but becomes more of a natural sound. Obviously, it's relative to the music you're doing. It's all different.

And so that's what you're trying to do then more than anything—trying to get something that's more of an ambient type of thing?

Allen Sides: Yeah, there's also a question of dryness versus liveness versus deadness in regards to monitor volume. Obviously, when you turn it down, your ambience determines how loud it sounds to you to some degree. And if you're monitoring at a loud level and it's very dry, it can be very impressive sounding. When you turn down, it might not be quite so full sounding, so obviously there's a balance there. I would say that I'm getting dryer these days.

That seems to be the trend, actually.

Allen Sides: I'm definitely getting back there, because I started in the late '60s R&B days, which were very dry.

Do you have a method for setting up your delays and reverbs?

Allen Sides: Yeah, I'm a big fan of tube stereo plates. I've got 25 plates here. And then I use this old Ampex mastering preview DDL for my predelay to my chambers. I have about 9 or 10 of these, and they're the greatest DDLs on the planet. Then I usually have API EQs across the sends.

I have some really great live chambers, too. I'm a big fan of the RMX16, not for drums, but for vocals and guitars and stuff. I love Nonlin for guitars and things. Let's say that you had a couple of discrete guitars that were playing different lines, and you try putting them in the middle and they get on top of each other. If you put them left and right, they're too discrete. The RMX non-lin set at 4 seconds with a 10 millisecond predelay and an API EQ on the send with about +4 at 12k shelf and −2 at 100Hz going into it does a wonderful job of creating a left/right effect, but it still spreads nicely. It works great for that.

Do you have an approach to panning?

Allen Sides: Yeah, I tend to do a lot of hard panning. [Laughs] I don't pan in much. I am really big on having things wide. Obviously, the reason for panning in is because there's tremendous value in returning to mono, particularly in reverb returns. I still do a lot of comparing between mono and stereo. No matter what anybody says, if you're in a bar, you're going to hear one speaker. There still has to be a relevance between the stereo and mono thing.

I tend to like things very wide. I just think you can't make it wide enough because I find that one of the biggest problems I have with the current digital formats is losing width. It never gets bigger; it only gets smaller and teenier and tinier. So I work so hard to use every possible bit of information I can, and it makes such a difference.

How about compression? Do you have an approach to that?

Allen Sides: Sometimes I use our Focusrite (console) setup, which has three different stereo busses that can combine, and take a mult of the initial totally clean program, and nail it to the wall to bring up all the little ambient stuff and just tuck that back into the main clean buss so that you can add this sustain that everybody wants without killing the attack. If I take one of my SSL limiters and do that thing that it does, of course it always suffers from a certain lack of impact. So a lot of times we want to get that sustain—particularly on a rocking track—but still want a hell of a punch. That's a way to do that.

I virtually never limit basses during the initial recording process. With players like Nathan East and Jimmy Johnson, who are so consistent and whose instruments sound so good and so well balanced in the track, all limiting would do is mess it up. But sometimes when you have a player in a band who's somewhat inconsistent and you need to bring it into balance, tasteful compression can be helpful, but you still want to leave dynamics. That's oftentimes one of the worst problems I encounter. There's no dynamics left; it's all gone.

It's squeezed to death.

Allen Sides: There's no impact, so I end up having to do as much as I can to put it back in. There's this box that isn't made anymore called the Marshall Time Modulator. You can set the Marshall Time Modulator so it's just on the verge of feedback, take a bass that's been limited to death, and it's possible to get the Marshall to expand the peaks. You set it so it's just on the verge of feeding back, and it'll actually push those peaks out. Amazing box. It's the only device I've ever seen that'll do that.

Have you ever used the Lang? Say you pull up the overheads and there's no highs above 8kHz and it's harsh because basically it's been recorded on the 24-track at +18. So if you take a nice set of EQs, maybe a GML, or some APIs, and boost the top end, it just gets harsher and doesn't really add highs. If you take a Lang, set it at 15k, then set it as narrow as the bandwidth will go and boost it, all of a sudden there is this silky 15k top end. If you set it narrow enough, it just ring-modulates and adds a beautiful silky 15k harmonic that did not exist on the program you boosted.

Or, say that you've got a vocal and you want to get that little air thing, but no matter what you try to do, it just gets harsh. The Lang is amazing. It's one of those boxes where you get something for nothing.

Do you have a monitor set up that you usually use, and what level do you listen back at?
Allen Sides: I must admit that I really do enjoy big speakers. I like to turn it up and have fun. I have no problem mixing on anything else, but I like having nice, accurate, big speakers that are fun to listen to that aren't harsh and that don't hurt my ears.

Generally speaking, when I put up the mix, I'll put it up at a fairly good level, maybe 105, and set all my track levels and get it punchy and fun sounding. Then I will probably reference on NS10s at a very modest level just to check my balance and go back and forth. The small speakers that I'm fond of now, the Genelecs 1032s, I can mix on totally without a problem. But I love my big speakers, and I have so much fun. [Laughs]

And if I listen loud, it's only for very short periods of time. It's rare that I would ever play a track from beginning to end loud. I might listen to 20 seconds or 30 seconds of it here and there, but when I'm actually down to really detailing the balance, I'll monitor at a very modest level.

Modest meaning how loud?
Allen Sides: I would say that at a level that we could have a conversation and you could hear every word I said.

Do you have any listening tricks like going to the back of the room, outside and listen through the door?
Allen Sides: Oh yeah, I think we all have that. You walk out to get a cup of coffee and you're listening to it outside in the hall and the realization strikes you, "How could I miss that?" because it's a different perspective. What I love is my car. With the automation we have today, I put it on in the car on the way home and any additional changes I hear, I just call them in and have the seconds print the updates.

How often do you have to go back and redo your mix or touch it up?
Allen Sides: I would say that about 10 percent of the time I have to go back and do that, so I have my guys document every single detail as best as I can. To be honest with you, sometimes it comes back and sometimes it doesn't, because even the different digital devices are different if it's

not the same unit. And if it's a song that really relies on a particular slap or effect or harmonizer or something that is really a major part of the ambiance of the song, a half dB level in an aux send is going to change the whole musical balance of a song. It just kills us to have a mix that we really are happy with and they say, "I love the mix—just change one thing," because they just don't understand. And then, of course, the joke of all time is to mix on an SSL or a VR in any given room, and then go to another room and put it up. Well, forget it. It's one thing putting it up on the same console, but the accuracy of the pots are so different from console to console.

How many versions of a mix do you usually do?
Allen Sides: Plenty. Invariably I will do the vocal mix to where I'm totally happy with it and then I'll probably do a quarter and half dB up and a quarter and half dB down. I'll print as many mixes as needed, depending on how difficult the artist is to please. Then if I need to, I'll chop in just the part I want. If there's a word or two, I'll just chop those words in. I really cover myself on mixes these days. I just do not want to have to do a mix again.

CHAPTER 33

Don Smith

Just one look at producer/engineer/mixer Don Smith's client list indicates his stature in the industry. With credits that read like a Who's Who of Rock & Roll, Don has lent his unique expertise to projects such as The Rolling Stones, Tom Petty, U2, Stevie Nicks, Bob Dylan, Talking Heads, The Eurythmics, The Traveling Wilburys, Roy Orbison, Iggy Pop, Keith Richards, Cracker, John Hiatt, The Pointer Sisters, and Bonnie Raitt, to name just a few.

Can you hear the mix before you start?
Don Smith: I can usually hear roughly what it should be. I start out with the basics of a good rough mix and then I try to tweak it from there. Sometimes I may hear something while I'm doing it—like a tape delay on the drums—that might change the character of the mix and make it turn into a different direction.

How do you start your mix?
Don Smith: Most of the time just drums and bass, then everything else. Then there were some records that I started with lead vocal then guitar and the drums would be last. With somebody like Tom Petty, his vocal is so important in the mix that you have to start with the vocal. So the vocals get roughed in, and you throw guitars around it. Then I might start back in the other direction, making sure that the drums and the foundation [are] solid. But I like to start with the vocal and guitar because it tells me what the song is about and what it's saying, then let everyone else support the song.

Do you have a method for setting levels?
Don Smith: Yeah, I'll start out with the kick and bass in that area (–7). By the time you put everything else in, it's +3 anyway. At least if you start that low, you have room to go.

Do you have an approach to using EQ?
Don Smith: Yeah, I use EQ different from some people. I don't just use it to brighten or fatten something up. I use it to make an instrument feel better. Like on a guitar—making sure that all the strings on a guitar can be heard. Instead of just brightening up the high strings and adding mud to the low strings, I may look for a certain chord to hear more of the A string. If the D string is missing in a chord, I like to EQ and boost it way up to +8 or +10 and then just dial through the different frequencies until I hear what they're doing to the guitar. So I'm trying to make things more balanced in the way they lay with other instruments.

Do you have a special approach to a lead instrument or vocals?
Don Smith: For vocals, just make sure that the song gets across. The singer is telling a story. He's gotta come through but not be so loud that it sounds like a Pepsi commercial. Sometimes you might want the vocal to sit back in the track more because it might make the listener listen closer. Sometimes you don't want to understand every word. It depends on the song. It's always different.

Do you build a mix up with effects as you go along?
Don Smith: I always build it up dry. I look at it like building a house. You've got to build a solid foundation first before you can put the decorations on. The same way with tracking. I very rarely use effects when I track. Just every now and again if an effect is an integral part of the track to begin with, then I'll record that.

What I've found is that if you really get it good butt naked, then when you dress it up, all it can do is get better. If you put on effects too early, then you might disguise something that's not right. I don't really have too many rules about it. I'll just do what feels good at that moment. Sometimes you get it butt naked and you don't need to put any effects on. It's pretty cool, so just leave it alone.

Do you have a method for adding effects?
Don Smith: I usually start with the delays in time, whether it's 1/8 note or 1/4 note or dotted value or whatever. Sometimes on the drums, I'll use delays very subtly. If you can hear them, then they're too loud, but if you turn them off, you definitely know they're gone. It adds a natural slap like in a room, so to speak, that maybe you won't hear but you feel. And, if the drums are dragging, you can speed the delays up just a nat so the drums feel like they're getting a lift. If they're rushing, you can do it the other way by slowing the delays so it feels like they're pulling the track back a bit.

A lot of times in my mixes, you won't hear those kinds of things because they're hidden. On the Stones *Voodoo Lounge* album, there's a song called "Out of Tears." There's these big piano chords that I wanted to sound not so macho and grand, so I put some Phil Spector kind of 15ips tape slap on it. It sounded kinda cool, so I tried some on the drums, and it sounded pretty cool there, too. By the end of it, I had it on everything, and it changed the whole song around from a big grandiose ballad to something more intimate. It was played on a Bosendofer but really wanted more of an upright, like a John Lennon "Imagine" type of sound.

Do you use tape slap a lot?

Don Smith: I use tape slap all the time. I use it more than I use digital delays. It's a lot warmer and much more natural, and the top end doesn't get so bright and harsh, so it blends in better. I vary-speed it to the tempo or whatever feels right. I usually use a 4-track with varispeed and an old mono Ampex 440 machine for vocals. The mono has a whole different sound from anything else. Sort of like the Elvis or Jerry Lee Lewis slap where it can be really loud but never gets in the way because it's always duller, yet fatter.

On the 4-track, I'll use two channels for stereo, like for drums, and send each slap to the opposite side. Then the other tracks I might use for guitars or predelay to a chamber or something. Sometimes I'll put Dolby on the 4-track to cut down the hiss or at least turn the gain way, way up 'cause you're not using much of it.

Do you have an approach to panning?

Don Smith: Yeah, it's kinda weird, though. I check my panning in mono with one speaker, believe it or not. When you pan around in mono, all of a sudden you'll find that it's coming through now and you've found the space for it. If I want to find a place for the hi-hat, for instance, sometimes I'll go to mono and pan it around, and you'll find that it's really present all of a sudden, and that's the spot. When you start to pan around on all your drum mics in mono, you'll hear all the phase come together. When you go to stereo, it makes things a lot better.

Do you have a set of monitors that you use all the time?

Don Smith: I have a set of Yamaha NS10s that I've had since '83, as well as a set of RORs from '80 or '81, which they stopped making. I tried all the different versions, but they never sounded the same afterwards. I bring a Yamaha 2101 amp with me sometimes.

What level do you listen at?

Don Smith: I like to listen loud on the big speakers to get started, and occasionally thereafter, and most of the time at about 90dB. When the mix starts to come together, it comes way down—sometimes barely audible. I turn it down way low and walk around the room to hear everything.

I mix a lot at my house now where I sit outside a lot on my patio. If I mix in a studio with a lounge, I'll go in there with the control room door shut and listen like that. I definitely get away from the middle of the speakers as much as possible.

How many mixes do you usually do?
Don Smith: I try to just do one mix that everybody likes, and then I'll leave and tell the assistant to do a vocal up and vocal down and all the other versions that they might want, which usually just sit on a shelf. I'll always have a vocal up and down versions because I don't feel like remixing a song once it's done.

How much gear do you bring with you?
Don Smith: Quite a bit. Mostly old stuff like Fairchilds, Pultecs, API EQs, Neve compressors, 1176s, an EMT 250. I've got just a handful of anything new, like a TC5000, two SPXs, and two SD3000s.

How much compression do you use?
Don Smith: I use a lot of it. Generally, the stereo buss itself will go through a Fairchild 670 (serial #7). Sometimes I'll use a Neve 33609 depending on the song. I don't use much; only a dB or 2. There's no rule about it. I'll start with it just on with no threshold just to hear it.

I may go 20:1 on a 1176 with 20dB of compression on a guitar part as an effect. In general, if it's well recorded, I'll do it just lightly for peaks here and there. I'll experiment with three or four compressors on a vocal. I've got a mono Fairchild to Neves to maybe even a dbx 160 with 10dB of compression to make the vocal just punch through the track.

Again, I don't have any rules. As soon as I think I've got it figured out, on the next song or the next artist, it won't work as well or at all.

CHAPTER 34

Ed Stasium

 Producer/engineer Ed Stasium is widely known for working on some of the best guitar albums in recent memory (including my own personal favorites by the Smithereens, Living Colour, and Mick Jagger), so I was really surprised to find the total breadth of his work. From Marshall Crenshaw to Talking Heads to Soul Asylum to Motorhead to Julian Cope to the Ramones and even to Ben Vereen, Ed has put his indelible stamp on their records as only he can.

Do you have a specific approach when you sit down to mix?
Ed Stasium: Unlike some other people who are specifically mixers, I've been fortunate in the fact that everything I produce I've been able to follow through on it with the mix. I'm a hands-on kind of producer/engineer guy.

Where do you start to build your mix from?
Ed Stasium: I put the vocals up first and then bring in the bass and drums. I bring up the whole kit at the same time and tweak it, but I'm not one to work on the kick drum sound for two hours. Also, I've recorded everything, so I know what's there and don't have to mess around much with anything.

How long does it take usually?
Ed Stasium: I would say maybe between 6 and 10 hours. I don't use a lot of effects. I use an EMT plate and a slap tape, but everything that you hear on the mix is basically like what's on the multitrack. I consider my technique very old school. I don't use a lot of digital reverb. If I use any kind of outboard gear, it's a Pultec or an LA-2A or LA-4A or a Fairchild or even

a Cooper Time Cube—that type of thing. I do use Drawmer gates on the reverb returns, just to keep them quiet.

Do you have an approach to using EQ? Do you find any frequencies that you always seem to be coming back to, like on a kick drum?
Ed Stasium: No. I approach it pretty haphazardly. I don't have any rules really. I just sort of move the knobs. I'd actually rather move the mic around and find whatever sounds good instead of resorting to extreme EQ.

Do you have an approach to panning?
Ed Stasium: My mixes are kind of mono, but not really. I pan tom-toms, but not to extremes—usually between 10 and 2 o'clock. Usually I have the drums in the middle, vocals in the middle, solos in the middle. I do pan out the guitars, though. If there's one guitar player, I'll do a lot of double tracking and have those split out on the sides. But if there's two guitar players, I'll just have one guy over on the left, one guy on the right. And if there is any double tracking on any of those, I'll split them a little bit, but I never go really wide with that.

Do you use a lot of compressors?
Ed Stasium: I like compression. I think of compression as my friend. What I do a lot is take a snare drum and go through an LA-2—just totally compress it—and then crank up the output so it's totally distorted, and edge it in a little bit behind the actual drum. You don't notice the distortion on the track, but it adds a lot of tone in the snare, especially when it goes [Makes an exploding sound]. Actually, something I've done for the last 20 years is to always split the kick drum and snare drum on a mult and take the second output into a Pultec into a dbx160VU and into a Drawmer 201 gate. Then I pretty much overemphasize the EQ and compression on that track and use it in combination with the original track.

How about effects? You say you don't use many, but you obviously use some. Do you get your mix up first and then add everything, or add effects as you go?
Ed Stasium: As I go. I usually have a couple of EMT140s to use. I always have a slap tape going on that I put in time with the tempo of the song.

Is the slap for an individual track, or is it specifically for predelay for the chambers?
Ed Stasium: It's usually on vocals. I always have a little bit of a slap on the vocals, and I might send some of that slap return to a chamber as well.

Do you have monitors that you take with you?
Ed Stasium: I have these little Aiwa speakers that I bought in 1983 in Atlanta. I always get my balances on those. I really like to listen at very low levels. Sometimes I try to have a pair of old JBL 4311s, 4312s, or 4310s,

because I still actually have the home version L100s in my house. And then there's always the Yamahas hanging around.

Do you have any listening tricks, like going out in your car?
Ed Stasium: I have this little stereo system I carry around with me with these Advent wedges called "Powered Partners" that are AV speakers. I have a little road case for them, and I bring them with me when I stay in hotels out of town. I do all my listening—even when I go home at night—on these.

Have you noticed any changes over the years in the way things are done, or the way you do things?
Ed Stasium: Yeah, especially with the onset of computers. I do a lot more riding of things—especially the vocal—and doing little different effect changes. It makes life easier in a way, but then it makes life more complicated because you can do so much more. It depends again on what you're doing. The Living Colour records were very complicated. We had a lot of different effects on the verse, different effects on the vocal—that kind of great stuff. When I mixed "Midnight Train to Georgia" back when I first started, we did that on a little 16-input, 16-track in somebody's basement in New Jersey. The drums were all on one track, and you just made sure you got the vocals right.

I remember the tracks were really packed on that song, so I just brought things in gradually. We started off with the piano, added the guitar, added the Hammond. But now, I'm riding every snare drum hit to make sure it cuts through, every little guitar nuance, little cymbal things, and the kick in certain places. I'll be riding everything.

"Midnight Train" sounds so clean…
Ed Stasium: That was a great console—a Langevin. I don't know what ever happened to it. I don't know where it came from, but it was in Tony Camillo's basement studio in New Jersey that we recorded that stuff on. The vocals were done in Detroit. I'm sure the drums were only on one track or two tracks at most. The Pips were double-tracked. You know, Gladys is right up in the front. We didn't use many effects on that because we didn't have any effects. It was a little basement studio, and all we had was a live chamber that was the size of a closet that was concrete with a speaker in there and a couple of microphones. That was the reverb on that record.

Figure 34.1
Eventide H910 Harmonizer (the first harmonizer—long out of production).

Same thing at Power Station (now sadly closed). I was mixing the third Ramones record, which was actually the first thing mixed at Power Station, while we were still building the place. We had that 910 Harmonizer [see Figure 34.1], a couple of Kepexs [see Figure 34.2], and no reverb at all. What we used for reverb on that whole record was the stairwell.

Figure 34.2
Valley People Kepex II noise gates in rack (long out of production).

How many mixes do you usually do?
Ed Stasium: I'll do a vocal up. Sometimes I do guitars up. It depends on what players are in the room. If the drummer's in the room, he'll say, "Hey, can I have more snare drum?" I'll say, "Oh yeah. We'll do an extra mix with more drums in it." And if the guitar player's in the room, he'll say, "I need to hear the guitars a little more." I'll say, "Okay, we'll put the guitars up," but I always use the real mix anyway. Just kidding everybody! [Laughs] It doesn't matter. You get so critical when you're mixing, and when it comes down to it, it's the darn song anyway. As long as the vocal's up there, it will sound pretty good. You won't even notice the little things a month later.

CHAPTER 35

Bruce Swedien

 Perhaps no one else in the studio world can so aptly claim the moniker of "Godfather of Recording" as Bruce Swedien. Universally revered by his peers, Bruce has earned that respect thanks to years of stellar recordings for the cream of the musical crop. His credits could fill a book alone, but legends like Count Basie, Lionel Hampton, Stan Kenton, Duke Ellington, Woody Herman, Oscar Peterson, Nat "King" Cole, George Benson, Mick Jagger, Paul McCartney, Edgar Winter, and Jackie Wilson are good places to start. Then comes Bruce's Grammy-winning projects that include Michael Jackson's *Thriller* (the biggest-selling record of all time), *Bad*, and *Dangerous*, and Quincy Jones's *Back on the Block* and *Jook Joint*. As one who has participated in the evolution of modern recording from virtually the beginning and one of its true innovators, Bruce is able to give insights on mixing from a perspective that few of us will ever have.

Do you have a philosophy about mixing that you follow?
Bruce Swedien: The only thing I could say about that is everything that I do in music—mixing or recording or producing—is music driven. It comes from my early days in the studio with Duke Ellington and from there to Quincy. I think the key word in that philosophy is what I would prefer to call responsibility. From Quincy (no one's influenced me more strongly than Quincy), I've learned that when we go into the studio, our first thought should be that our responsibility is to the musical statement that we're going to make and to the individuals involved. And I guess that's really the philosophy that I follow.

Responsibility in that you want to present the music in its best light?
Bruce Swedien: To do it the best way that I possibly can. To use everything at my disposal to not necessarily re-create an unaltered acoustic event, but to present either my concept of the music or the artist's concept of the music in the best way that I can.

Is your concept ever opposed to the artist's concept?
Bruce Swedien: It's funny, but I don't ever remember running into a situation where there's been a conflict. Maybe my concept of the sonics of the music might differ at first with the artist, but I don't ever remember it being a serious conflict.

I would think that you're hired because of your overall concept.
Bruce Swedien: I have a feeling that's true, but I'm not really sure. I think probably my range of musical background helps a lot in that I studied piano for eight years and as a kid I spent a lot of time listening to classical music. So when it comes to depth of musical experience, I think that's one reason that people will turn to me for a project.

Do you think that starting out without the benefit of the vast amount of technology that we have today has helped you?
Bruce Swedien: Oh, definitely. Absolutely. No question. And I think what's helped me more is that I was the right guy in the right place at the right time at Universal in Chicago. Bill Putnam, who was my mentor and brought me from Minneapolis as a kid, saw or heard something in me that I guess inspired some confidence. From there I got to work with people like Duke Ellington, Count Basie, Woody Herman, Stan Kenton, Oscar Peterson, and so on. One of the thrilling parts about the late '50s at Universal in Chicago was that I literally learned microphone technique with Count Basie and Duke Ellington, and these guys were in love with the recording process.

Really? I was under the impression they only recorded because they had to.
Bruce Swedien: No. Absolutely not. Now there were some band leaders that were that way, although I can't think of anybody offhand, but most of them just loved being there. The guy that I think was most formative in my early years as a kid was probably Count Basie. I did a lot of records with that band.

How were you influenced?
Bruce Swedien: I came into the industry at that level as a real youngster. In 1958, I was only 20 years old, and I started right out working with Stan Kenton, and a couple of years later Count Basie, Duke Ellington, Quincy, and so on. But I was not in love with the status quo that was part of the recording industry at the time. The goal of music recording in the late '50s was to present the listener with a virtually unaltered acoustic event, and

that wasn't terribly exciting to me. I loved it, but I wanted my imagination to be part of the recording.

Another guy who bumped into that who I didn't work with but I got to meet in the early '60s at Universal was Les Paul. There was one record that I remember that came out when I was in high school in 1951 that changed popular music forever, and it was Les Paul and Mary Ford's "How High the Moon," which was an absolutely incredible thing. I couldn't wait to get to the record store to buy it so I could try to figure out what that was all about. At that point in time, I think a whole segment of the record-buying public made a left turn in that the records of the day were pretty much, as I said, an unaltered acoustic event, and we were trying to put the listener in the best seat in the house. But all of a sudden, this record came along without a shred of reality in it, and a whole segment of the record-buying public said, "This is what we want."

That being said, can you hear that sonic space in your head before you start to mix?
Bruce Swedien: No. That's the wonderful part about it.

Is your approach to mixing each song generally the same then?
Bruce Swedien: I'll take that a step further and I'll say it's never the same, and I think I have a very unique imagination. I also have another problem in that I hear sounds as colors in my mind. Frequently when I'm EQing or checking the spectrum of a mix or a piece of music, if I don't see the right colors in it, I know the balance is not there.

Wow! Can you elaborate on that?
Bruce Swedien: Well, low frequencies appear to my mind's eye as dark colors, black or brown, and high frequencies are brighter colors. Extremely high frequencies are gold and silver. It's funny, but that can be very distracting. It drives me crazy sometimes. There is a term for it, but I don't know what it's called.

What are you trying to do then, build a rainbow?
Bruce Swedien: No, it's just that if I don't experience those colors when I listen to a mix that I'm working on, I know that there's either an element missing or that the mix values aren't satisfying.

How do you know what proportion of what color should be there?
Bruce Swedien: That's instinctive. Quincy has the same problem. It's terrible! Drives me nuts! But it's not a quantitative thing. It's just that if I focus on a part of the spectrum in a mix and don't see the right colors, it bothers me. I have a feeling it's a disease, but people have told me it isn't.

How do you go about getting a balance? Do you have a method?
Bruce Swedien: No, it's purely instinctive. Another thing that I've learned from Quincy, but started with my work with Duke Ellington, is to do my mixing reactively not cerebrally. When automated mixing came along, I got really excited because I thought, "At last, here's a way for me to pre-serve my first instinctive reaction to the music and the mix values that are there." You know how frequently we'll work and work and work on a piece of music, and we think, "Oh boy, this is great. Wouldn't it be great if it had a little more of this or a little more of that?" Then you listen to it in the cold gray light of dawn, and it sounds like shit. Well, that's when the cerebral part of our mind takes over, pushing the reactive part to the background, so the music suffers.

Do you start to do your mix from the very first day of tracking?
Bruce Swedien: Yes, but again I don't think that you can say any of these thoughts are across the board. There are certain types of music that grow in the studio. You go in and start a rhythm track and think you're gonna have one thing, and all of a sudden it does a sharp left and it ends up being something else. While there are other types of music where I start the mix even before the musicians come to the studio. I'll give you a good example of something. On Michael's *History* album, for the song "Smile, Charlie Chaplin," I knew what that mix would be like two weeks before the musi-cians hit the studio.

From listening to the demo?
Bruce Swedien: No. It had nothing to do with anything except what was going on in my mind because Jeremy Lubbock, the orchestra arranger and conductor, and I had talked about that piece of music and the orchestra that we were going to use. I came up with a studio setup that I had used with the strings of the Chicago Symphony many years before at Universal where the first violins are set up to the left of the conductor and the second violins to the right, the violas behind the first fiddles, and the celli behind the second fiddles, which is a little unusual. So I had that whole mix firmly in mind long before we did it.

So sometimes you do hear the final mix before you start.
Bruce Swedien: Sometimes, but that's rare.

Where do you generally build your mix from?
Bruce Swedien: It's totally dependent on the music. Always. But if there was a method of my approach, I would say the rhythm section. You usu-ally try to find the motor and then build the car around it.

Some people say they always put the bass up first, some from the snare, some the overheads…
Bruce Swedien: No, I don't think I have any set way. I think it would spoil the music to think about it that much.

I guess you don't have any kind of method for setting balances.
Bruce Swedien: Starting the bass at –5 or something? Boy, that would be terrible. I couldn't do that if my life depended on it.

Do you have a method for panning?
Bruce Swedien: I don't think I have any approach to it. I generally do whatever works with the music that I'm doing.

So it's just something that hits you when you're doing it?
Bruce Swedien: Yeah, that's really the way it works. It'll be an idea, whether it's panning or a mix value, or an effect, or whatever, and I'll say, "Ooh, that's great. I'm gonna do that."

What level do you usually monitor at?
Bruce Swedien: That's one area where I think I've relegated it to a science. For the nearfield speakers, I use Westlake BBSM8s, and I try not to exceed 85dB SPL. On the Auratones, I try not to exceed 83. What I've found in the past few years, I use the big speakers less and less with every project.

Are you listening in mono on the Auratones?
Bruce Swedien: Stereo.

Do you listen in mono much?
Bruce Swedien: Once in awhile. I always check it because there's some places where mono is still used.

I love the way you sonically layer things when you mix. How do you go about getting that?
Bruce Swedien: I have no idea. If I knew, I probably couldn't do it as well. It's purely reactive and instinctive. I don't have a plan. Actually, what I will do frequently when we're layering with synths and so on is to add some acoustics to the synth sounds. I think this helps in the layering in that the virtual direct sound of most synthesizers is not too interesting, so I'll send the sound out to the studio and use a coincident pair of mics to blend a little bit of acoustics back with the direct sound. Of course, it adds early reflections to the sound, which reverb devices can't do. That's the space before the onset of reverb where those early reflections occur.

So what you're looking for more than anything is early reflections?
Bruce Swedien: I think that's a much-overlooked part of sound because there are no reverb devices that can generate that. It's very important. Early reflections will usually occur under 40 milliseconds. It's a fascinating part of sound.

When you're adding effects, are you using mostly reverbs or delays?
Bruce Swedien: A combination. Lately, though, I have been kinda going through a phase of using less reverb. I've got two 7-foot high racks full

of everything. I have an EMT250, a 252, and all the usual stuff. All of it I bought new. No one else has ever used them. It's all in pretty good shape, too.

Do you have any listening tricks?
Bruce Swedien: You know what? Since I moved from California (I live in Connecticut now, and I'm not going back), one of the things that I miss is my time in the car. I had a Ford Bronco with an incredible sound system, and I still kinda miss that great listening environment.

Do you do all your work at your facility now?
Bruce Swedien: No, wherever they'll have me. I love it here, but my studio's dinky. I have an older little 40-input Harrison and a 24-track. The Harrison is a wonderful desk. It's a 32 series, and the same as the one I did *Thriller* on. [See Figure 35.1.] Actually, I think that's one of the most underrated desks in the industry. It's all spiffied up with a beautiful computer and Neve summing amps. It's just fabulous.

Figure 35.1
Harrison 32 Series console (circa 1980).

Didn't you used to have a couple of Neves put together?
Bruce Swedien: I did have a beautiful Neve, but after I finished Michael's *History* album and Quincy's *Jook Joint*, I was kind of burned out and very, very tired, so I told my wife as we were having breakfast one morning, "Honey, I'm gonna get rid of this damn studio at home, and I don't ever want to have another at home." Six months later, I was buying a console. I guess once a junkie, always a junkie.

How long does it usually take you to do a mix?
Bruce Swedien: That can vary. I like to try not to do more than one song a day unless it's a real simple project, and then I like to sleep on a mix and keep it on the desk overnight. That's one of the advantages of having my little studio at home.

I know that a lot of your projects are really extensive in terms of tracks.
Bruce Swedien: But that's not so much true anymore. I start a mix tomorrow here at home for EMI in Portugal of a Portuguese band. It's all on one 24-track tape.

How many versions of a mix do you do?

Bruce Swedien: Usually one. Although when I did "Billy Jean," I did 91 mixes of that thing, and the mix that we finally ended up using was mix 2. I had a pile of half-inch tapes to the ceiling. And we thought, "Oh man, it's getting better and better." [Laughs]

Do you have an approach to using EQ?

Bruce Swedien: I don't think I have a philosophy about it. What I hate to see is an engineer or producer start EQing before they've heard the sound source. To me, it's kinda like salting and peppering your food before you've tasted it. I always like to listen to the sound source first, whether it be on tape or live, and see how well it holds up without any EQ or whatever.

That being the case, do you have to approach things differently if you're just coming in to do the mix?

Bruce Swedien: Not usually. But I'm not really crazy about listening to other people's tapes, I gotta tell you that. But I consider myself fortunate to be working, so that's the bottom line. [Laughs]

Do you add effects as you go?

Bruce Swedien: There's probably only two effects that I use on almost everything, and that's the EMT 250 and the 252. I love those reverbs. There's nothing in the industry that comes close to a 250 or a 252.

What are you using the 252 on?

Bruce Swedien: I love the 252 on vocals with the 250 program. It's close to a 250, but it's kinda like a 250 after taxes. It's wonderful, but there's nothing like a 250.

What do you do to make a mix special?

Bruce Swedien: I wish I knew. I have no idea. But the best illustration of something special is when we were doing "Billie Jean," and Quincy said, "Okay, this song has to have the most incredible drum sound that anybody has ever done, but it also has to have one element that's different, and that's sonic personality." So I lost a lot of sleep over that. What I ended up doing was building a drum platform and designing some special little things like a bass drum cover and a flat piece of wood that go between the snare and the hat. And the bottom line is that there aren't many pieces of music where you can hear the first three or four notes of the drums and immediately tell what piece of music it is. But I think that is the case with "Billy Jean," and that I attribute to sonic personality. But I lost a lot of sleep over that one before it was accomplished.

Do you determine that personality before you start to record?

Bruce Swedien: Not really. But in that case, I got to think about the recording setup in advance. And, of course, I have quite a microphone collection that goes with me everywhere (17 anvil cases!), and that helps a little bit in that they're not beat up.

Are most of the projects that you do these days both tracking and mixing?
Bruce Swedien: I don't know what's happened, but I don't get called to record stuff very much these days. People are driving me nuts with mixing, and I love it, but I kinda miss tracking. A lot of people think that since I moved to Connecticut I retired or something, but that's the last thing I'd want to do. You know what Quincy and I say about retiring? Retiring is when you can travel around and get to do what you want. Well, I've been doing that all my life. I love what I do, and I'm just happy to be working. So that's the bottom line.

CHAPTER 36

John X

Yes, his effects are loaded, and he's not afraid to use them. John X. Volaitis is one of the new breed of engineers who's thrown off his old-school chains and ventured into the world of remixes (known to some as Techno, Trance, Industrial, Ambient, or any one of about 10 other different names). Along with his partner Danny Saber, John has done remixes for such legends as David Bowie, U2, Marilyn Manson, the Rolling Stones, Black Sabbath, Garbage, Korn, Limp Bizkit, and a host of others. As you'll see, the X man's methods are both unique and fun.

When people send you tapes for remixes, what are they actually sending you?
John X: Far too often, they send us the entire multitrack when all we need is one track of that. Usually you could just send the lead vocal, time code, and a start time and tempo, because half the time we'll change the key and the tempo anyway. David Bowie's "Little Wonder," for instance, we did in almost half time. That means you're pretty much throwing out most of the original tracks because you can't use any of that stuff to begin with.

Sometimes that's inappropriate, though. We did one for U2, "Staring at the Sun," which they're really happy with. Part of why I think they're happy is the fact that we didn't butcher them at all. We kept a little piece of everybody because they're a band. The one thing you learn is that when you remix for a band, you can't have the singer and the guitar player in the track but not have the bass player and the drummer in it because it creates total warfare for them that's gonna make them say, "Look, let's not use that." So you find one little thing, like some thick fill that the drummer did or the bass player making some noise at the beginning of the song, and use that. Maybe it's the only thing that you can really loop and get into the track and make it dancey, but it's something that's gonna let them say, "Hey man, that's me." As long as they know they're in there, they're fine.

One special thing I've noticed about the remixes is that if you don't have a really great vocal performance to begin with, you're screwed. The same old rule still applies. If you got a good performance on somebody, you can almost do anything to it and it's still good. With somebody like Bowie or Bono, those guys are "the" cats, so it sounds great right off.

Where do you build your mix from?
John X: I generally have to start with the loops. You've got to find the main loop or the combination of loops that creates the main groove. Sometimes the loops may have a lot of individual drums, but they're usually not crucial rhythmic elements. They can be accents, and they can be stuff that just pops up in a break here and there.

Do you use a lot of compression?
John X: I use it a lot. Not always in great amounts, but I tend to try to get some handle on the peaks. Loops I rarely mess with. If somebody's got a loop and a certain groove that they like, I almost always leave those things alone because they start getting real squirrelly if you mess with them. All of a sudden, the groove can change radically. Anything else, I don't mind slammin' the hell out of as long as it sounds the way I want it to sound. I don't even have a rule about it.

What's your approach to panning?
John X: I try not to waste the sides on anything that's not really, really actively stereo, like a lot of stereo patches that come out of people's keyboards. To me, most of those are boring. They're not really doing anything, and they're a waste of the sides, so I'll just tuck them up a little bit. I'll have them left and right but not always hard. What I always try to do is keep my effects and delays or my radical panning stuff hard left and right, which makes it feel like the more radical stuff is projecting a little bit further than the rest of the band. It just gives a different sort of depth perception.

What about adding effects? Do you add them as you go along, or do you get a balance and then add them?
John X: I do both. I love effects. For years, I acted as a total purist. "I'm gonna bypass everything in the room and go to tape." That's really cool for some stuff, but what it was doing was getting me into a mindset where I couldn't even think about putting effects on stuff with any real imagination. All I was coming up with was sort of the same thing you always hear on conservative albums. Now, as far as I'm concerned, I'll go haywire with that stuff. I'll record effects on tracks, and if I don't like them, I'll just erase them. It's no big deal.

That sounds chaotic, but usually I'm trying to accomplish something very special. For example, sometimes I'll mult the lead vocal to a few different channels. Then each will be EQed completely differently, some compressed, some de-essed severely and sent to long reverbs, and some super-filtered and sent to some weird pitch modulation stuff. Then I'll flip around from syllable to syllable throughout the verses and have the entire effect structured around the voice constantly shifting, yet leave something consistent from the main vocal track. As far as the amount of dry vocal, that's arbitrary. Sometimes, you find some spots where you feel like it's right and you leave it there and then just sort of tune in that other stuff so it becomes something natural. But sometimes it's something special to where anyone who listens to it can't even figure out what the hell is on there. You don't have enough time to identify the flanger because by the time you think it might be a flanger, it's already turned into three other effects. You have to do it in such a way so it's not a distraction and it's not defeating the lead vocalist, though.

Do you have a method for setting up your effects?
John X: Yeah, I go right for the Eventide stuff first. I'm definitely a snob that way. I go for the 4000, the 3500, the 3000. Then I'm gonna go into the 480s and stuff, depending on what the people have in them. I actually like the 224X [see Figure 36.1] with the Resonant Chords. I love that patch and use that thing a lot, and I use the PCM70 with their "Rhyme in C-minor BPM, Rhyme in C-major BPM" patch a lot also. You can generate pitches with a nice resonance but be able to tune the pitches to the key of your track and set the delay time almost instantly. I've taken some really dud parts and just really brought them to life with those. I've been making loops with them, too, like tuned drum loops that are really usable. I definitely go for the weird stuff first. I only put up maybe one reverb. Reverb has a way of piling up underneath your track, so there's a lot more of it underneath the track than there is on top of it. I'll usually try to keep the amount of reverb down to one special item for a distance perspective kind of thing, just to let you know that someone's back there, but not so much to drown the band. I prefer the shorter, weirder stuff, definitely.

Figure 36.1
Lexicon 224X digital reverb (long out of production).

What do you bring to the studio with you?
John X: I have a bunch of mostly funky gear. A lot of stuff I bring is not engineer related; it's more music related. I'll bring some weird toys like an ancient AKAI sampler that has knobs on the front that lets me do all kinds of weird stuff. I have some weird vocal processors like the Digitech Vocalist VH5, which I use quite often, and a Korg version that was made

years ago. It's a really super-cheesy vocorder with some weird key-bending stuff that you can do. Other than that, I bring a Lexicon Vortex, and a bunch of weird little pedals. That's about it. I like to bring the stuff you know you're not going to find in a control room.

Since you're building up the track from scratch, how long does it take you on a remix?

John X: Usually we try to do them in two days. My partner, Danny Saber, will go in the first day, and he'll do his musical arrangement, such as playing all the parts and laying out the loops and all that stuff. The second day is mine, and that's it. Sometimes it slips into three, depending on how elaborate I get on that second day.

When I'm mixing, you don't really get the impression that people are working in there. The vibe is whatever it is because that's my day, it's my show, and I can do what I want with it. I rarely stress out about anything, and it's always gonna be complete mayhem and chaos. My main assistant has to be wearing a lab coat that says "Patch Boy" on it, and I have my own dark blue one. We've found that giving the assistants those lab coats gives them a really new sense of importance. At first we were joking about it, but now it's like, "Damn, look at these guys! They have become serious." If you ask them a question, they're right on it! [Laughing] And the best thing is when clients come in who've never worked with us, the assistants could tell them anything, and they believe them because they're wearing that lab coat. It's like, "The doctor just told me that this is the way it's gonna go down, so I believe [him]." The whole thing is really fun!

Glossary

5.1 A speaker system that uses three speakers across the front and two stereo speakers in the rear, along with a subwoofer.

ambience The background noise of an environment.

attack The first part of a sound. On a compressor/limiter, this is a control that affects how that device will respond to the attack of a sound.

attenuation A decrease in level.

Augsburger George Augsburger of Perception Inc. in Los Angeles is one of the most revered studio designers. He also designs large studio monitors, each having dual 15-inch woofers and a horn tweeter.

automation A system that memorizes and then plays back the position of all faders and mutes on a console.

bandwidth The number of frequencies that a device will pass before the signal degrades. A human being can supposedly hear from 20Hz to 20kHz, so the bandwidth of the human ear is 20Hz to 20kHz.

bass management A circuit that utilizes the subwoofer in a 5.1 system to provide bass extension for the five main speakers. The bass manager steers all frequencies below 80Hz into the subwoofer along with the LFE source signal. *See also* LFE.

bass redirection Another term for bass management.

bit rate   The transmission rate of a digital system.

buss   A signal pathway.

chamber (reverb)   A method to create artificial reverberation using a tiled room with a speaker and several microphones placed in the room.

chorus   A type of signal processor in which a detuned copy is mixed with the original signal, creating a fatter sound.

codec   Compressor/decompressor. A codec is a software algorithm that encodes and decodes a particular file format. .wav, .aiff, and .mp3 are examples of codecs.

comb filter   A distortion produced by combining an electronic or acoustic signal with a delayed copy of itself. The result is peaks and dips introduced into the frequency response. This is what happens when a signal is flanged. *See also* flanging.

competitive level   A mix level that is as loud as your competitor's mix.

controller   An external hardware device that controls the parameters of a computer application.

cut   To decrease, attenuate, or make less.

cut pass   A playback of the song in which the engineer programs only the mutes into the automation to clean up the mix.

data compression   A method of taking multiple digital data streams (as in 6-channel surround sound) and combining them into a single data stream for more efficient storage and transmission.

DAW   Digital Audio Workstation. A computer with the appropriate hardware and software needed to digitize and edit audio.

DDL   Digital delay line. This is the same as a digital delay. *See also* delay.

decay   The time it takes for a signal to fall below audibility.

delay   A type of signal processor that produces distinct repeats (echoes) of a signal.

Distressor   A compressor made by Emperical Labs that's noted for its distinctively aggressive sound.

Dolby Digital   A data compression method, otherwise known as AC-3, that uses psycho-acoustic principles to reduce the number of bits required to represent the signal. Bit rates for 5.1 channels range from 320kbps for sound on film to 384kbps for digital television and up to 448kbps for audio use on DVD. AC-3 is also what's known as a lossy compressor that relies on psychoacoustic modeling of frequency and temporal masking effects to reduce bits by eliminating those parts of the signal thought to be inaudible. The bit rate reduction achieved at a nominal 384kbps is about 10 to 1. *See also* lossy compression.

documentation   The session notes and track sheets for a song.

downmix   To automatically extract a stereo or mono mix from an encoded surround mix.

DTS   A data compression method developed by Digital Theater Systems using waveform coding techniques. It takes six channels of audio (5.1) and folds them into a single digital bit stream. This differs from Dolby Digital in that the data rate is a somewhat higher 1.4Mbps, which represents a compression ratio of about 4 to 1. DTS is also known as a lossy compression. *See also* lossy compression.

DTV   Digital television.

element   A component or ingredient of the sound or groove.

Elliptical EQ   A special equalizer built especially for vinyl disc mastering that takes excessive bass energy from either side of a stereo signal and directs it to the center. This prevents excessive low-frequency energy from cutting through the groove wall and destroying the master lacquer.

equalizer   A tone control that can vary in sophistication from very simple to very complex. *See also* parametric equalizer.

exciter   An outboard effects device that uses phase manipulation and harmonic distortion to produce high-frequency enhancement of a signal.

flanging   The process of mixing a copy of the signal back with itself, but gradually and randomly slowing down the copy to cause the sound to "whoosh" as if it were in a wind tunnel. This was originally done by holding a finger against a tape flange (the metal part that holds the tape on the reel)—hence the name.

Fletcher-Munson curves   A set of measurements that describes how the frequency response of the ear changes at different sound pressure levels. For instance, we generally hear very high and very low frequencies much better as the overall sound pressure level is increased.

groove   The pulse of the song and the way the instruments dynamically breathe with it.

harmonizer   Originally developed and trademarked by Eventide, the harmonizer has become a generic term for pitch shifting, either to tune an instrument (usually a vocal) or as an effect similar to chorusing.

headroom   The amount of dynamic range between the normal operating level and the maximum output level, which is usually the onset of clipping.

hi-pass filter   A filter that allows only the high frequencies to pass. The frequency point where it cuts off is usually either switchable or variable.

hypercompression   Adding too much compression to a track, leaving it sounding lifeless and unexciting.

LFE   Low-Frequency Effects channel. This is a special channel of 5 to 120Hz information primarily intended for special effects such as explosions in movies. The LFE has an additional 10dB of headroom to accommodate the required level.

lossy compression   A data compression method that uses psychoacoustic principles to reduce the number of bits required to represent the signal. Lossy compression relies on psychoacoustic modeling of frequency and temporal masking effects to reduce bits by eliminating those parts of the signal thought to be inaudible.

lo-pass filter   A filter that allows only the low frequencies to pass. The frequency point where it cuts off is usually either switchable or variable.

make-up gain   A control on a compressor/limiter that applies additional gain to the signal. This is required because the signal automatically decreases when the compressor is working. Make-up gain "makes up" the gain and brings it back to where it was prior to compression.

mastering   The process of turning a collection of songs into a record by making them sound like they belong together in tone, volume, and timing (spacing between songs).

MLP   Meridian Lossless Packing. This is a data compression technique designed specifically for high-quality (96kHz/24-bit) sonic data. MLP differs from other data compression techniques in that no significant data is thrown away, thereby claiming the "lossless" moniker. MLP is also a standard for the 96kHz/24-bit portion of the new DVD-Audio disc.

modulate The process of adding a control voltage to a signal source to change its character. For example, modulating a short slap delay with a .5Hz signal produces chorusing. *See also* chorus.

Mute A parameter or control that temporarily silences the audio.

parametric equalizer A tone control in which the gain, frequency, and bandwidth are variable.

overdubbing The process of recording new material while listening to material that has been previously recorded. *See* also Selsync.

pan pot Short for pan potentiometer, which is the electronic name for the hardware control on a recording console that sets the audio panning.

phantom image The effect in a stereo system whereby, if the signal is of equal strength in the left and right channels, the resultant sound appears to come from between them.

phase shift The highly undesirable process during which some frequencies (usually those below 100Hz) are slowed down ever so slightly as they pass through a device. This is usually exaggerated by excessive use of equalization.

plate (reverb) A method to create artificial reverberation using a large steel plate with a speaker and several transducers attached directly to it.

predelay A variable length of time before the onset of reverberation. Mixing engineers often use predelay to separate the source from the reverberation so they can hear the source more clearly.

Prologic Dolby's sophisticated algorithm that processes stereo material to reproduce 4- or 5-channel surround sound.

Pultec An equalizer that Western Electric sold during the '50s and '60s that is highly prized today for its smooth sound.

punchy A description for a quality of sound that infers good reproduction of dynamics with a strong impact. The term sometimes means emphasis in the 200Hz and 5kHz areas.

Q Bandwidth of a filter or equalizer.

ratio A control on a compressor/limiter that determines how much compression or limiting will occur when the signal exceeds threshold.

range On a gate or expander, a control that adjusts the amount of attenuation that will occur to the signal when the gate is closed.

recall   A system that memorizes the position of all controls and switches on a console. The engineer must still physically reset the pots and switches back to their previous positions as indicated on a video monitor.

release   The last part of a sound. On a compressor/limiter, this is a control that affects the way that device responds to the release of a sound.

return   Inputs on a recording console especially dedicated for effects devices such as reverbs and delays. The return inputs are usually not as sophisticated as normal channel inputs on a console.

reverb   A type of signal processor that reproduces the spatial sound of an environment (that is, the sound of a closet or locker room or inside an oil tanker).

SDDS   Sony Dynamic Digital Sound. This is Sony's digital delivery system for the cinema. The 7.1 system features five speakers across the front, stereo speakers on the sides, and a subwoofer.

Selsync   Selective synchronization. This is the process of using the Record head on a tape machine to do simultaneous playback of previously recorded tracks while recording. This process is now called overdubbing.

sibilance   A rise in the frequency response in a vocal in which the 5kHz is excessive, resulting in an overemphasis of *S* sounds.

slate   A comment added to a tape or track to identify it. In the early days of tape, a 50Hz slate tone was added before each take of a song to easily identify its beginning as the tape was rewinding.

Spatializer   A process developed by Spatializer Laboratories that uses psychoacoustic algorithms to give the listener the impression that he is immersed in sound.

SPL   Sound pressure level.

sub   Subwoofer.

subwoofer   A low-frequency speaker that has a frequency response from about 25Hz to 120Hz.

synchronization   The condition by which two devices—usually storage devices such as tape machines, DAWs, or sequencers—are locked together in respect to time.

tape slap   A method to create a delay effect by using the repro head of a tape machine (which is located after the record head in the tape path).

test tones   A set of tones used to calibrate a playback system. In the days of tape, they were added to a tape to help calibrate the playback machine.

threshold   The point at which an effect takes place. On a compressor/limiter, for instance, the Threshold control adjusts the point at which compression will take place.

track sharing   The condition by which a single track shares more than one instrument. For instance, this might happen when a percussion part is playing on a guitar solo track in the places where the guitar has not been recorded. This is usually used when the number of available tracks is limited.

TV mix   A mix without the vocals so that the artist can sing live to the back tracks during a television appearance.

unity gain   When the output level of a process or processor exactly matches its input level.

varispeed   A parameter on tape recorders that varies the speed of the playback.

Vocal Stressor   A signal processor made by the now-defunct ADR company that combined a compressor, EQ, and de-esser, all tuned in such a way as to make a vocal stand out in the mix.

Delay Chart

BPM	1/4 Note	1/8 Note	1/16 Note	1/32 Note	1/4 Triplet	1/8 Triplet	1/16 Triplet	Dotted 1/4	Dotted 1/8	Dotted 1/16
75	800.0	400.0	200.0	100.0	533.6	266.8	133.4	1200.0	600.0	300.0
76	789.5	394.7	197.4	98.7	526.6	263.3	131.6	1184.2	592.1	296.1
77	779.2	389.6	194.8	97.4	519.7	259.9	129.9	1168.8	584.4	292.2
78	769.2	384.6	192.3	96.2	513.1	256.5	128.3	1153.8	576.9	288.5
79	759.5	379.7	189.9	94.9	506.6	253.3	126.6	1139.2	569.6	284.8
80	750.0	375.0	187.5	93.8	500.3	250.1	125.1	1125.0	562.5	281.3
81	740.7	370.4	185.2	92.6	494.1	247.0	123.5	1111.1	555.6	277.8
82	731.7	365.9	182.9	91.5	488.0	244.0	122.0	1097.6	548.8	274.4
83	722.9	361.4	180.7	90.4	482.2	241.1	120.5	1084.3	542.2	271.1
84	714.3	357.1	178.6	89.3	476.4	238.2	119.1	1071.4	535.7	267.9
85	705.9	352.9	176.5	88.2	470.8	235.4	117.7	1058.8	529.4	264.7
86	697.7	348.8	174.4	87.2	465.3	232.7	116.3	1046.5	523.3	261.6
87	689.7	344.8	172.4	86.2	460.0	230.0	115.0	1034.5	517.2	258.6
88	681.8	340.9	170.5	85.2	454.8	227.4	113.7	1022.7	511.4	255.7
89	674.2	337.1	168.5	84.3	449.7	224.8	112.4	1011.2	505.6	252.8
90	666.7	333.3	166.7	83.3	444.7	222.3	111.2	1000.0	500.0	250.0
91	659.3	329.7	164.8	82.4	439.8	219.9	109.9	989.0	494.5	247.3
92	652.2	326.1	163.0	81.5	435.0	217.5	108.8	978.3	489.1	244.6
93	645.2	322.6	161.3	80.6	430.3	215.2	107.6	967.7	483.9	241.9
94	638.3	319.1	159.6	79.8	425.7	212.9	106.4	957.4	478.7	239.4
95	631.6	315.8	157.9	78.9	421.3	210.6	105.3	947.4	473.7	236.8
96	625.0	312.5	156.3	78.1	416.9	208.4	104.2	937.5	468.8	234.4
97	618.6	309.3	154.6	77.3	412.6	206.3	103.1	927.8	463.9	232.0

BPM	1/4 Note	1/8 Note	1/16 Note	1/32 Note	1/4 Triplet	1/8 Triplet	1/16 Triplet	Dotted 1/4	Dotted 1/8	Dotted 1/16
98	612.2	306.1	153.1	76.5	408.4	204.2	102.1	918.4	459.2	229.6
99	606.1	303.0	151.5	75.8	404.2	202.1	101.1	909.1	454.5	227.3
100	600.0	300.0	150.0	75.0	400.2	200.1	100.1	900.0	450.0	225.0
101	594.1	297.0	148.5	74.3	396.2	198.1	99.1	891.1	445.5	222.8
102	588.2	294.1	147.1	73.5	392.4	196.2	98.1	882.4	441.2	220.6
103	582.5	291.3	145.6	72.8	388.5	194.3	97.1	873.8	436.9	218.4
104	576.9	288.5	144.2	72.1	384.8	192.4	96.2	865.4	432.7	216.3
105	571.4	285.7	142.9	71.4	381.1	190.6	95.3	857.1	428.6	214.3
106	566.0	283.0	141.5	70.8	377.5	188.8	94.4	849.1	424.5	212.3
107	560.7	280.4	140.2	70.1	374.0	187.0	93.5	841.1	420.6	210.3
108	555.6	277.8	138.9	69.4	370.6	185.3	92.6	833.3	416.7	208.3
109	550.5	275.2	137.6	68.8	367.2	183.6	91.8	825.7	412.8	206.4
110	545.5	272.7	136.4	68.2	363.8	181.9	91.0	818.2	409.1	204.5
111	540.5	270.3	135.1	67.6	360.5	180.3	90.1	810.8	405.4	202.7
112	535.7	267.9	133.9	67.0	357.3	178.7	89.3	803.6	401.8	200.9
113	531.0	265.5	132.7	66.4	354.2	177.1	88.5	796.5	398.2	199.1
114	526.3	263.2	131.6	65.8	351.1	175.5	87.8	789.5	394.7	197.4
115	521.7	260.9	130.4	65.2	348.0	174.0	87.0	782.6	391.3	195.7
116	517.2	258.6	129.3	64.7	345.0	172.5	86.3	775.9	387.9	194.0
117	512.8	256.4	128.2	64.1	342.1	171.0	85.5	769.2	384.6	192.3
118	508.5	254.2	127.1	63.6	339.2	169.6	84.8	762.7	381.4	190.7
119	504.2	252.1	126.1	63.0	336.3	168.2	84.1	756.3	378.2	189.1
120	500.0	250.0	125.0	62.5	333.5	166.8	83.4	750.0	375.0	187.5
121	495.9	247.9	124.0	62.0	330.7	165.4	82.7	743.8	371.9	186.0
122	491.8	245.9	123.0	61.5	328.0	164.0	82.0	737.7	368.9	184.4
123	487.8	243.9	122.0	61.0	325.4	162.7	81.3	731.7	365.9	182.9
124	483.9	241.9	121.0	60.5	322.7	161.4	80.7	725.8	362.9	181.5
125	480.0	240.0	120.0	60.0	320.2	160.1	80.0	720.0	360.0	180.0
126	476.2	238.1	119.0	59.5	317.6	158.8	79.4	714.3	357.1	178.6
127	472.4	236.2	118.1	59.1	315.1	157.6	78.8	708.7	354.3	177.2
128	468.8	234.4	117.2	58.6	312.7	156.3	78.2	703.1	351.6	175.8
129	465.1	232.6	116.3	58.1	310.2	155.1	77.6	697.7	348.8	174.4
130	461.5	230.8	115.4	57.7	307.8	153.9	77.0	692.3	346.2	173.1
131	458.0	229.0	114.5	57.3	305.5	152.7	76.4	687.0	343.5	171.8
132	454.5	227.3	113.6	56.8	303.2	151.6	75.8	681.8	340.9	170.5
133	451.1	225.6	112.8	56.4	300.9	150.5	75.2	676.7	338.3	169.2
134	447.8	223.9	111.9	56.0	298.7	149.3	74.7	671.6	335.8	167.9
135	444.4	222.2	111.1	55.6	296.4	148.2	74.1	666.7	333.3	166.7
136	441.2	220.6	110.3	55.1	294.3	147.1	73.6	661.8	330.9	165.4
137	438.0	219.0	109.5	54.7	292.1	146.1	73.0	656.9	328.5	164.2

BPM	1/4 Note	1/8 Note	1/16 Note	1/32 Note	1/4 Triplet	1/8 Triplet	1/16 Triplet	Dotted 1/4	Dotted 1/8	Dotted 1/16
138	434.8	217.4	108.7	54.3	290.0	145.0	72.5	652.2	326.1	163.0
139	431.7	215.8	107.9	54.0	287.9	144.0	72.0	647.5	323.7	161.9
140	428.6	214.3	107.1	53.6	285.9	142.9	71.5	642.9	321.4	160.7
141	425.5	212.8	106.4	53.2	283.8	141.9	71.0	638.3	319.1	159.6
142	422.5	211.3	105.6	52.8	281.8	140.9	70.5	633.8	316.9	158.5
143	419.6	209.8	104.9	52.4	279.9	139.9	70.0	629.4	314.7	157.3
144	416.7	208.3	104.2	52.1	277.9	139.0	69.5	625.0	312.5	156.3
145	413.8	206.9	103.4	51.7	276.0	138.0	69.0	620.7	310.3	155.2
146	411.0	205.5	102.7	51.4	274.1	137.1	68.5	616.4	308.2	154.1
147	408.2	204.1	102.0	51.0	272.2	136.1	68.1	612.2	306.1	153.1
148	405.4	202.7	101.4	50.7	270.4	135.2	67.6	608.1	304.1	152.0
149	402.7	201.3	100.7	50.3	268.6	134.3	67.1	604.0	302.0	151.0
150	400.0	200.0	100.0	50.0	266.8	133.4	66.7	600.0	300.0	150.0
151	397.4	198.7	99.3	49.7	265.0	132.5	66.3	596.0	298.0	149.0
152	394.7	197.4	98.7	49.3	263.3	131.6	65.8	592.1	296.1	148.0
153	392.2	196.1	98.0	49.0	261.6	130.8	65.4	588.2	294.1	147.1
154	389.6	194.8	97.4	48.7	259.9	129.9	65.0	584.4	292.2	146.1
155	387.1	193.5	96.8	48.4	258.2	129.1	64.5	580.6	290.3	145.2
156	384.6	192.3	96.2	48.1	256.5	128.3	64.1	576.9	288.5	144.2
157	382.2	191.1	95.5	47.8	254.9	127.5	63.7	573.2	286.6	143.3
158	379.7	189.9	94.9	47.5	253.3	126.6	63.3	569.6	284.8	142.4
159	377.4	188.7	94.3	47.2	251.7	125.8	62.9	566.0	283.0	141.5
160	375.0	187.5	93.8	46.9	250.1	125.1	62.5	562.5	281.3	140.6

Index

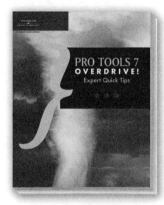

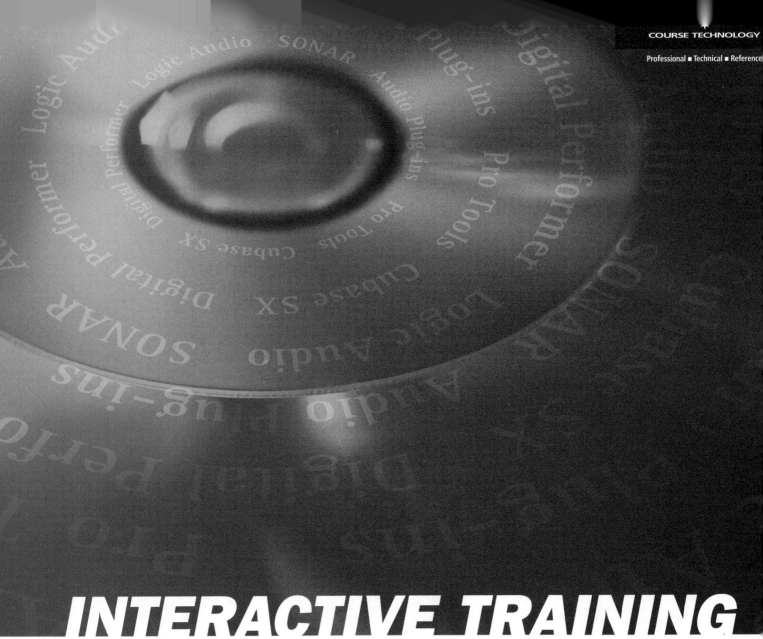

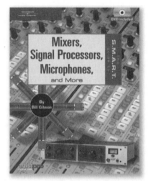

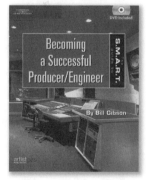

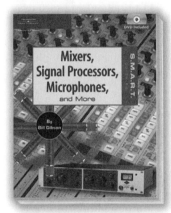
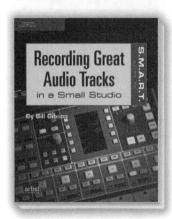
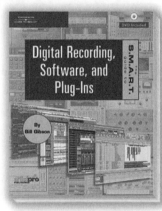

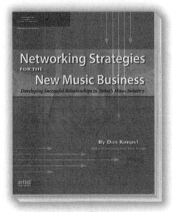